So Longeth My Soul

In memory of Freda Nicholls (1931–2022)
Wise spiritual mentor and loving friend

So Longeth My Soul

A Reader in Christian Spirituality

Joanna Collicutt

scm press

© Joanna Collicutt 2024

Published in 2024 by SCM Press
Editorial office
3rd Floor, Invicta House,
110 Golden Lane,
London EC1Y 0TG, UK

www.scmpress.co.uk

SCM Press is an imprint of Hymns Ancient & Modern Ltd
(a registered charity)

Hymns Ancient & Modern® is a registered trademark of
Hymns Ancient & Modern Ltd
13A Hellesdon Park Road, Norwich,
Norfolk NR6 5DR, UK

British Library Cataloguing in Publication data
A catalogue record for this book is available
from the British Library

ISBN 978-0-334-06310-0

Typeset by Regent Typesetting
Printed and bound in Great Britain by
CPI Group (UK) Ltd

Contents

Preface

This book has been several years in the making. It has arisen from my experience of teaching Christian spirituality to people training for ministry in the Church of England, and more specifically from three modules from Durham University's Common Awards in Theology, Mission and Ministry: 'Texts and traditions in Christian spirituality', 'Aspects of spirituality and ministry' and 'Christian theology, ritual and pastoral care'. The classes were sources of rich insights drawn from engaging discussion with intelligent and prayerful students, but they also revealed their limited exposure to the primary texts themselves. Several students told me that they had perhaps one or two favourite writers, but beyond this did not know where to start in reading and evaluating these sources.

This is something that is also true for a lot of ordinary Christians (including myself for many years). However, there are exceptions, and Freda Nicholls, to whom this book is dedicated, was an extraordinary ordinary Christian who was quietly steeped in the texts and traditions of Protestant, Catholic and Orthodox Christianity. I was her priest, but she was my teacher.

The book introduces readers with little prior knowledge to the range of Christian spiritual writings from the end of the apostolic age until the late nineteenth century. I have not ventured into more recent times as there seems to be much less of a problem in accessing twentieth- and twenty-first-century writers such as Evelyn Underhill, Simone Weil, Thomas Merton and so on. Even within this limit, the coverage is indicative rather than comprehensive: several key thinkers, such as Evagrios of Pontus, John Donne, Søren Kierkegaard or Catherine of Siena, do not appear. The chapters are arranged according to a number of psychological themes rather than on the basis of historical epoch or spiritual tradition, and texts have been selected primarily on the basis of their fit with these themes. (I have also tried to keep a reasonable balance between Catholic and Protestant, and east and west, and to include a variety of literary genres.)

The rather unusual thematic structure is aimed at helping readers engage with the texts in a way that is spiritually enriching and psychologically useful, and to encourage them to think about ways of drawing others in, perhaps by presenting the key ideas in more contemporary form. The rationale for the chosen themes (each connected in a different way with human bereavement) is presented in Part I, together with a consideration of the inherent challenges of engaging with historically distant texts, and some guidance on navigating these challenges and getting the most from them. Part II is devoted to the readings themselves, most of which are sufficiently long to give a flavour of the writer's thinking. Nevertheless, each is only a small sample of the output of its writer, and the topic in question may not be fully representative of their major concerns. So, for example, while there are readings from Josephine Butler and Thomas Aquinas in a section on social justice, this topic dominated Butler's thought but was only part of Thomas' broader theological and philosophical agenda. This, of course, relates to a second aim of the book which is to encourage its readers to read more by or about the authors they encounter here. Suggestions for further reading are provided at the end of each chapter. A concluding chapter with a single reading returns to the theme of waiting well for the return of Christ, the foundational idea of the book.

Where possible, the most accessible translations have been used. Some translations convey the literal sense of the text accurately but others capture its spirit better. Where there has been a choice, I have generally favoured the latter. In order to engage well with these texts a sense of where they come in the history and geography of the Church and the world is useful. I have therefore included a time and place table (pp. 244–6) which makes this clear and helps locate the readings in relation to each other. From this it can be seen that, with the rise of Christendom, there is a relentless shift in the preserved written sources northwards and westwards, mirroring the geographic shift in centres of scholarship and faith, and the development in modes and channels of communication.

This book has grown out of many conversations, and I cannot now recall all the individuals who have knowingly or unknowingly offered helpful insights. I would, nevertheless, like to thank colleagues and students at Ripon College Cuddesdon, particularly Grant Bayliss, Eddie Howells, Michael Lakey and George Meyrick; my tutor at King's College London, Rebecca Gill; and my colleague in parish ministry, Mark Thomas. I also owe a debt to Salisbury Diocese: to Colin Heber-Percy and the people of Pewsey Deanery, and to James Woodward and students at Sarum College for their hospitality in allowing me to present some of the material as part of their learning and development programmes.

A number of scholars, translators and religious communities have been generous with permissions and advice as I requested approval to reproduce work authored by themselves or deceased colleagues and loved ones. These are all acknowledged on pages 247–51, but I would particularly like to thank Father John Anthony McGuckin for sharing his scholarship on Symeon the New Theologian.

Much of the groundwork for the book took place during the lockdown of 2021, during which Alister McGrath and I were delighted to discover that, after 40 years of marriage in which we didn't see much of each other, we still get on rather well. I am deeply grateful to him for his translations of three of the readings, and for much more.

Part I

Like as the hart desireth the water-brooks:
so longeth my soul after thee, O God.
Psalm 42.1 (Book of Common Prayer)

1

The Vital Testimony of the Ancients

This book is a collection of readings from classic texts of Christian spirituality drawn from the early years after the close of the New Testament to the end of the nineteenth century. Its aim is to offer the reader a way into these texts that enables them to be received as living and relevant for both personal spirituality and ministry. In my experience people beginning the study of Christian spirituality have an ambivalent attitude to primary sources from the past. On the one hand they are intrigued by the mysterious 'otherness' of their language (examen, shewings, interior castle, hesychasm etc.) and the promise that this very 'otherness' may take them into exciting uncharted territory. On the other hand, they lack the confidence to navigate this territory, so that what begins as strangely intriguing can quickly become 'just too weird'.

In this vein it has been said that primary sources on Christian spirituality fall into the class of literature that 'everyone wants to have read but no one wants to read'.[1] That may be going too far; some people on first encountering these texts seem to relish their archaic and arcane aspects, treating them somewhat like literary fantasies. There is nothing wrong with this, especially if it goes beyond simple diversion and opens the door to forms of self-transcendence. But I would want to argue that a lot more is required to do them full justice; otherwise there is a danger of 'silencing the ancients: of refusing the vital testimony they can give on great questions of who we humans are, why we act as we do, and how we may wisely direct our short and often painful lives'.[2] This book is an invitation to listen and attend well to some of this 'vital testimony'.

From action to contemplation

In my 2015 book *The Psychology of Christian Character Formation* I presented the Christian life as a transformative process of 'growing up into Christ',[3] a phrase that reflects both resemblance and union. The book was mainly concerned with the former: developing a Christ-like character through conscious imitation of him (1 Corinthians 11.1). It focused on the cultivation of virtue,

---

1 A. McGrath, 1999, *Christian Spirituality*, Oxford: Blackwell, p. 135, quoting Mark Twain.

2 D. Halperin, 1995, 'Methodological reflections on psychoanalysis and Judaic studies: A response to Mortimer Ostow' in M. Ostow (ed.), *Ultimate Intimacy: The psychodynamics of Jewish mysticism*, London: Karnac, p. 184.

3 J. Collicutt, 2015, *The Psychology of Christian Character Formation*, London: SCM Press.

and thus emphasized the active side of Christian spirituality, at times drawing on classic texts such as the Rule of St Benedict. The present book could be described as a companion volume that concentrates on these texts themselves, and with a more experiential and contemplative focus.

While the active and contemplative are not so easily separated as this might seem to imply, the shift from an early focus on virtue to a later focus on contemplation is a pattern repeatedly found and even explicitly advocated in several classic texts, summed up by Evelyn Underhill: 'First, there are the virtues to be acquired: those "ornaments of the Spiritual Marriage" with which no mystic can dispense ... the rebuilding of character – as the preparation of the contemplative act.'[4] This order does not indicate that concerns of character and virtue are less important than divine contemplation; rather it is to assert that they are foundational to it. You cannot go straight to mystical union without passing the 'Go' of good character. The contemplative life is not an escape from the challenging world of embodied human relationships but something that emerges from it[5] and speaks back into it.

The shift in emphasis from imitation to contemplation is then not so much about advancing up the rungs of a ladder beyond spiritual basics (though some of the writers in this book do talk in such terms); it is more like moving around a circle and exploring another perspective to give a full account of 'what is going on'. It represents a move from considering the Christian spiritual life as one of following Christ to one of encountering Christ, from knowing about to knowing, from a 'Me and Him' relationship to what Martin Buber called an 'Ich und Du' (I and Thou) relationship.[6]

The phrase 'I and Thou' reminds us that the contemplative gaze of the believer is not directed at an object (however exalted) but at *a person who meets our gaze*, an experience beautifully, if unintentionally, captured by Monteverdi's famous secular love duet *Pur ti miro* ('I gaze upon you').[7] Paul describes this in more theologically robust terms as receiving 'the light of the knowledge of the glory of God in the face of Jesus Christ' (2 Corinthians 4.6b). For Paul at least, any 'I and Thou' encounter with the triune God takes the form of a meeting with the second person of the Trinity, a key point to which I shall shortly return.

---

4 E. Underhill, 1922, 'Introduction' in *The Cloud of Unknowing*, London: John Watkins, p. 6.

5 This is because imitating Christ is about more than just copying his habits of life; ultimately it is about identifying with his person. See J. Collicutt, 2019, *When You Pray*, Oxford: Bible Reading Fellowship, pp. 9–10.

6 M. Buber, 2013, *I and Thou*, London: Bloomsbury.

7 It can be heard here: '"Pur ti miro", Claudio Monteverdi | TENET's "UNO + ONE"', *Youtube*, https://www.youtube.com/watch?v=LDzAEB03MZs, accessed 10.01.2024.

Is God dead?

The context in which the Christian life happens is the gospel – the ultimate good news story that in the life, death, and raising of Jesus of Nazareth, God acted to reconcile all things to himself, and that now in and through the Spirit Christians are 'being transformed from one degree of glory to another' (2 Corinthians 3.18). Christians believe that God came to be with us in Jesus and, because of the resurrection, God is still with us in Jesus. Lest we forget that fact, most Anglican collects end with the assertion that Jesus is alive.

But our lived experience may be different. Sometimes it takes the eyes of a child to notice this and the naiveté of a child to name it. Many years ago my (then) little niece asked me with great seriousness, 'Joanna, is God dead?'. 'What makes you think that?' I questioned, hoping to buy some time. She replied, 'Well, because when we go to his house he's never home.' Somewhat thrown, I explained that God was indeed there but in a different and special sort of way. She didn't look convinced.

Later, I told her mother, who ran through some possible amusing alternative responses that included, 'He's just popped out to the shops, but he'll be back later.' It seemed to me that in saying this she had unknowingly put her finger on the heartbeat of the Christian dilemma: Jesus came but then he went away; Jesus is with us now but not yet; or, in the words of those Anglican collects, 'who is alive *and reigns with you* …' – not dead but inaccessible in heaven. Both the individual Christian and the church live in a constant state of tension between the presence and absence of Jesus. This means that much of our spiritual experience takes the form of yearning for something half-remembered that is just beyond our grasp, or seeking after something that we have mislaid, at least temporarily.

The Christian story of salvation presents the human condition more generally in these terms, framing it as 'paradise lost'. In the beginning human beings lived in intimacy with God in a garden with the tree of life at its centre (Genesis 2.9). The Fall resulted in their banishment from this state with no hope of accessing the tree of life (Genesis 2.24) – that is, until the coming of Christ.

Human spiritual awakening has then traditionally been understood as an inchoate desire for this prelapsarian life. It can present as a seeking after parental intimacy and connectedness; a longing for liberation from oppression; a search for true identity; a desire to shake off the shackles of the ego; a quest for ultimate understanding and meaning; a deep need to go home:

Greatly saddened was the Tree of Life
when it beheld Adam stolen away from it;
it sank down into the virgin ground and was hidden
– to burst forth and appear on Golgotha;

Humanity, like birds that are chased,
took refuge in it that it might return them to their proper home.[8]

However, the Christian is not promised a return to Eden but is instead offered the prospect of the heavenly city of the New Jerusalem whose gates stand open (Revelation 21.25), with the tree of life at its centre, its fruit now available to all (Revelation 22.2). The writer to the Hebrews suggests that this vision is also for those who died in faith before Christ (Hebrews 11.13–16), and emphasizes that 'in these last days' (Hebrews 1.1) there is no more need for anyone to look back with regret or nostalgia.

And yet we do.

Marana tha

That description of the New Jerusalem in Revelation ends with a cry of unconsummated longing that forms the conclusion to the Christian Bible as a whole: 'The one who testifies to these things says, "Surely I am coming soon." Amen. Come, Lord Jesus!' (Revelation 22.20). This is obviously a future-oriented sentiment, but its roots lie in the past; for the call is not for a first meeting with a stranger but for a reunion with someone already known:

> … the Aramaic phrase '*Marana tha*' (Our Lord, come!), presumably originating in the Palestinian church …both expressed a prevalent need or wish and also maintained a sense of expectation.
> … these very first Christians … remembered what it was like to know Jesus the first time around … They were bereaved … When you lose someone you love, the hope of a reunion is what keeps you going.[9]

This perhaps accounts for the feeling of wistfulness, the sense of having lost something precious, that can be found in the pages of the New Testament, and the repeated exhortations by its writers to look forward in hope rather than backwards in grief. Just as the human condition can be understood as a longing for Eden, the Christian condition can be understood as a longing for Emmanuel. This longing must have been acutely painful for those who knew Jesus of Nazareth (it is almost palpable in John's description of the brief encounter between Jesus and Mary Magdalene by the garden tomb); many later Christians too have experienced a form of grief for the Jesus they never met.

---

8 Ephrem the Syrian, *Hymns of Virginity XVI*, tr. S. Brock.
9 J. Duff and J. Collicutt McGrath, 2006, *Meeting Jesus: Human responses to a yearning God*, London: SPCK, pp. 2–3.

In his book *The Shadow of the Galilean*,[10] the New Testament scholar Gerd Theissen explores this idea. The book tells the fictional story of Andreas, a Galilean Jew who reluctantly finds himself working as a spy for Pontius Pilate. His task is the surveillance of local troublemakers or possible political insurgents and, as he goes about it, he keeps running into people who know Jesus, both enemies and followers. Little by little Andreas finds himself being drawn to this mysterious figure through hearing snippets of his teaching, meeting people who have been healed by him, and witnessing the transformation in the lives of some of his clandestine disciples. The suspense builds as Andreas comes nearer and nearer to meeting Jesus himself, and this appears to be inevitable as he arrives at Pilate's headquarters in Jerusalem during Passover. But the meeting never happens; the nearest Andreas gets is to see the lifeless body of Jesus on the cross from a distance. Like Christians down the centuries, he has to be content with traces of Jesus, with the shadow of Galilean.

'He is not here'[11]

The Gospels were written a generation after the death of Jesus, drawing on the recollections of those who had known him for an audience who had never met him (1 Peter 1.8). They clearly recognize the Christian dilemma, what another New Testament scholar Markus Bockmuehl refers to as 'the dialectic of the present and the absent Jesus',[12] and each addresses it in a different way. John is the most explicit, devoting four chapters to Jesus' farewell discourses as he prepares his followers for his departure and comforts them with the promise of the Holy Spirit: 'It is to your advantage that I go away, for if I do not go away, the Advocate will not come to you; but if I go, I will send him to you' (John 16.7b). For John, Jesus has gone but the Spirit has come in some sense in his place.

Matthew, the evangelist who uses the term 'Emmanuel' at the beginning of his Gospel (Matthew 1.23), ends it with Jesus' deeply paradoxical parting farewell assertion that 'I am with you always, to the end of the age' (Matthew 28.20b). Matthew places much less emphasis on the Spirit and instead locates the continuing presence of Jesus in the gathered Christian community – the *ekklēsia* (e.g. Matthew 18.20), especially its weak or suffering members (Matthew 25.40).

Luke at the end of his Gospel gives a clear account of Jesus' physical ascension heavenwards, repeating it at the opening of Acts, this time including the details of an impenetrable cloud and the confirmation by two angels that he

---

10 G. Theissen, 1987, *The Shadow of the Galilean*, London: SCM Press.
11 Matthew 28.6; Mark 16.6; Luke 24.5.
12 M. Bockmuehl, 2017, 'The personal presence of Jesus in the writings of Paul', *Scottish Journal of Theology*, 70(1), 39–60, p. 55.

has gone (Luke 24.51; Acts 1.9–11). Like John, Luke presents the departure of Jesus as a prelude to the coming of the Spirit, but in the Emmaus Road story he also identifies 'the breaking of the bread' as a place of encounter with the elusive risen Christ, which he links with the continuing practice of the first Christians after the ascension (Luke 24.35; Acts 2.42). As in John's Gospel, a continuing sense of the presence of Christ is closely connected with the act of remembering, an important motif in the Emmaus Road story.

Here there is also a connection with Mark, whose Gospel ends abruptly with the angel's statement that 'he is not here' plus the direction to return to Galilee with a reminder of Jesus' earlier words (Mark 16.6–7; see 14.28). Mark's emphasis on returning to where it all started brings to mind the opening words of his Gospel: 'The beginning…' (*archē*). The angel's words invite the reader to follow the disciples back to where the Good News *began* and to encounter Jesus afresh in the text with the benefit of hindsight. The last words of this Gospel are 'for they were afraid'; there is no sense of closure or resolution here, just the instruction to go back. This is something that survivors of trauma or bereavement involuntarily find themselves doing: going over it all, questioning, re-processing, seeking significance with hindsight.

Paul never met Jesus of Nazareth, yet he too struggled with a tension between the felt presence of the risen-and-ascended Christ in his life and a sense that he was also absent:

> For to me, living is Christ and dying is gain. If I am to live in the flesh, that means fruitful labour for me; and I do not know which I prefer. I am hard pressed between the two: my desire is to depart and be with Christ, for that is far better. (Philippians 1.21–23)

> But if Christ is in you, though the body is dead because of sin, the Spirit is life because of righteousness … Christ Jesus, who died, yes, who was raised, who is at the right hand of God, who indeed intercedes for us. (Romans 8.10, 34b)

This is never fully resolved for him; like Luke he associates the presence of Jesus with the Lord's Supper (1 Corinthians 10.16); like Matthew, he finds him in the gathered community (1 Corinthians 12.27); like John, he sees him as represented by the Spirit (Philippians 1.19). In all these ways Jesus is experienced in a mediated or indirect form, seen 'in a mirror, dimly' (1 Corinthians 13.12). Yet it seems that Paul has also had experiences more like direct 'I-and-Thou' encounters that might be described as mystical (Galatians 1.12; 2 Corinthians 12.2–4), in which the Christ Jesus who is at the right hand of God briefly became accessible to him, as he was for Stephen (Acts 7.56).[13]

The first Christians mourned a Jesus they had loved and lost, but who also continued to be with them in manifold ways, some of which are mentioned

---

13 C. Rowland, 2002, *The Open Heaven*, Eugene, OR: Wipf & Stock, p. 383.

above. Subsequent generations continue to inhabit this presence–absence tension. All look forward to an ultimate meeting when we shall 'see face to face' and 'know fully' (1 Corinthians 13.12). In this sense all Christians are in a quasi-bereaved state. Yet, just as in human bereavement, we have ways in which we can maintain the relationship with our loved one and, unlike the situation in human bereavement, we have the Holy Spirit to help us in this. The Holy Spirit makes the presence of Christ a felt reality; or to put it in more theological language, his work is both psychological (comforting, encouraging and reminding the believer who misses Jesus) *and* ontological (mediating Jesus' presence and bestowing spiritual gifts). Finally, like Paul and Stephen before him, we may catch a direct glimpse of the exalted Christ.

What has all this got to do with classic texts of Christian spirituality?

Christian spirituality is fundamentally eschatological; the life of faith is about inhabiting Jesus' absence well as we eagerly await his return in glory. Many of Jesus' own parables deal with this theme, especially the series in Matthew 25.[14] Christian spiritual practices and systems, whether active or contemplative, can be understood as part of this greater agenda. Many focus on making Christ more psychologically accessible to the believer as she waits; some engage directly with the absence of Christ in its own right; some take a more mystical path, offering insights from heavenly visions or instructions on cultivating receptivity to such experiences. It is remarkable how Christocentric the spiritual practices of the Church have been throughout her history.

I want to suggest that approaching the classic texts of Christian spirituality as rich resources crafted to help the reader manage the felt absence or inaccessibility of Jesus will make them more comprehensible. This is because the challenge of living well in the context of the loss of a loved one is a universal human experience. It may be expressed somewhat differently in different cultures and aeons, but it is a fundamental thread that has the capacity to connect people from widely different historical and geographical contexts through their common humanity. This is perhaps why these texts are often taken up by people who are in the acute stages of human grief; the yearning for Christ and the mourning for a beloved human companion become intertwined. Here are two examples, one biblical, the other from a classic text, that are frequently chosen for funeral readings:

> 'Do not let your hearts be troubled. Believe in God, believe also in me. In my Father's house there are many dwelling places. If it were not so, would I have told you that I go to prepare a place for you? And if I go and prepare

---

14 The wise and foolish bridesmaids, the talents, the sheep and the goats.

a place for you, I will come again and will take you to myself, so that where I am, there you may be also.'[15]

He did not say, 'You shall not be perturbed, you shall not be troubled, you shall not be distressed', but he said, 'You shall not be overcome.'[16]

One of the things about bereavement that has only been articulated in the last 20 years or so, is the way that people move seamlessly to and fro between deep engagement with emotion and practical activities concerned with getting on with life without the deceased, which often includes finding ways to honour them.[17] The former may involve 'yearning for the deceased, looking at old photos, imagining how he or she would react, or crying about the death of the loved person'.[18] The latter can include making sure that their values are respected, maintaining or completing their projects, following their instructions, doing 'what she would have wanted'. Here we see a parallel with the relationship between spirituality, mission and social justice. Waiting well for Jesus' return involves seamless moves between attentiveness to his person (as in the case of the wise bridesmaids), contributing to the advance of his kingdom (as in the case of wise use of talents), and behaving with mercy and compassion (as in the case of the sheep vs the goats).

As has already been noted, there is a lot more to Christian mission[19] and spirituality than bereavement. Nevertheless, the bereavement analogy highlights the way that mission and spirituality are interconnected parts of something bigger, even two sides of the same coin. This has not always been obvious in the history of Christianity, which has tended to split spirituality off from the rest of life, a move described by the late theologian and social activist Robert McAfee Brown as 'the great fallacy'.[20] McAfee Brown instead argues for what he calls a 'withdrawal and return' model in which spiritual practices enable the individual or community to get on with life in the 'real world' more effectively because its reality is discerned more clearly: 'The best way to understand "withdrawal and return", therefore, is to see it not as an oscillation between two different worlds, but as a way of *concentrating for a time on a part of the single world that we inhabit.*'[21]

15 John 14.1–3.

16 Julian of Norwich, 2015, *Revelations of Divine Love*, B. Windeatt (tr.), Oxford: Oxford University Press.

17 M. Stroeb and H. Schut, 1999, 'The dual process model of bereavement', *Death Studies*, 23, pp. 197–224.

18 Stroeb and Schut, 'The dual process model', p. 212.

19 I am using the term 'mission' to include striving for social justice (as in the 'Five marks of mission'; see 'Marks of Mission', *Anglican Communion*, https://www.anglicancommunion.org/mission/marks-of-mission.aspx, accessed 10.01.2024).

20 R. McAfee Brown, 1988, *Spirituality and Liberation: Overcoming the great fallacy*, Louisville, KY: Westminster John Knox Press.

21 McAfee Brown, *Spirituality and Liberation*, p. 47.

The phrase 'a single world that we inhabit' connects with a basic assumption of this book: even in the face of significant cultural differences across time and place, human beings share some basic commonalities in the way they relate to the created world, each other, and the divine. All have been created in the image of God and all have the capacity to recognize and respond to him. Reading classic Christian spiritual texts from 'other' cultures and ages requires that *both* the cultural differences *and* the human commonalities be acknowledged and negotiated, something explored further in the next chapter.

One consequence of this mix of diversity and commonality is mess. Insights from spiritual traditions in different times and places can seem to overlap, replicate, or link with each other, to say similar things in slightly different ways or even to 'reinvent the wheel'. This is one reason that a strictly historical or denominational approach to spiritual texts and traditions may be less helpful than an approach that explores the themes they have in common.

These similarities between different Christian traditions (or even different religions) do not only arise from direct influences of one on another or from their shared biological or cultural heritage; they relate to the nature of reality. Christians believe that there is an underlying coherence to this reality, held together as it is by Christ (Colossians 1.17), which may be helpfully thought of as dynamic, full of interconnections, and multilayered.[22] It is manifested and rediscovered repeatedly by human beings in their different contexts, coming at it from different angles, with different local agendas, full of their foibles and fallibilities, yet all participating in the same God-given truth:

> It was a hard thing to undo this knot.
> The rainbow shines, but only in the thought
> Of him that looks. Yet not in that alone,
> For who makes rainbows by invention?
>
> And many standing round a waterfall
> See one bow each, yet not the same to all,
> But each a hand's breadth further than the next.
> The sun on falling waters writes the text
> Which yet is in the eye or in the thought.
> It was a hard thing to undo this knot.[23]

---

22 See, for example, D. Bohm and B. Hiley, 1995, *The Undivided Universe: An ontological interpretation of quantum theory*, London: Routledge.

23 G. M. Hopkins, 1990 (1864), 'It was a hard thing to undo this knot', N. McKenzie (ed.), *The Poetical Works of Gerard Manley Hopkins*, Oxford: Oxford University Press, p. 24.

2

Approaching the Text I: Understanding its Nature

In the previous chapter I suggested that it may be helpful to look at Christian spirituality through the lens of bereavement. One important aspect of bereavement and mourning is the significance of time. We remember the date of our loved one's death, often marking the anniversary in special ways; we evaluate the well-being of a bereaved person in terms of time since death – 'It's too soon', 'Shouldn't she be over it by now?' and so on. W. H. Auden's famous poem 'Funeral blues' even begins, 'Stop all the clocks' and goes on to describe the cruel interruption of something that was assumed to 'last for-ever'.[1] Like birth, death is a physical, embodied event located in real time, something that changes the world.

In a similar way the birth, life, death and resurrection of Jesus have con-ventionally been referred to by scholars as 'The Christ *event*'; something that happened in real time – a fact rather than a concept. This point is repeatedly made by Rowan Williams in his book *The Wound of Knowledge*; the reality communicated in Christian spiritual writings is not the stuff of abstract and eternal logic, but something revealed in the light of 'a brief set of contingent events in Palestine' 2,000 years ago.[2] The Christ event is like the sun in Hopkins' poem, making rainbows in the minds of the faithful.

This means that reading classic texts of Christian spirituality always involves facing the challenge of history. They are to be received not as time-less messages that have dropped out of the sky but as historically located human documents, reaching back to Jesus but also reaching out to readers down the centuries.

Receiving the texts involves *understanding* where they are coming from and *interpreting* their implications for here and now. Understanding requires, among other things, knowledge of the language and culture of the writer in order to achieve an empathetic entering into his or her perspective. Interpre-tation – bringing the writer's perspective into conversation with that of the reader – is more complex; it is sometimes described in terms of the merg-ing of two horizons.[3] This is where considerations of history really bite: first because with 'classic' texts the main thing that separates the two horizons is

---

1 W. H. Auden, 1940, *Another Time*, New York: Random House, p. 78.

2 R. Williams, 1979, *The Wound of Knowledge*, London: Darton, Longman & Todd, p. 1.

3 H. Gadamer, 1989, *Truth and Method*, London: Sheed & Ward. See also P. Sheldrake, 1995, *Spirituality and History*, London: SPCK, chapter 7.

time – 'The past is a foreign country; they do things differently there'[4] – and second because the Christian reader is constrained to interpret the texts in the light of the historical Christ event attested by the New Testament.

In this chapter I will set out the main issues to be considered in trying to understand these texts, moving on to issues of interpretation in the following chapter. These, together with themes arising from the phenomenon of bereavement, form the framework for the presentation of the texts themselves in Part II.

The text is written by someone

Sometimes the identity of the author is clear and there are quite a lot of biographical details available. However, the biographies of 'spiritual giants' should be read critically, as they tend to be written by followers who idealize them, may be redacted by the ecclesiastical magisterium to fit its own agenda, or even written by their enemies or critics to discredit them. Examples: the autobiography of Thérèse of Lisieux (1873–97) was heavily edited by her Carmelite order with the agenda of her rapid canonization; contemporary accounts of the life of Marguerite Porete (1250–1310) were based on the prosecution documents at her trial for heresy.

> Consider the human being behind the text; their personal history contributes to it, whether or not that history is known to us.

Sometimes a work has traditionally been attributed to one individual but was actually written by someone else, known or unknown. Example: 'The prayer of St Francis' that begins 'Lord, make me an instrument of your peace' was not written by Francis of Assisi (c.1181–1226) and is likely to date from as recently as the early twentieth century.

Sometimes a work is anonymous, or the author is named but there are minimal biographical details. Examples: the author of *The Cloud of Unknowing* is (appropriately) unknown; Julian of Norwich (c.1343–c.1416) is a shadowy figure, and it remains unclear whether Julian was her baptismal name or simply that of her local church.

Anonymous works can nevertheless have a strong 'authorial voice'; we feel we know the person behind the text even when we know next to nothing about them.

---

4 L. P. Hartley, 1953, *The Go-between*, London: Hamish Hamilton, p. 1.

The text bears witness to something: it is both reactive and purposeful

In chapter 4 of Acts, Peter and John are brought before the Sanhedrin and ordered not to speak about Jesus. They respond, 'Whether it is right in God's sight to listen to you rather than to God, you must judge; for we cannot keep from speaking about what we have seen and heard' (Acts 4.19–20). They simply feel compelled to bear witness no matter what the consequences. This compulsion to speak (or write) is a common human response to a significant experience or encounter, especially one that seems in some sense to reveal truth.[5] In this case there is much less interest in what the audience thinks than in simply 'getting it out there'.

But bearing witness can also be more purposeful and less reactive, concerned with the impact on the hearer or reader. Towards the end of John's Gospel, the writer, who describes himself as a 'witness' throughout, says, 'These are written so that you may come to believe that Jesus is the Messiah, the Son of God, and that through believing you may have life in his name' (John 20.31).

Christian spiritual texts are usually a combination of these two aspects of witness. They are a reaction to an experience (often profound and significant), indeed may even be a means of processing the experience – working it through on paper; *and* they are usually written with a purpose in mind – such as teaching, evangelism, or self-defence. Example: the

Think about how both aspects of bearing witness are manifest in the text.

Confessions of Augustine of Hippo (354–430) appears to be an account of his faith journey in which he works through his experiences, but it was also probably intended to encourage and instruct young converts to Christianity and may have been a form of self-defence against charges of heterodoxy.

The text has a language and a genre

Most classic texts of Christian spirituality were not written in English, so translation is an issue, especially for poetry. They are also naturally archaic versions of the language in question. Example: John of the Cross (1542–91) wrote his poem 'Dark night of the soul' in sixteenth-century Spanish, and each English translation (some of which are themselves quite old) has its own distinctive 'flavour'. Even relatively modern English has changed its meaning over time: 'suffer the little children' (Matthew 19.14, KJV) means 'allow them' not 'make them suffer'; 'indifferently administer justice' (Holy

---

5 M. Crossley, 2000, *Introducing Narrative Psychology: Self, trauma and the construction of meaning*, Buckingham: Open University Press.

Communion Service from the *Book of Common Prayer*) means 'be impartial' not 'be mediocre'.

In addition, spiritual writers may intentionally use a version of the language that was out of date even in their own time; this is because the presence of archaic turns of phrase can lend the text a sense of 'otherness' (hence the enthusiasm in many quarters for the language of the King James Bible). Example: the *Philokalia* is a collection of Greek spiritual texts dating from the fourth to the fifteenth centuries that was collected, edited and published in 1782. It was compiled

> Be aware of the original language and of whether there are other translations that present the text differently. Notice the genre and how this influences the writing.

at a time when Greek identity and heritage was in danger of being lost in the culture (and real) wars between the Venetian and Ottoman empires. It looks back to 'better times', aiming both to conserve ancient spiritual writings and to assert a distinctive Greek identity. To further this agenda the writings were not presented in the modern Greek of the day, but that of the patristic period, which actually pre-dated many of them.

It is also important to consider the genre of a text: is it a letter, a sermon, a poem, an instruction manual, a court document? The genre gives a clue as to whether the writer is employing metaphor, allegory and 'poetic licence' or speaking more literally. Example: some of the more famous sayings of Meister Eckhart (1260–1328) are taken from his self-defence to charges made against him by the Inquisition in Cologne, a more guarded genre than, say, a personal journal.

The text emerged in a context

The text was occasioned by something – an extraordinary event or a more apparently mundane experience that acted as a tipping point in a process that had been building for some time. What was it that made the author sit down and write (or stand up and dictate) the text at that particular moment? Perhaps she or he had a mystical experience and had to record its details before its impression faded; perhaps a religious superior ordered or a patron invited them to write; perhaps they came out of teaching a class of novices thinking, 'This won't do! I need to write an instruction manual.'

> Find out what was going on in the writer's life, community or society more widely at the time of writing.

Often we do not know the answer, but it is worth reflecting on the question, which is part of the broader issue of context. This context will have physical, social and political dimensions that may be highly relevant to the content of the text. The text may exemplify the prevailing culture, or protest against it, or simply draw images and concepts from it.

Examples: *The Cloud of Unknowing* is written in English rather than the conventional Latin, perhaps to subvert the perceived dogmatic authoritarianism of the Roman church of the time; Thomas Traherne (1636–74) wrote *The Kingdom of God* at the time of the Restoration of the monarchy to England after seven years of what had essentially been a republic, and questions of what constitutes proper kingly governance were on the minds of many.

The theological context should not be overlooked. All Christian spiritual writings have an implicit theology and are sometimes dominated by an important theological idea. To separate spirituality from the intellectual aspects of the Christian life is as mistaken as the splitting of spirituality and mission discussed in Chapter 1. Example: as the dogma of the Trinity, and in particular the nature of Christ, became crystallized in the church councils of the third and fourth centuries, the idea of the uniqueness of Christ, his ascended location and the ontological gulf between God and human beings was re-emphasized and consolidated. This theological context is expressed psychologically in the perception that, despite the incarnation, God is distant and inaccessible. Spiritual writings of this period, for example Gregory of Nyssa's *Life of Moses*, are concerned with finding a way back to the God who is 'other', often invoking images of ladders or bridges.

Another important aspect of context is the balance of power in the religious institutions of the day. It has often been observed that bearing witness to spiritual experiences can be a way of subverting the existing ecclesiastical hierarchy, bypassing its authority structures by claiming direct communication from God himself. This surely accounts for the fact that, while there are no women among the officially recognized teachers of theological dogma in the history of the Church before the twentieth century (and few then), they are much more visible in the history of Christian spiritual writings. Whether consciously or not, you choose the genre and rhetorical style that will give you a voice. Example: Hildegard of Bingen (1098–1179) executed substantial theology in the form of spiritual writing in her three volumes of *Visionary Theology*.

Sometimes this issue of who has authority to speak spills on to the text, as in the writings of María de Jesús de Ágreda (1602–65), who experienced visions of the Virgin Mary encouraging her not only to inhabit her role as Abbess of her convent with confidence, but also to set out the insights gained through these visions in a book. Maria writes, 'I alone am given understanding of things, and I must create for myself the words to explain what I understand,'[6] an astonishing claim in the context of the patriarchal authoritarianism of seventeenth-century Spanish Catholicism.

---

6 Ágreda, *Mística cuidad de Dios*, Libro I, 28 translated by H. Bowman.

The text means something

'Come, we shall have some fun now!' thought Alice. 'I'm glad they've begun asking riddles. – I believe I can guess that,' she added aloud. 'Do you mean that you think you can find out the answer to it?' said the March Hare.

'Exactly so,' said Alice.

'Then you should say what you mean,' the March Hare went on.

'I do,' Alice hastily replied; 'at least – at least I mean what I say – that's the same thing, you know.'

'Not the same thing a bit!' said the Hatter. 'Why, you might just as well say that "I see what I eat" is the same thing as "I eat what I see"!'[7]

It is obvious that the text *has* a meaning; people generally do not waste time on meaningless words. But, as this extract from *Alice in Wonderland* shows, it can be much less obvious *what* that meaning is. 'I believe I can guess' *could* mean 'I think I can find the answer'; but it could equally mean, 'I have faith in my capacity to speculate.' Furthermore, does the meaning reside in the words, or the mind of the speaker or hearer, or in some meeting point between them all?

Much ink has been spilt by philosophers and literary theorists on these questions,[8] but for our purposes it is helpful to identify three main sorts of meaning, which I shall refer to as the 'propositional meaning', the 'implicational meaning' and the 'emergent meaning'. These terms have their origins in cognitive psychology, a discipline less concerned with constructing abstract theories of reading, and more concerned with the ways real people actually engage with texts.[9]

> Be attentive to different sorts of meanings and the different ways of decoding them.

1. *Propositional meaning* is what the text says on the surface (its plain meaning) plus references and allusions that would have been obvious to its intended audience. Understanding the propositional meaning begins with knowing the range of possible meanings of the words and idiomatic phrases used in that language and culture. In nineteenth-century Britain, 'I believe I can guess' could mean a number of things but there are limits; it can't mean, 'I am taking a plane to Miami next week.'

---

7 L. Carroll, 1865, *Alice's Adventures in Wonderland*, London: Macmillan, pp. 97–8.

8 For a further exploration see A. Thistleton, 2009, *Hermeneutics: An introduction*, Grand Rapids, MI: Eerdmans.

9 For a fuller discussion see J. Collicutt, 2012, 'Bringing the academic discipline of psychology to bear on the study of the Bible', *Journal of Theological Studies*, 63, pp. 1–48; for a worked example of emergent meaning see M. Croasmun, 2017, *The Emergence of Sin: The cosmic tyrant in Romans*, New York: Oxford University Press.

The next thing to consider is the immediate context; the March Hare (who is very pernickety about plain meaning) is able to infer the meaning of Alice's words because he knows she has just been asked a riddle and is intent on bringing logic to bear on it. We can also take a broader perspective; if we are familiar with the writer's general world view and the wider cultural context then we will be alert to what is implied, what is alluded to, and what is intimated by *not* saying something. Thus, because it is well known that 'Lewis Carroll' (Charles Dodgson) was an academic mathematician who specialized in logic, it becomes clear that this passage is playing with, even parodying, the logical syllogisms studied in introductory university courses at the time.

It can be seen that working out the propositional meaning(s) of a text involves conscious reflection and rational problem-solving skills.

2. *Implicational meaning* refers to the non-verbal aspects of the text. In direct speech this would involve tone of voice and additional gestures. Written texts convey this in different ways including the rhythm of the phrases, the colouring of the words and the pattern of the argument. Some of this can easily get 'lost in translation' but the mark of a good translation is the degree to which it preserves at least some of these features of the original text (consider how well different translations of Psalm 23.4 'do the job'). Implicational meaning is primarily about feelings and social relationships – precisely the stuff that can be difficult to express in straight propositions, and also the stuff of spirituality. This is often best communicated through metaphor and symbol; thus, poetry is strong on implicational meaning and weaker on propositional meaning.

The passage from *Alice in Wonderland* does not use explicit verbal references to the character of the March Hare (though knowledge of the springtime behaviour of hares and the title of the chapter from which the passage is taken strongly indicate that he is 'mad'). Instead, in a few short lines, we are able to comprehend its implicational meaning: the hare is a pedant, a rather rude and abrupt one at that, and we are left with a feeling of confusion and disorientation, as if we are being played with. We might well conclude that this is how Alice feels, though again we are not explicitly told this.

By its nature implicational meaning is more subjective and ambiguous than propositional meaning, intuited rather than deduced; but it nevertheless requires careful attention. Example: the negative and paradoxical language used by writers such as Pseudo-Dionysius may be 'a strategy to destabilise ordinary modes of thought' and thus opening up a 'new mode of consciousness'.[10]

3. *Emergent meaning* refers to the deeply intriguing observation that some events, concepts, or images seem to mean more than the writer or original

---

10 L. Nelstrop, 2009, *Christian Mysticism: An introduction to contemporary theoretical approaches*, Farnham: Ashgate, p. 65.

readers thought they meant, something that has been described as 'carrying surplus meaning'.[11] Here meaning is 'not conceived as something static or fixed but rather as an ongoing process, "unfolding like a plant out of a seed"'.[12] This is at the heart of typological understandings of the Bible that hold that, while all events before Christ are what they are, some also point forward to him. Thus the 'suffering servant passages' of Isaiah 40—55 are about an unnamed individual or community living at the time of the return from the Babylonian exile; but as time passes – and note again the significance of time – further layers of meaning emerge, the ultimate meaning being Jesus.

The original meaning remains true, but more is revealed. While the emergent meaning is more expansive than the original meaning, it is always faithful to it, as the plant is to its seed. This understanding of meaning is not only rich; for the Christian it affirms the continuity and coherence of divine revelation across time in the story of God's people and its endpoint in Christ. Example: John of the Cross relies heavily on the Song of Songs in his writings, but he doesn't seem to see it as simply a vivid extended metaphor for the love between the believer and Christ (an allegory); instead, he treats the story of a historical human being (traditionally understood to be Solomon) as something like an embryo, and in crafting his own version, carefully reveals the fuller Christological meaning that had always been there.

The concept of emergent meaning alerts us to the fact that it is not enough to ask what a writer meant to say (important as this question is). They may have been saying more than they realized; if Solomon did indeed write Song of Songs, it is pretty certain that Jesus was not on his mind at the time, but it could still be 'about' Jesus.

There are several ways of making sense of this rather strange phenomenon of the text meaning more than the writer meant. The first relates to our common human psychology referred to in Chapter 1 (what is 'in our heads'): perhaps the writer is unknowingly tapping into one or more of the archetypes that, according to C. G. Jung,[13] populate the human collective unconscious and hold surplus meaning. Another possibility relates to the nature of reality also asserted in Chapter 1 (what is 'out there'): perhaps the intended meaning is like the tip of an iceberg, made up of networks of further meanings, not accessible to the original writer but gradually becoming visible to later readers who know more about the world. Finally, from a theological perspective, we might say that emergent meaning can be a mark of the Holy

---

11 T. Fabiny, 1992, *Figura and Fulfillment: Typology in the Bible, art, and literature*, Eugene, OR: Wipf & Stock, p. 23.

12 Fabiny, *Figura and Fulfillment*, p. 31, quoting Northrop Frye.

13 The analytic psychologist Carl Gustav Jung proposed that all human beings have both a 'personal unconscious' that is unique to each individual and a 'collective unconscious' that is the same for all. This collective unconscious is structured around certain themes or tropes that he termed 'archetypes'. For example, the 'tree of life' motif may be such an archetype. These archetypes are common to all human beings, but they are expressed in different ways in different cultures. For a helpful account see M. Palmer, 1997, *Freud and Jung on Religion*, London: Routledge, chapter 8.

Spirit at work, growing the mustard seed into a tree and 'guid[ing] you into all the truth' (John 16.13).

Emergent meaning stands at the threshold between understanding a text and interpreting it because it refers both to where the writer is coming from and the often-unanticipated afterlife of their writings in the hands and minds of others. This raises the thorny issue of how one decides whether that afterlife is legitimate. Example: the political agendas of the compilers of the *Philokalia* (p. 115), were clearly not in the minds of the original writers centuries earlier. Furthermore, while that first 1782 translation made the texts inaccessible to people outside of an inner circle of scholars, extracts were rapidly translated into other languages and it has become hugely popular in generic spiritual movements of many faith traditions and none. This would no doubt have greatly troubled those eighteenth-century compilers, if not the earlier writers on whom they drew. Do these afterlives represent the emergence of the full meaning(s) of the *Philokalia* texts or their misunderstanding and misappropriation?

This chapter has set out some ways to guard against misunderstanding the nature of a text and to receive it as faithfully as we can. In the last example the focus began to shift to the next task, which is to work out what *the text might be saying to us here and now*, doing something with it and becoming part of its afterlife while trying as best we can not to misappropriate it. This is a move from empathetic listening to more active conversation. The contours of this conversation are the subject of the next chapter.

3

Approaching the Text II:
Interpreting its Significance

One of the risks of coming to a better understanding of the nature of a text, including where the author is coming from, is that we may conclude that it is not for us. This is especially true if we find that the original context is very specific (for example, a monastic community) or if the intended audience is quite different from ourselves. The words of the author of the *Cloud of Unknowing* might deter many:

> I do not desire that this book be seen by worldly chatterers, public self-praisers or fault-finders, newsmongers, gossips or scandal-mongers, or detractors of any kind, for it was never my intention to write of such matters for them. And so I do not wish them, or anyone driven by mere curiosity, whether educated or uneducated, to concern themselves with it.[1]

Addressing this issue, Edward Howells observes that present-day readers may be put off classic spiritual texts simply because they are not members of a religious order, have only limited time to devote to prayer and cannot honestly describe themselves as free of the usual human vices.[2] But he then counters this by demonstrating the way that these texts nevertheless draw or even 'hook' such readers in, so that already 'I am to some extent "inside the text", even if I doubt that I am among the stated audience.'[3] The reach of these texts is often greater than it first appears.

One helpful way of looking at this is through the story of Mary of Bethany in chapter 10 of Luke's Gospel. Jesus is visiting the home of Martha and her siblings; he is engaged in some sort of discourse and the most likely scenario is that he is reclining at table with a group of male companions. In such settings the participants would be in a circle facing each other, with their feet facing outwards (hence the ease in which an uninvited guest could approach and wash Jesus' feet in an earlier episode in the same Gospel). This would be a closed circle, with those serving moving about the periphery. So, Mary, who is described as 'sat at the Lord's feet' (v.39), is unlikely to have been addressed face to face but is instead eavesdropping on teaching directed at

---

1 *The Cloud of Unknowing*, Prologue, tr. A. C. Spearing.
2 E. Howells, 2014, 'Personal experience and critical distance in the interpretation of spiritual texts', *The Way*, 53, pp. 7–16.
3 Howells, 'Personal experience', p. 12.

others. Yet crucially Jesus praises her for allowing herself to be hooked in by his words.

As present-day readers we may stand outside the original circle of the conversation, and it is good to recognize this; but we can still legitimately engage in spiritual eavesdropping and continue the conversation ourselves.

To be continued ...

At the end of Chapter 1, I presented the idea that reality is coherent, made by the God whose creative act is one of careful ordering (Genesis 1; Isaiah 45.18–19; 1 Corinthians 14.33). The seven-day narrative of Genesis 1 makes it clear that this ordering is not confined to space and matter but also extends to time. In creation God doesn't just set in motion a train of disconnected events; he begins a story. This story has the Christ event at its centre, but it then continues and we are graciously invited to become part of it.

> The writer and reader are part of the same story.

One of the ways in which we draw closer to God is to bring our story into conversation with his. Some Christians talk enthusiastically of being part of 'God's plan', and there is something in this; but the phrase does have rather passive and instrumental connotations, as if God is simply using us. The idea that 'our story becomes God's story' does better justice to the collaborative way that the Spirit works with us (Romans 8.16),[4] and the richness of our relationship with God that involves rest and play as well as work.[5]

The storied nature of the Christian life is mirrored in the narrative form of the Gospels. Each Gospel offers a way for the reader to make its story their own and then to continue it. (Their engagement with the 'dialectic of the present and the absent Jesus' discussed in Chapter 1 is part of this bigger agenda.) Mark presents itself as the *beginning* of the good news and leaves the ending open for the reader to make something of it; Luke tells the story of the Emmaus road, leaving the identity of one of the disciples unknown, inviting the reader to step into that place and continue the journey; in John's Gospel, Jesus looks beyond his immediate audience and says, 'Have you believed because you have seen me? Blessed are those who have not seen and yet have come to believe' (John 20.29). Of all the Gospels, Matthew makes the most of the order and continuity of God's story, repeatedly speaking of Jesus as the fulfilment of signs and prophecies from the history of God's people (Matthew 5.17). This 'fulfilment' is not simply about predictions 'coming true' but of

---

4 Psychological research (e.g. Pargament et al., 1998) also indicates that approaching God with a collaborative rather than passive attitude is associated with higher levels of well-being.

5 J. Collicutt, 2015, *The Psychology of Christian Character Formation*, London: SCM Press, p. 107.

shadows and sketches being *filled* out or up.[6] The 'great commission' of Matthew 28 is an instruction to continue this story to its ultimate fulfilment.

If we understand that we are part of a bigger story that is coherent and continuous we can approach historically and culturally distant texts with more confidence. They may be located in a different part of the story from ours, but it is one story – the story of the church; and we are tasked with continuing it, not reinventing it.

The search for significance

In their powerful book *Mighty Stories, Dangerous Rituals*, Herbert Anderson and Edward Foley argue that 'ordinary people yearn for a union between God's story and their story'.[7] We might think of this yearning as one way that the Image of God makes itself felt in the lives of human beings.

Paul, addressing the Athenians in Acts chapter 17, talks about the human search for God that has been planted in our nature. We are helped in this search by what some have called 'signals of transcendence'.[8] For Paul, these consist of the majesty and providence of nature (Acts 14.17; Romans 1.19–20) together with the impulse to be *deisidaimōn* (v.22), a word that is usually translated 'religious' but corresponds quite well to what we today would call 'spiritual'. In this speech Paul presents human spirituality as a kind of untutored instinct – a groping for God who is close at hand waiting to be found (Acts 17. 27). Augustine of Hippo takes up this theme, infusing it with a more interpersonal tone in his famous lines 'You have made us for yourself, and our heart is restless, until it rests in you.'[9]

Psychologists who study religion and spirituality have seen this search as part of a wider seeking after meaning in life, and it is interesting that Paul's speech about the search for God is in response to the Athenians' stated desire 'to know what it *means*' (v. 20). Research indicates that this seeking after meaning is made up of two strands: global comprehensibility – finding a metaphysical system or metanarrative with which to make sense of life as a whole; and personal significance – understanding what this particular situation means for me here and now.[10] The mention of particular situations draws to our attention the fact that the search is not a constant part of our

---

6 John also makes much of fulfilment and offers a vivid depiction of 'filling up' in the water jars in the wedding at Cana in John 2. See also T. Fabiny, 1992, *Figura and Fulfillment: Typology in the Bible, art, and literature*, Eugene, OR: Wipf & Stock, pp. 20–22.

7 H. Anderson and E. Foley, 2019, *Mighty Stories, Dangerous Rituals*, Minneapolis, MN: Fortress Press, p. 41.

8 P. Berger, 1969, *A Rumor of Angels: Modern society and the rediscovery of the supernatural*, New York: Doubleday.

9 Augustine, *Confessions*, I. i (1), tr. H. Chadwick.

10 C. Park, 2010, 'Making sense of the meaning-making literature', *Psychological Bulletin*, 136, pp. 257–301.

mental life but comes to the fore in specific circumstances, particularly points of crisis, positive or negative: a new baby, a major bereavement, diagnosis with a serious illness, the beginning or ending of a romantic relationship, the loss of a job. This is captured beautifully in the story of the prodigal son, whose spiritual sense is (re)awakened at the point when he has lost everything (Luke 15.16–18).

Such situations lead us to question our existing assumptions, often in consultation with others (in real life or virtually through reading or the internet), and to reorder our world. Sometimes this reordering takes us back to where we were before and restores our equilibrium; sometimes we find that our world has been reordered in a new way. These two pathways have been described respectively as 'conservation of significance' and 'transformation of significance'.[11] The re-ordering involves re-thinking, but many other processes will also be at work; we go about it

> ... by sticking close to someone who seems to hold meaning and will just be there while we journey into challenging thought-places. Another way is through story; we might think of living the Christian life as a process in which God's story and our story come together. A third way is through creativity – artistry and craft. Here we work out meaning through action and we may use symbols.[12]

This understanding of human spirituality has a number of implications. First it takes us back to the issue touched on in Chapter 1 that mission and spirituality are closely linked. People draw near[13] to God at crisis points in their lives, and it is at these points that they are most likely to connect with the message of the gospel. Second, it draws our attention to the fact that many of the classic texts of Christian spirituality were written at times of crisis or in the context of trauma; they are part of the writer's personal meaning-making and were often written to help others find significance in the face of adversity and deprivation. Finally, the fact that the

> Interpreting a text involves asking how it speaks into the search for personal significance.

most profound ways of finding significance are not through propositional thinking but through relationship, story, the creation and curating of beauty, and a deeper connection with nature goes some way to explaining the power of classic spiritual texts which so often exhibit these very qualities.

---

11 K. Pargament, 2001, *The Psychology of Religion and Coping: Theory, research, practice,* New York: Guilford, pp. 106–10; E. Howells and P. Tyler, 2010, *Sources of Transformation: Revitalising Christian spirituality,* London: Continuum.

12 J. Collicutt, L. Moore, M. Payne and V. Slater, 2019, *Seriously Messy: Making spaces for families to talk together about death and life,* Oxford: Bible Reading Fellowship, p. 40.

13 'Now the tax collectors and sinners were all *drawing near* [*engizō*] to hear him' (Luke 15.1, RSV).

How the text achieves its impact

The kind of academic reading of a text that tells us everything about its origins and components, without supporting a personal engagement in which we can discover and savour the *meaning in relation to our own experience*, is unsatisfying.[14]

The degree to which a spiritual text will speak personally to a reader or reading community is related to its capacity to connect with their situated search for significance. This can happen in several possible ways, five of the most important of which are outlined below.

Spiritual texts often act on our emotions and bodily senses, connect with our situation, emphasize a personal encounter with God, wow us with their beauty and take us to a different thought-world.

1. *The text may engage emotion* through aspects of its implicational meaning (p. 18). The processing of implicational meaning appears to involve different brain pathways from those processing propositional meaning; in particular information from the autonomic nervous system (the guts) plays its part, giving the attained knowledge a physical and emotional tone. This is the stuff of heart-felt conviction or stomach-sinking doubt. Engagement with implicational meaning is thus highly embodied.[15]

Embodied knowing is not just about psychology and biology; it is theologically important because it connects with our understanding of the Christ event as 'incarnation'. The fact that the Word became flesh, lived a bodily life and had a resurrection body tells us that the human body is of vital significance in God's story; it is not an incidental detail to be discarded at the end of all things, but a key aspect of life with God now and in the future. So we would expect spiritual texts both to connect with the bodies of their readers and to offer a deeper appreciation of the incarnation. In precisely this way, Howells claims that the achievement of Bernard of Clairvaux's *Sermon on the Song of Songs* 'is to situate the incarnation in our own experience'.[16]

2. *The text may seem to speak into the reader's situation.* This, of course, is part of the way so many biblical texts achieve their impact: who has not at one time or another walked 'through the valley of the shadow of death' (Psalm 23.4, see p. 18), or looked up at the night sky and felt small (Psalm 8.3–4), or got themselves into a mess with no clear way out (Luke 15.16; 16.3)? This is even there in the extract from *Alice in Wonderland* quoted in Chapter 2: who has not

---

14 Howells, 'Personal experience', p. 8. My italics.

15 For a full discussion see F. Watts, 2021, *A Plea for Embodied Spirituality: The role of the body in religion*, London: SCM Press, p. 92.

16 Howells, 'Personal experience', p. 14.

at one time or another been subjected to the barbs of a supercilious pedant? Furthermore, the suggestion in *Alice* that pedantry can be a form of 'madness' offers a new way of viewing such experiences, and with it the possibility of healing. So the text can go beyond affirming the reader through an apparent connection with their situation to having an impact on that situation by reframing it.

3. *The text may include 'I and Thou' language*,[17] drawing the reader into – as it were – an intimate conversation with God. As a very new Christian aged about 14, I came across a book in my parents' bedroom entitled *The Imitation of Christ*. As my father was an atheist, I assumed that the book was an atheist apologetic and that the title referred to Christ as some sort of counterfeit – only an 'imitation' of the ultimate good. Imagine my surprise on opening it and finding extended conversations between the fifteenth-century monk, Thomas Kempis, and Christ himself! These had a profound effect on me. Astonishingly, Christ's way of speaking to Thomas in his cell felt very like the way I had experienced him when praying in my own teenage bedroom, surrounded by pop star fan magazines and the latest affordable beauty products. The book gave me the confidence to continue to talk to Christ in this intimate way – and to expect an answer!

4. *The text may be beautiful*. The human response to beauty is poorly understood and has been the subject of much debate. Recently philosophers and neuroscientists have rediscovered and developed the idea that this response is not just a pleasurable sensory or emotional experience, but a means by which substantive knowledge is gained and significance discovered.[18]

Beauty itself is a very elusive quality – it seems to slip through our fingers as soon as we try to define it. The Bible says little about beauty as we would understand it; instead it uses related concepts such as integrity, fittingness, splendour and pleasantness. In a BBC documentary broadcast in 2009 the art critic Matthew Collings identified ten aspects of beauty.[19] Notable among these were a collection of qualities that relate to order, unity and coherent organization through patterns. These qualities seem to be fundamental to the biblical concepts of integrity and fittingness. So, part of the perceived beauty of some classic spiritual texts (or the illuminated manuscripts we associate with them) may relate to the way they communicate a sense of coherence,[20]

---

17 See p. 4.

18 See, for example, B. Gaut, 2003, 'Art and knowledge' in J. Levinson (ed.), *The Oxford Handbook of Aesthetics*, Oxford: Oxford University Press, pp. 436–50; S. Zeki, 2011, *Splendors and Miseries of the Brain: Love, creativity, and the quest for human happiness*, Oxford: Wiley-Blackwell; A. O'Hear, 2011, 'Ruskin and the distinction between aesthesis and theoria', *The Fortnightly Review*, https://fortnightlyreview.co.uk/2011/04/ruskin-crown/, accessed 29.07.21.

19 M. Collings, 2012, *What is Beauty?* BBC/Simply media (DVD).

20 A. Antonovsky, 1993, 'The structure and properties of the Sense of Coherence Scale', *Social Science & Medicine*, 36, pp. 725–33.

both in the outer world itself and between that world and the human beings who inhabit it.

Jesus uses the word *kalos* (sometimes translated 'beautiful') to describe the actions of the woman who anoints his head at the beginning of his passion (Matthew 26.10 and Mark 14.6 RSV). He is saying that the woman's deed befits his kingly status and his imminent death, and thus demonstrates her deep understanding of both. Here insight, embodiment and fittingness come together in an act of careful ordering that reflects God's creative nature.

In a Christmas newspaper piece Sam Wells similarly brings together the incarnation, embodied action and beauty: 'Christmas is about being material- istic. About seeing each other's flesh and blood – humanity, fear, anger, exasperation. And letting the light of hope, generosity and courage shine through, in acts of goodness, truth and beauty.'[21]

Yet beauty can also stop us in our tracks, suppressing all action and causing us to gaze or listen with awe and wonder. Collings acknowledged this in his analysis, talking of the way that beauty can open the door to transcendence by showing us that there is far more to reality than we had previously seen, transfiguring the ordinary so that it becomes extraordinary. Which brings us to the next point.

5. The text may enable self-transcendence, offering a different mode with which to engage in the search for significance. This has already been touched on in the previous chapters: the beauty, strangeness or sheer otherness of some classic spiritual texts can shift the reader out of the ordinary ways of being in the world, including ordinary forms of thinking. These qualities can allow us to step aside from the chatter in our heads or the immediate demands of our emotions into a more contemplative or mindful state of consciousness. Commenting on the aesthetic dimension, Thomas Merton writes:

> Art enables us to find ourselves and lose ourselves at the same time. The mind that responds to the intellectual and spiritual values that lie hidden in a poem, a painting, or a piece of music, discovers a spiritual vitality that lifts it above itself, takes it out of itself, and makes it present to itself on a level of being that it did not know it could ever achieve.[22]

The radically different way of being in the world opened up by such states of consciousness offers a new field in which and a new means by which to search for significance.[23] Nevertheless, in contemplation we do not leave the body or even the mind, but we stand in a new relationship with the ego; we are for a while free of its constraints, subjecting ourselves to reality rather than attempting to understand it, master it, or bend it to our agenda. The

---

21 *Evening Standard*, 21.12.17.

22 T. Merton, 1955, *No Man is an Island*, London: Burns & Oates, p. 35.

23 Howells, 'Personal experience', p. 13.

highly psychological nature of this move from discursive ego-driven thinking, through reflection and wonder to pure contemplation and back again is
vividly described by Augustine of Hippo in his *Confessions*:

> Our minds were lifted up by an ardent affection towards eternal being
> itself. Step by step we climbed beyond all corporeal objects and the heaven
> itself … we ascended even further by internal reflection and dialogue and
> wonder at your works, and we entered into our own minds. We moved
> beyond them so as to attain to the region of inexhaustible abundance where
> you feed Israel eternally with truth for food … we touched it in some small
> degree by a moment of total concentration of the heart … we returned to
> the noise of human speech where a sentence has both a beginning and an
> ending.[24]

Reading with awareness and discipline

As the extract from Augustine illustrates, classic Christian spiritual texts can
be very powerful. The previous section outlined the main ways in which
this power is exercised, drawing to our attention the way that our emotions,
bodies, life story or situation, interpersonal yearnings, aesthetic sensibilities
and desire for transcendence may be engaged as we read them. We should
welcome all of this but also be prepared to interrogate it critically as we try
and interpret what the text has to say for me/us. Are we connecting with
the text and its writer or projecting our stuff on to it? Are we taking a 'pick
and mix' approach, concentrating on the bits that attract us and defending
against the more challenging aspects? Are we accepting its content uncritic-
ally because the form of communication is so compelling? Are we glorying
in something radical and cutting-edge or being misled by absurd ravings?
In the history of the church spiritual writings have often been controversial
precisely because of their tendency to stretch the boundaries of orthodoxy;
this is part of their power, but it is good to be aware that the stretch may
sometimes be too far.

One way of avoiding potential interpretative pitfalls, already noted in
Chapter 2, is to ask how a text accords with the first witnesses to the Christ
event recorded in the New Testament; to try and detect biblical influences
on the text or explore the way that it does or doesn't stand in some sort of
continuity with the biblical writers. The conversation with the text then

> Christians are obliged to
> read spiritual texts in the
> light of the New Testament.

becomes three-way and the interpretation has some external accountability.
For example, the extract from Augustine above has very strong resonances

---

24 *Confessions*, IX. x (24), tr. H. Chadwick.

with Paul's account of his heavenly ascent in 2 Corinthians 12; it might be fruitful to examine points of similarity and difference between the two.

Another possible conversation partner is life in the world outside church. An interpretation that speaks only to Christians – 'At last I know what perichoresis means!' – is limited in its missional value. Also, if the text is a window into a greater coherent reality one would expect to find some echoes in the wider world. The most likely conversation partners would be the creative arts; over the years my students have detected and explored meaningful connections between classic Christian spiritual writers and the work of creative artists as diverse as Stormzy, John Tavener, Leonard Cohen, Maya Angelou, Max Richter, Ennio Morricone; Jacob Epstein, Anthony Gormley, Caroline MacKenzie; Jackson Pollak, William Utermohlen, Peter Monamy, Michael Radcliffe; U. A. Fanthorpe, William Morris, Michael Morpurgo and J. B. Priestley.

Less obviously, science can also be a fruitful conversation partner. As will be evident, I find many points of connection between these texts and the science of psychology. More specifically, as explained in Chapter 1, I believe that the psychology of separation and bereavement may be particularly relevant because Christian spirituality is about waiting well for the return of the Christ for whom we yearn. The readings in Part II are therefore organized into a series of chapters, each of which deals with a different theme related to waiting well in the context of loss. Each chapter opens with a number of quotations from the Bible. The order of the chapters broadly reflects the time-course of grief from the acute phase, through periods of struggle, to a place of relative peace; but of course, the trajectory of every bereavement is different and the human response rarely proceeds in a linear manner, so this ordering of chapters is in no sense prescriptive and they can each be read as addressing stand-alone themes.

These themes form the warp through which the weft of key interpretative questions can be woven. The issues addressed by these questions have been the subject of the last two chapters, flagged in the text boxes as they went along. The questions are summarized overleaf. For each reading, answers to the factual questions are provided; the more open and personal questions are then presented as prompts.

Questions

- Who is the author?

- When was it written?

- What was the original language and which translation is this?

- What was the social, political and personal context?

- How does reading the text make me feel?

- What do I understand the meaning to be? Could I paraphrase it in a couple of sentences?

- Having done this, are there things that I can't make sense of?

- Does the text connect with aspects of my own situation?

- What is the writer trying to achieve?

- What features of the text make it impact on me as a reader?

- Has reading the text enriched and or challenged my theology?

- Can I find connections – resonances with or influences from – the Bible?

- Are there any possible dangers in the line of thinking and/or practice that is being explored?

- Is there a work of secular art (classic or popular) that expresses similar or related ideas? Or helps me to continue the conversation with the text in a way that may draw others in?

Part II

Therefore, since we are surrounded by so great a cloud
of witnesses … let us run with perseverance the race that is set
before us, looking to Jesus the pioneer and perfecter of our faith,
who for the sake of the joy that was set before him endured
the cross, disregarding its shame, and has taken his seat at the
right hand of the throne of God.
(Hebrews 12.1–2)

4

Lamenting

Jesus began to weep.
(John 11.35)

'A little while, and you will no longer see me, and again a little while, and you will see me. … Very truly, I tell you, you will weep and mourn.'
(John 16.16, 20a)

A great number of the people followed him, and among them were women who were beating their breasts and wailing for him.
(Luke 23.27)

… God anointed Jesus of Nazareth with the Holy Spirit and with power; how he went about doing good and healing all who were oppressed by the devil, for God was with him. We are witnesses to all that he did both in Judea and in Jerusalem. They put him to death by hanging him on a tree…
(Acts 10.38–39)

Thomas, who was called the Twin, said to his fellow disciples, 'Let us also go, that we may die with him.'
(John 11.16)

For to me, living is Christ and dying is gain. If I am to live in the flesh, that means fruitful labour for me; and I do not know which I prefer. I am hard pressed between the two: my desire is to depart and be with Christ, for that is far better…
(Philippians 1.21–23)

The word 'lament' is most simply defined as 'to express or feel sorrow for',[1] but lamenting is both broader in scope and deeper in intensity than this. It is perhaps the most obvious response to loss, expressing not only consternation at what/who has been lost, but also a desire for things to be made right. Its origins lie in the cries of our earliest years, the immediate primal reaction to events beyond our control. Yet it can also be an intentional means of exerting some control, or at least re-establishing a sense of equilibrium in the midst of disorientation and disaster, a formal ritual of mourning.

---

1 Oxford English Dictionary.

There are several aspects to lament. It is a means of venting emotion, a cathartic unlocking of repressed feelings. It involves protest, either at the facts with which we are confronted or at the kind of world order in which such things happen; the words 'Oh no!' are one of the commonest responses to witnessing or first hearing of the death of a loved one, carrying within them the seeds of lament. It can thus be a form of self-assertion, of refusing to be silenced, and thus an expression of power.

Lament is also increasingly being seen as a way of making meaning,[2] offering a framework within which to process significant existential issues by posing 'Why?' questions. It can involve high degrees of creativity, especially where it becomes a more formalized genre within a tradition. It is also intimately associated with narrative, the weaving of events into a story, bearing witness and speaking truth.[3] Often those lamenting are drawn into the story, asking themselves whether they could or should have acted differently, expressing contrition or remorse for the part they may have played.

While lament begins as a response to an acute recent loss, it can come to be repeated regularly in order to ensure that the deceased, and especially the circumstances of their death, are not forgotten (as in Holocaust memorial ceremonies). Pathos, in word, gesture or music, is often invoked to refresh the emotional intensity and lessen the risk of simply 'going through the motions'.

Traditionally lament has been seen as the work of women and eulogizing as the work of men, illustrated in the quotations from Luke 23 and Acts 10 at the beginning of the chapter. But Peter's eulogy in Acts 10 is primarily an act of witness, and the Greek word for witness, *martureō*, is the origin of our English word 'martyr' (as Peter would eventually become).

There is an aspect of lament, not often talked about in Western society, which involves the urge to throw oneself into the grave or on to the funeral pyre of one's loved one. It's a form of intense identification with, commitment to, and attachment to the deceased, an acknowledgement that life has no meaning without them and a desire to be reunited in some better place. We may find this troubling, but there is a tacit acknowledgement of the phenomenon in the remark sometimes made after the death of one partner in a life-long devoted pairing, 'He won't be long after her.'

This chapter is therefore divided into two sections. The first contains spiritual texts of lament that bear witness to the death of Christ in words; the second contains texts that are more culturally dissonant to us, texts that present bearing witness through martyrdom as a desirable – even essential – aspect of Christian discipleship.

---

2 M. E. Lewis Hall, L. Shannonhouse, J. Aten, J. McMartin and E. Silverman, 2018, 'Religion-specific resources for meaning-making from suffering: Defining the territory', *Mental Health, Religion & Culture*, 21, pp. 77–92.

3 R. N. Nakashima Brock and R. A. Parker, 2008, *Saving Paradise: How Christianity traded love of this world for crucifixion and empire*, Boston, MA: Beacon Press, p. 51.

4.1 Bearing witness in words

To Mary and her Son
Blathmac, Son of Cú Brettan (eighth century)

Author Blathmac appears to have been a priest of noble family. His precise dates are unknown but he is thought to have been active in the middle of the eighth century.

Language Early Old Irish. The poem is part of a collection of seventeenth-century manuscripts in the National Library in Dublin studied and translated for the first time in 1964 by James Carney.

Date Eighth century.

Genre and context This poem is a form of keening. Keening involved the public performance of a specially composed poem or song over the deceased. This Irish tradition is very early and may even be pre-Christian, and it is associated with women. However, there is evidence that it was strictly regulated by the Irish church from as early as the sixth century, with greater tolerance being shown for male bards keening over deceased males of high social status. It has elements of both eulogy and lament. It would usually include praise for the dead man's beauty, virtues and fine ancestry, and the cursing of his enemies and their weapons. Blathmac's lament is not one of self-examination and remorse but simply the expression of deep dismay at the loss of the beautiful beloved from this world, a desire to honour him and, as the poem progresses, a longing to come close to him through his mother.

To Mary and her son

Come to me, loving Mary,
that I may keen with you your very dear one;
Alas! The going to the cross of your son,
that great jewel, that beautiful champion.

That with you I may beat my two hands
for your fair son's captivity.
Your womb has conceived Jesus –
it has not marred your virginity.

You have conceived him and no sin with man,
you brought him forth without ailing wound;
without grief he strengthened you (fair grace!)
at the time of his crucifixion.

I ask: Have you heard of a son like this,
one who could do these three things?
Such has not come upon the thighs of women
and such will not be born.

The first-begotten of God, the Father, in heaven
is your son, Mary, virgin;
he was begotten in a pure conception
through the power of the septiform Spirit.

No father has found, Mary,
the like of your renowned son;
better he than prophet, wiser than druid,
a king who was bishop and full sage.

His form was finer than that of other beings,
his stout vigour greater than any craftsman's,
wiser he than any breast under heaven,
juster than any judge.

More beautiful, more, pleasant, bigger than other boys
since he was in his swaddling clothes;
it was known what would come of him,
a being for the saving of multitudes.

Noble the being born from you!
You were granted, Mary, a great gift:
Christ, son of the Father in heaven,
him have you borne in Bethlehem.

May I have from you my three petitions,
beautiful Mary, little white-necked one;
get them, sun amongst women,
from your son who has them in his power.

That I may be in the world till old
serving the Lord who rules starry heaven,
and that then there be a welcome for me
into the eternal, ever-enduring kingdom.

That everyone who uses this as a vigil prayer
at lying down and at rising,
that it may protect him from blemish in the other world
like breastplate and helmet.

Everyone of any sort shall recite it
fasting on Friday night,
provided only that it be with full-flowing tears,
Mary, may he not be for hell.

When your son comes in anger
with his cross on his reddened back,
that then you will save
any friend who shall have keened him.

For you, beautiful Mary,
I shall go as guarantor:
anyone who says the full keen,
he shall have his reward.

I call you with true words,
Mary, beautiful queen,
that we may have talk together
to pity your heart's darling.

So that I may keen the bright Christ
with you in the most heartfelt way,
shining precious jewel,
mother of the great Lord.

Were I rich and honoured
ruling the people of the world to every sea,
they would all come with you and me
to keen your royal son.

There would be beating of hands
by women, children and men,
that they might keen on every hill-top
the king who made every star.

I cannot do this. With heartfelt feeling
I will bewail your son with you
if only you come at some time
on a visit to me.

Come to me, loving Mary,
you, head of unsullied faith,
that we may have talk together
with the compassion of unblemished heart.

Prayer to Christ and *Meditation on Human Redemption* (extracts)
Anselm of Canterbury (c.1033–1109)

Author Anselm of Canterbury is also known as Anselm of Aosta, his birth-place in northern Italy. At the age of 25 he entered the Benedictine monastery of Bec in Normandy and was elected abbot in 1078. England had come under Norman rule in 1066, and in 1093 Anselm was appointed Archbishop of Canterbury. He became caught up in disputes about the relationship between the church and state (under William Rufus and then Henry I), facing strong opposition from the monarchy to the reforming and centralizing agenda of Pope Gregory VII that he was trying to advance. The situation became so difficult that Anselm spent several years effectively in exile but returned to Canterbury two years before his death. Anselm was a prolific and sophisti-cated writer on philosophy, theology and spirituality. His most famous works include *Why God Became Man*, the *Proslogion* (containing a philosophical proof for the existence of God) and some of his many prayers and meditations, two of which are reproduced below.

Language Latin. This translation is by Benedicta Ward SLG from contempor-ary manuscripts.

Date *Prayer to Christ* c.1070–80; *Meditation on Human Redemption* c.1100.

Genre and context The *Prayer to Christ* is unusual in being directed to Christ in his own right rather than as the Father's mediator. Addressing Christ directly in prayer had been strongly discouraged after the fourth century for fear of elevating one person of the Trinity above the others, but the practice re-emerged and became very popular from the twelfth century, and this prayer is an early harbinger of that development. Both this prayer and the later *Meditation on human redemption* were written for educated lay people as well as monks and nuns to use in personal devotion. In these laments Anselm aims to stir up longing for God, through grief at 'not having seen Christ after the flesh'[4] in the prayer, and wonder at the costliness of redemp-tion in the meditation. The meditation can be seen as a worked example of the seeking after God aspired to in the prayer. It is presented as an affect-laden process of thinking out loud in order to make meaning out of the horror of Christ's death, that lands in a place of composure, even of joy; and it informs a theology of atonement.

---

4 B. Ward, 1973, *The Prayers and Meditations of St Anselm*, London: Penguin, p. 27. Ward goes on to note the 'dialectic of the absent and present God' that is a feature of the prayer precisely as discussed in Chapter 1 of this book.

Prayer to Christ
(final two stanzas)

Most kind lover of men,
'the poor commits himself to you,
or you are the helper of the orphan'.
My most safe helper,
have mercy upon the orphan left to you.
I am become a child without a father;
my soul is like a widow.
Turn your gaze and behold my tears
which I offer to you till you return.
Come now, Lord, appear to me and I will be consoled;
show me your face and I shall be saved;
display your presence and I have obtained my desire;
reveal your glory and my joy will be full.
'My soul thirsts for you, my flesh longs after you,'
my soul thirsts for God, the fountain of life;
'when shall I come to appear before the presence of God?'
My consoler, for whom I wait, when will you come?
that I might see the joy that I desire;

that I might be satisfied with the appearing of your glory
for which I hunger;
that I might be satisfied with the riches of your house
for which I sigh;
that I might drink of the torrent of your pleasures
for which I thirst.

Lord, meanwhile let my tears be my meat day and night,
until they say to me, 'Behold your God,'
until I hear, 'Soul behold your bridegroom.'
Meanwhile, let me be fed with griefs,
and let my tears be my drink;
comfort me with sorrows.
Perhaps then my Redeemer will come to ne,
for he is good;
he is kind, he will not tarry;
to whom be glory for ever. Amen.

Meditation on Human Redemption

Christian soul, brought to life again out of the heaviness of death, redeemed and set free from wretched servitude by the blood of God, rouse yourself and remember that you are risen, realize that you have been redeemed and set free. Consider again the strength of your salvation and where it is found …

What then is the strength and power of your salvation and where is it found? Christ has brought you back to life. He is the good Samaritan who healed you. He is the good friend who redeemed you and set you free by laying down his life for you. Christ did all this. So the strength of your salvation is the strength of Christ.

Where is the strength of Christ? 'Horns are in his hands, there is his strength hid.' Indeed horns are in his hands, because his hands were nailed to the arms of the cross. But what strength is there in such weakness, what height in such lowliness? What is there to be venerated in such abjection? Surely something is hidden by this weakness, something is concealed by this humility. There is something mysterious in this abjection. O hidden strength: a man hangs on a cross and lifts the load of eternal death from the human race; a man nailed to wood looses the bonds of everlasting death that hold fast the world. O hidden power: a man condemned with thieves saves men condemned with devils, a man stretched out on the gibbet draws all men to himself. O mysterious strength: one soul coming forth from torment draws countless souls with him out of hell, a man submits to the death of the body and destroys the death of souls …

But, Lord, you gave yourself up to death that I might live; how can I be happy about a freedom which is not wrought without your chains? How can I rejoice in my salvation, which would not be without your sorrows? How can I enjoy a life which meant your death? Shall I rejoice with those who by their cruelty made you suffer? For unless they had done it you would not have suffered, and if you had not suffered these good things would not have been mine. But if I grieve because of their cruelty, how can I also rejoice in the benefits that I only possess because of your sufferings? Their wickedness could have done nothing unless you freely permitted it, nor did you suffer except because in love you willed it. Thus I must condemn their cruelty, imitate your death and sufferings, and share them with you, giving thanks for the goodness of your love. And thus may I safely rejoice in the good that thereby comes to me.

Now, little man, leave their cruelties to the justice of God, and think of what you owe your Saviour. Consider what he was to you, what he did for you, and think that for what he did for you he is the more worthy to be loved. Look into your need and his goodness, and see what thanks you should render him, and how much love you owe him …

Stabat Mater
Unknown Italian author (twelfth–thirteenth century)

Author Authorship is unknown but the strongest contender is Jacopone da Todi (c.1230–1306), an Umbrian Franciscan friar, who had a life marked by great suffering, even by the standards of the time. Following the loss of his wife under traumatic circumstances, he joined a branch of the Franciscan order known for its extreme rigour and self-mortification. He was excommunicated by the authoritarian Pope Boniface and imprisoned in appalling conditions for six years, though eventually pardoned by Pope Benedict XI four years before his death.

Language Latin. The nineteenth-century translation below (linguistically free but close to the original in metre and rhyme) is by Denis Florence MacCarthy.

Date c.thirteenth century.

Genre and context This appears to have originally been written for personal devotion, but its widespread popularity meant that it eventually became incorporated into the Missal as a hymn for liturgical use at Passiontide and for feasts celebrating the Virgin Mary. It has been set to music several times, for example by Pergolesi, Palestrina and Vivaldi. During the medieval period there was an explosion of devotion to Christ as the 'Man of Sorrows', focusing on his passion and horrific death, evident in visual art and literature; attention was also paid to the suffering of his mother expressed in the *Pietà* of visual art. At a period dominated by pandemics and wars it seems that great comfort was taken from an identification with the mourning of Mary.

His mother was standing

By the cross, on which suspended,
With his bleeding hands extended,
Hung that Son she so adored.

Stood the mournful Mother weeping,
She, whose heart, its silence keeping,
Grief had cleft as with a sword.

Oh, that Mother's sad affliction –
Mother of all benediction –
Of the sole-begotten One;

Oh, the grieving, sense-bereaving,
Of her heaving breast, perceiving
The dread sufferings of her Son.

What man is there so unfeeling,
Who, his heart to pity steeling,
Could behold that sight unmoved?

Could Christ's Mother see there weeping,
See the pious Mother keeping
Vigil by the Son she loved?

For his people's sins atoning,
She saw Jesus writhing, groaning,
'Neath the scourge wherewith he bled:

Saw her loved One, her consoler,
Dying in His dreadful dolour,
Till at length his spirit fled.

O thou Mother of election,
Fountain of all pure affection,
Make thy grief, thy pain, my own;

Make my heart to God returning,
In the love of Jesus burning,
Feel the fire that thine has known.

Blessed Mother of prediction,
Stamp the marks of crucifixion
Deeply on my stony heart.

Ever leading where thy bleeding
Son is pleading for my needing,
Let me in His wounds take part.

Make me truly, each day newly
While life lasts, O Mother, duly
Weep with Him, the Crucified.

Let me, 'tis my sole demanding,
Near the cross, where thou art standing,
Stand in sorrow at thy side.

Queen of virgins, best and dearest,
Grant, oh, grant the prayers thou hearest,
Let me ever mourn with thee;

Let compassion me so fashion
That Christ's wounds, His death and passion
Be each day renewed in me.

Oh, those wounds, do not deny me;
On that cross, oh, crucify me;
Let me drink His blood, I pray:

Then on fire, enkindled, daring,
I may stand without despairing
On that dreadful judgment-day.

May that cross be my salvation;
Make Christ's death my preservation;
May His grace my heart make wise;

And when death my body taketh,
May my soul when it awaketh
Ope in heaven its rapture eyes.

The Little Book of Eternal Wisdom (extract)
Henry Suso (1295–1366)

Author Henry Suso (Heinrich Seuse) was born in the region of Lake Konstanz in Germany and is said to have entered the Dominican priory there in his early teens. Five or so years later he experienced a vision which led him to pursue a life of extreme asceticism and self-mortification. From 1324 to 1327 he studied in Cologne with Meister Eckhart, the great mystical theologian of the Middle Ages (see chapter 7), and some of his later works were devoted to a defence of Eckhart's controversial ideas. He seems to have had a large following among German-speaking Christians, both religious and lay, especially those with a mystical form of spirituality, and his writings spread rapidly as a result. His works include *The Little Book of Truth*, *Life of the Servant* and many letters.

Date c.1328–30

Language German (*Das Büchlein der ewigen Weisheit*). Suso later expanded this and translated it into Latin as *Horologium Sapientiae*. The nineteenth-century anonymous translation below is from a German edition.

Genre and context The book was written not long after Suso's period of study in Cologne, though it shows a much greater interest in the humanity of Christ than the writings of Meister Eckhart. It is a lyrical meditation on Christ's passion presented as a dialogue between the believer and the dying Christ. Like the *Stabat Mater*, it also focuses on Mary's grief. The extract below is extraordinary in its attempt to connect empathetically with Christ's subjective experience. The book seems to have been envisaged as an aid to personal devotion and would have been gladly received by groups from the renewal movements that were springing up in the Rhineland at that time, broadly referred to as 'The Friends of God'.

The Little Book of Eternal Wisdom
Chapter XVIII: How it was with him at that hour
in regard of his interior man

The Servant Eternal Wisdom! the more one reflects on Thy measureless Passion, the more unfathomable it appears. Thy extremity was so very great UNDER the cross, but still more so ON the cross, according to Thy exterior powers which, at that hour, felt all the pangs of bitter death. But, gentle Lord, how was it with Thy interior Man, with Thy noble Soul? Had it no consolation, no sweetness like other martyrs' souls, so as to mitigate its cruel sufferings? Or, when did Thy sufferings come to an end?

Eternal Wisdom Now, hearken to a misery of miseries, such as thou never yet didst hear of. Although My soul, according to her highest powers, was at that time wrapt in the vision and enjoyment of the pure divinity, noble as, in truth, she is, behold, the lower powers of My exterior and interior nature were yet wholly abandoned to themselves, even to the very last drop of infinite bitterness of suffering, without any consolation, so that no torment was ever equal to it. And as I was thus left entirely helpless and forsaken, with running wounds, with weeping eyes, with extended arms, with the veins of My body on the rack, in the agony of death, then it was that I lifted up My voice in lamentation, and cried out miserably to My Father: My God, My God, why hast Thou forsaken Me.? And still in all this, My will was united in eternal conformity with His will. And when all My blood was poured out, and all My strength exhausted, behold, I was seized by a bitter thirst, because of My mortal agony. But I thirsted still more for the salvation of man. Then did they reach Me vinegar and gall to quench the burning thirst of My parched mouth. And when I had accomplished the work of human redemption, I cried out: It is finished! I was entirely obedient to My Father, even unto death. My Spirit I commended into His hands, saying: Into Thy hands I commend My Spirit. And then My noble Soul separated from My body, both of which yet remained unseparated from the divinity! After this a sharp spear was thrust into My right side; forthwith a stream of precious blood gushed out, and with it a fountain of living water. Behold, My child, in an extremity so pitiable as this did I redeem thee, and all the elect, and did save thee by the living sacrifice of My innocent blood from everlasting death.

The Servant Alas! tender and loving Lord and Brother, with what sorrowful, what bitter toil didst Thou not reap me in! Alas!, noble Lord, how ardently didst Thou love me, how generously didst Thou redeem me! Woe is me, Thou fair Wisdom, how shall I ever be in a condition to acknowledge Thy love and Thy sufferings? If I had Samson's strength, Absalom's beauty, Solomon's wisdom, and the riches and greatness of all kings, my only wish would be to devote them to Thy praise and service. But, Lord, I am nothing, and therefore can do nothing. O Lord, how am I to thank Thee?

Eternal Wisdom If thou hadst the tongues of all the angels, the good works of all mankind, and the powers of all created beings, thou yet couldst not thank Me, nor requite Me, for the least pang which I suffered for the love of thee.

The Servant Tender Lord, inform and teach me, then, how I may become pleasing to Thee by means of Thy grace, since no one is able to make Thee a return for the tokens of Thy love.

Eternal Wisdom Thou shouldst often set My sorrowful cross before thy eyes, and let My bitter torments penetrate to thy heart, and shape thy own sufferings after them. If I allow thee to pine and wither in disconsolate affliction and dryness, without any sweetness, thou shouldst not seek after strange consolation. Let thy cry of misery rise to thy heavenly Father with a renunciation of thyself and all thy desires, according to His Fatherly will. The bitterer thy suffering is from without, and the more resigned thou art from within, the more like art thou to Me, and the more dear to My heavenly Father, for herein the most pious are put to the strongest proof. What though thy desires may have a thirsty craving to seek satisfaction and delight in something that might be pleasant to them, yet shouldst thou forego it for My sake, and thus will thy thirsty mouth be steeped with Me in bitterness. Thou shouldst thirst after the salvation of men. Thy good works thou shouldst direct to a perfect life, and persevere to the end. Thy will must be subject, thy obedience prompt to thy superiors; thy soul, and all that belongs to it, thou must surrender into thy heavenly Father's hands, and thy spirit must ever be dying out of time into eternity, in prefiguration of thy last journey. Behold, thus will thy cross be shaped after My miserable cross, and worthily accomplished in it. Thou shouldst wholly lock thyself up with My love-wounded heart in My open side, and dwell there, and seek there thy resting-place. Then will I wash thee with the waters of life, and deck thee out with My precious blood, in purple. I will associate Myself to thee, and unite thee with Myself eternally.

The Servant Lord, never was there any magnet so powerful in attracting hard iron to itself, as Thy love-fraught Passion, thus presented to my soul, is powerful to unite to itself all hearts. Alas! Thou loving Lord, draw me now by means of love and sorrow away from this world to Thee on Thy cross, fulfil in me the closest resemblance to Thy cross, so that my soul may enjoy Thee in Thy highest glory.

The St Matthew Passion of J. S. Bach (opening chorus)
Christian Friedrich Henrici (1700–1764)

Author Christian Friedrich Henrici wrote under the pen name 'Picander'. He was a Lutheran poet and librettist, who was commissioned by J. S. Bach to write the words for several of his choral works.

Language German (my translation).

Date c.1727. It is not clear when the first performance of the *Passion* took place, and the words may have been adapted from a pre-existing poem from the early 1720s.

Genre and context The piety of late medieval German writers such as Suso was taken up into the spirituality of the Reformation. Lament over Christ's passion continued, but the focus shifted from sympathy for him to remorse for the human sin that had brought such suffering upon him. The Matthew Passion can be seen as one very long liturgical lament. It was written nearly two centuries after the German Reformation, but it looks backward to it, using Luther's translation for the biblical sections. Henrici also drew on earlier Lutheran sermons by Heinrich Müller (1631–75) and reached even further back to Anselm in crafting some of the laments. True to the genre, the extract below which opens the work gives a prominent place to women. The women are presented as an amalgam of the daughters of Jerusalem of Luke 23, whom Jesus instructs to weep *for themselves*, and the bridesmaids of Matthew 25.

Come you daughters

Come, you daughters, help me lament,
Look! *At whom?* The Bridegroom.
Look at him! *How?* As a lamb!
Look! *At what?* See patience.
Look! *Where?* At our blame.
Look at him from love and grace,
Bearing his own wooden cross.
Come, you daughters, help me lament,
Look! *At whom?* The Bridegroom.
Look at him! *How?* As a lamb!

Oh blameless Lamb of God
Slaughtered on the trunk of the cross,
Always found patient,
Even though you were despised.
You have borne all sin,
Otherwise we must have despaired.
Have pity on us, Oh Jesus!

4.2 Bearing witness in martyrdom

The desire to die and be with Christ is characteristic of the very early years of the church when Christ's death was almost a living memory and crucifixion still a common form of punishment across the Roman empire. There was no need to dwell imaginatively on crucifixion: it was a present reality.

This desire could often be realized as Christians faced repeated, if sporadic, periods of brutal persecution in the first four centuries. Martyrdom has many aspects: it subverts the narrative of those in power, it unites the believer with Christ, it is a form of sacrifice to God, it increases solidarity and commitment in the community of faith.

Letter to the Romans (extract)
Ignatius of Antioch (d. early second century)

Author Ignatius was the bishop of Antioch at the turn of the first century. Almost nothing is known about him apart from his letters, but the third-century Christian writer Eusebius describes him as a follower of the Apostle John and whose appointment as bishop was at the Apostle Peter's direction. His enthusiasm about the role of bishops is reflected in his taking the name Theophorus ('God-bearing'). He is said to have been martyred in Rome during the persecution of the Emperor Trajan.

Language Greek. This letter was enormously popular because of its inspirational effect on suffering Christians. It rapidly became available in several languages and appears to have been embellished over time. Careful critical scholarship from the seventeenth to the nineteenth centuries was able to reconstruct the likely original. The version below is Kirsopp Lake's early twentieth-century translation.

Date Very early second century.

Genre and context Ignatius wrote seven letters during his final journey from Antioch to Rome. Six were on matters of church order and doctrine. The *Letter to the Romans* is about his anticipated martyrdom. He asks the Christians in Rome not to try and prevent his desired fate but instead to support him in and through it.

Letter to the Romans

Ignatius, who is also called Theophorus, to her who has obtained mercy in the greatness of the Most High Father, and of Jesus Christ his only Son; to the Church beloved and enlightened by the will of him who has

---

willed all things which are, according to the love of Jesus Christ, our God, which also has the presidency in the country of the land of the Romans...

3. You never have envied anyone, you taught others. But I desire that those things may stand fast which you enjoin in your instructions. Only pray for me for strength, both inward and outward, that I may not merely speak, but also have the will, that I may not only be called a Christian, but may also be found to be one. For if I be found to be one, I can also be called one, and then be deemed faithful when I no longer am visible in the world. Nothing visible is good, for our God, Jesus Christ, being now in the Father, is the more plainly visible. Christianity is not the work of persuasiveness, but of greatness, when it is hated by the world.

4. I am writing to all the Churches, and I give injunctions to all men, that I am dying willingly for God's sake, if you do not hinder it. I beseech you, be not 'an unseasonable kindness' to me. Suffer me to be eaten by the beasts, through whom I can attain to God. I am God's wheat, and I am ground by the teeth of wild beasts that I may be found pure bread of Christ. Rather entice the wild beasts that they may become my tomb, and leave no trace of my body, that when I fall asleep I be not burdensome to any. 'Then shall I be truly a disciple of Jesus Christ, when the world shall not even see my body. Beseech Christ on my behalf, that I may be found a sacrifice through these instruments …'

5. … Grant me this favour. I know what is expedient for me; now I am beginning to be a disciple. May nothing of things seen or unseen envy me my attaining to Jesus Christ. Let there come on me fire, and cross, and struggles with wild beasts, cutting, and tearing asunder, rackings of bones, mangling of limbs, crushing of my whole body, cruel tortures of the devil, may I but attain to Jesus Christ!

6. The ends of the earth and the kingdoms of this world shall profit me nothing. It is better for me to die in Christ Jesus than to be king over the ends of the earth. I seek Him who died for our sake. I desire Him who rose for us. The pains of birth are upon me. Suffer me, my brethren; hinder me not from living, do not wish me to die. Do not give to the world one who desires to belong to God, nor deceive him with material things. Suffer me to receive the pure light; when I have come thither I shall become a man. Suffer me to follow the example of the Passion of my God. If any man have him within himself, let him understand what I wish, and let him sympathise with me, knowing the things which constrain me.

To the Martyrs and *On Baptism* (extracts)
Tertullian (c.155–220)

Author Tertullian was a native of Carthage in North Africa. He appears to have converted to Christianity in mid-life. He was a prolific writer and Christian apologist, possibly with a background in law. He was deeply concerned with maintaining the rigorous purity of the Church, and in later life was drawn to the ascetic Montanist movement.

Language Latin. There are several fifteenth-century manuscripts of *To the Martyrs*. *On Baptism* is based on a twelfth-century manuscript. The version below is Charles Dodgson's nineteenth-century translation.

Date c.200. *To the Martyrs* is probably the earlier of the two.

Genre and context Christians in North Africa suffered significantly more persecution than in other parts of the Roman Empire. Infamous executions, for example those of Felicity and Perpetua, meant that there was a particular concern with martyrdom in this part of the early church. *To the Martyrs* is a formal letter written to comfort Christians who were in prison awaiting execution. *On Baptism* is a sermon or treatise written to counter the teaching of a female gnostic preacher who had argued that martyrdom was unimportant and unnecessary in the life of faith. In this extract Tertullian presents martyrdom as a form of baptism.

To the Martyrs
Chapter III

Grant now, O blessed, that even to Christians the prison is unpleasant; yet we were called to the warfare of the living God in our very response to the sacramental words. Well, no soldier comes out to the campaign laden with luxuries, nor does he go to action from his comfortable chamber, but from the light and narrow tent, where every kind of hardness, roughness and unpleasantness must be put up with. Even in peace soldiers inure themselves to war by toils and inconveniences – marching in arms, running over the plain, working at the ditch, making the *testudo**, engaging in many arduous labours. The sweat of the brow is on everything, that bodies and minds may not shrink at having to pass from shade to sunshine, from sunshine to icy cold, from the robe of peace to the coat of mail, from silence to clamour, from quiet to tumult. In like manner, O blessed ones, count whatever is hard in this lot of yours as a discipline of your powers of mind and body. You are about to pass through a noble struggle, in which the living God acts the part of superintendent, in which the Holy Ghost is your trainer, in which the prize

---

is an eternal crown of angelic essence, citizenship in the heavens, glory everlasting. Therefore your Master, Jesus Christ, who has anointed you with His Spirit, and led you forth to the arena, has seen it good, before the day of conflict, to take you from a condition more pleasant in itself, and has imposed on you a harder treatment, that your strength might be the greater. For the athletes, too, are set apart to a more stringent discipline, that they may have their physical powers built up. They are kept from luxury, from daintier meats, from more pleasant drinks; they are pressed, racked, worn out; the harder their labours in the preparatory training, the stronger is the hope of victory. And they, says the apostle, that they may obtain a corruptible crown (1 Corinthians 9:25). We, with the crown eternal in our eye, look upon the prison as our training-ground, that at the goal of final judgment we may be brought forth well disciplined by many a trial; since virtue is built up by hardships, as by voluptuous indulgence it is overthrown.

* A human shield formed by soldiers standing in a circle with their shields. *Ed.*

On Baptism
Chapter XVI. Of the Second Baptism – With Blood

We have indeed, likewise, a second font (itself withal one with the former) of blood, to wit; concerning which the Lord said, 'I have to be baptized with a baptism,' when He had been baptized already. For He had come by means of water and blood (1 John 5.6), just as John has written; that He might be baptized by the water, glorified by the blood; to make us, in like manner, called by water, chosen by blood. These two baptisms He sent out from the wound in His pierced side, in order that they who believed in His blood might be bathed with the water; they who had been bathed in the water might likewise drink the blood. This is the baptism which both stands in lieu of the fontal bathing when that has not been received, and restores it when lost.

The Life of Cyprian (extract)
Attributed to Pontius the Deacon (d. c.262)

Author Nothing is known of Pontius other than that he was a companion of Cyprian, Bishop of Carthage (c.210–258). Pontius' name does not appear on the manuscript itself, but authorship was attributed to him by Jerome (see Chapter 7) in the fourth century. Cyprian himself was a late convert to Christianity, was baptized in 245 and three or four years later appointed bishop. He controversially went into hiding during the Decian persecution in the 250s and yet took a harsh line with those who had avoided martyrdom by agreeing to sacrifice to Roman gods. In 256 persecution broke out again under the Emperor Valerius, and this time Cyprian publicly resisted the authorities. He was imprisoned, tried, convicted and beheaded.

Language Latin. This is from Robert Ernest Wallis' nineteenth-century translation.

Date Late third century. There were numerous manuscripts circulating from early times.

Genre and context This is often described as 'the first Christian biography', but it can also be understood as a sermon or eulogy. In this section Pontius gives an account of Cyprian's martyrdom under the local proconsul Galerius Maximus.

The Life of Cyprian

17. And thus, therefore, the judge reads from his tablet the sentence which lately in the vision he had not read – a spiritual sentence, not rashly to be spoken – a sentence worthy of such a bishop and such a witness; a glorious sentence, wherein he was called a standard-bearer of the sect, and an enemy of the gods, and one who was to be an example to his people; and that with his blood discipline would begin to be established. Nothing could be more complete, nothing more true, than this sentence. For all the things which were said, although said by a heathen, are divine. Nor is it indeed to be wondered at, since priests are accustomed to prophesy of the passion. He had been a standard-bearer, who was accustomed to teach concerning the bearing of Christ's standard; he had been an enemy of the gods, who commanded the idols to be destroyed. Moreover, he gave example to his friends, since, when many were about to follow in a similar manner, he was the first in the province to consecrate the first-fruits of martyrdom. And by his blood discipline began to be established; but it was the discipline of martyrs, who, emulating their teacher, in the imitation of a glory like his own, themselves also gave a confirmation to discipline by the very blood of their own example.

18. And when he left the doors of the praetorium, a crowd of soldiery accompanied him; and that nothing might be wanting in his passion, centurions and tribunes guarded his side. Now the place itself where he was about to suffer is level, so that it affords a noble spectacle, with its trees thickly planted on all sides. But as, by the extent of the space beyond, the view was not attainable to the confused crowd, persons who favoured him had climbed up into the branches of the trees, that there might not even be wanting to him (what happened in the case of Zacchaeus), that he was gazed upon from the trees. And now, having with his own hands bound his eyes, he tried to hasten the slowness of the executioner, whose office was to wield the sword, and who with difficulty clasped the blade in his failing right hand with trembling fingers, until the mature hour of glorification strengthened the hand of the centurion with power granted from above to accomplish the death of the excellent man, and at length supplied him with the permitted strength. O blessed people of the Church, who as well in sight as in feeling, and, what is more, in outspoken words, suffered with such a bishop as theirs; and, as they had ever heard him in his own discourses, were crowned by God the Judge! For although that which the general wish desired could not occur, viz. that the entire congregation should suffer at once in the fellowship of a like glory, yet whoever under the eyes of Christ beholding, and in the hearing of the priest, eagerly desired to suffer, by the sufficient testimony of that desire did in some sort send a missive to God, as his ambassador.

Confessions (extract)
Patrick of Ireland (late fourth–fifth century)

Author All that is known about Patrick (always self-identified as Patricius) is based on his two authentic pieces of writing, the *Confessions* and *Letter to the Soldiers of Coroticus*. He grew up in England in a Romano-British middle-class Christian family. At the age of 16 he was captured by human traffickers and taken to Ireland as a slave. After six years he escaped and returned home, but ten years later experienced a vision calling him back to Ireland as an evangelist. After studying with monastic communities in France, he was ordained and returned to Ireland, eventually serving as a bishop.

Language Latin. Manuscripts date back to as early as the eighth century and there are also early Irish versions. The translation below is by Padraig McCarthy.

Date Fifth century.

Genre and context The *Confessions* is, on the face of it, a spiritual auto-biography but, like those of Augustine (Chapter 12), also has the character of a personal defence. In this case, it appears that Patrick had been accused of heterodoxy and/or financial irregularity by fellow Christians. Patrick's writings display a dogged perseverance in the face of adversity and opposition, and an austerely ascetic approach to faith, often alluding to Paul's writings on these topics. The extracts below come towards the end of the work, as Patrick reflects on martyrdom and prepares himself for the end of his earthly life.

Confessions
37–8, 56–9

If I be worthy, I am ready even to give up my life most willingly here and now for his name. It is there that I wish to spend my life until I die, if the Lord should grant it to me. I am greatly in debt to God. He gave me such great grace, that through me, many people should be born again in God and brought to full life. Also that clerics should be ordained everywhere for this people who have lately come to believe, and who the Lord has taken from the ends of the earth. This is just what he promised in the past through his prophet …

Now I commend my soul to my most faithful God. For him I perform the work of an ambassador, despite my less than noble condition. However, God is not influenced by such personal situations, and he chose me for this task so that I would be one servant of his very least important servants. So I shall make a return to him for all that he has given to me. But what can I say, or what can I promise to my Lord? There is nothing I have that is not his gift to me. But he knows the depths of my heart, my very gut feelings! He knows that it is enough that I desire very much, and am ready for this, that he would grant me to drink of his chalice, just as he was pleased to do for others who loved him. For this reason, may God not let it come about that I would suffer the loss of his people who have become his in the furthermost parts of the earth. I pray that God give me perseverance, and that he grant me to bear faithful witness to him right up to my passing from this life, for the sake of my God. If I have ever imitated anything good for the sake of my God whom I love, I ask that he grant me to be able to shed my blood with these converts and captives – even were I to lack a grave for burial, or my dead body were to be miserably torn apart limb from limb by dogs or wild beasts, or were the birds of heaven to devour it. I declare with certainty that if this were to happen, I would have gained both my soul and my body.

There is no doubt whatever that we will rise on the appointed day in the brightness of the sun, that is, in the glory of Christ Jesus our redeemer. We shall be like children of the living God and co-heirs of Christ and to be fashioned in his image, since it is from him and through him and in him that we are to reign.

Further reading

Anselm of Canterbury: Teacher of prayer by Benedicta Ward SLG. Oxford: Fairacres Publications, 2018.

Bach Among the Theologians by Jaroslav Pelikan. Eugene, OR: Wipf & Stock, 1986.

Mediaeval Irish Lyrics by James Carney. Gerrards Cross: Colin Smythe, 1985.

Practicing Lament by Rebekah Eklund. Eugene, OR: Cascade Books, 2021.

Saint Patrick Retold: The legend and history of Ireland's patron saint by Roy Flechner. Princeton, NJ: Princeton University Press, 2019.

Stabat Mater: The mystery hymn by Desmond Fisher. Leominster: Gracewing Publications, 2015.

Tertullian, Cyprian, and Origen on the Lord's Prayer by Alistair Stewart-Sykes. London: SPCK, 2004.

Three Friends of God: Records from the lives of John Tauer, Nicholas of Basle, Henry Suso by Frances Bevan, 1887 (various editions available on the internet).

5

Attending to the Body

But Jesus said, 'Let her alone; why do you trouble her? She has performed a good service for me … She has done what she could; she has anointed my body beforehand for its burial.'
(Mark 14.6, 8)

When it was evening, there came a rich man from Arimathea, named Joseph, who was also a disciple of Jesus. He went to Pilate and asked for the body of Jesus; then Pilate ordered it to be given to him. So Joseph took the body and wrapped it in a clean linen cloth and laid it in his own new tomb, which he had hewn in the rock. He then rolled a great stone to the door of the tomb and went away.
(Matthew 26.57–60)

The women who had come with him from Galilee followed, and they saw the tomb and how his body was laid. Then they returned, and prepared spices and ointments. On the sabbath they rested according to the commandment. But on the first day of the week, at early dawn, they came to the tomb, taking the spices that they had prepared. They found the stone rolled away from the tomb, but when they went in, they did not find the body.
(Luke 23.55—24.3)

Shun fornication! Every sin that a person commits is outside the body; but the fornicator sins against the body itself. Or do you not know that your [pl.] body [sing.] is a temple of the Holy Spirit within you, which you have from God, and that you are not your own? For you were bought with a price; therefore glorify God in your body.
(1 Corinthians 6.18–20)

The cup of blessing that we bless, is it not a sharing in the blood of Christ? The bread that we break, is it not a sharing in the body of Christ? Because there is one bread, we who are many are one body, for we all partake of the one bread.
(1 Corinthians 10.16–17)

Lament can happen anywhere, but it is particularly associated with the body of the deceased; lament over the body is a key part of many funeral rituals. Lament then is not simply a verbal and emotional outpouring; it is part of the proper treatment of human remains as they are laid to rest. All societies take great care with the dignified disposal of human remains because the body is held to be important, even if the spirit of the deceased is understood to have departed. When there is no body to dispose of (as in some accidental deaths, suicides or murders) grief is intensified, marked by chronically unresolved feelings and compulsive psychological or even physical searching (John 20.15).

If there is no body, there is no evidence that the person ever existed. This was part of the horror of crucifixion; the body was generally left on the cross to be devoured by scavenging animals, and the victim's identity thus erased. This is why Matthew takes such trouble in his account of the deposition of Jesus' body, emphasizing that it was wrapped in clean linen and laid intact in the pristine tomb of a high-status individual: however horrible Jesus' death, at least he had a decent burial. It is an indication that Jesus' material bodily identity was taken extremely seriously by the first Christians.

Tending the body of the deceased and laying it to rest is the last human-to-human service that we can perform and the last act of physical connection with them. For the Christian there is then the hope of a reunion with our loved one's resurrection body, something anticipated in the Gospel accounts of reunions with the risen Christ. But, as noted in Part I, these were short-lived: like our deceased loved ones, Christ is now absent in body.

Yet, paradoxically, in the history of Christian spirituality there has been a continuing strong instinct to offer devotion to his body as a means of easing the pain of this absence. Sometimes this has been metaphorical, for instance the fourth-century church father Jerome writes, 'The Lord's body is wrapped not in gold and jewels and silk, but in a pure linen shroud. This signifies that he wraps Jesus in clean linen who receives him with a pure mind.'[1] More often the focus has been on material aspects of embodiment.

Human cultures have a strong tendency to treat social and individual bodies as standing in a symbolic relationship to each other, with the latter often seen as a microcosm of the former: 'There is a continual exchange of meanings between the two kinds of bodily experience so that each reinforces the categories of the other'.[2] This goes some way to explaining the seemingly perplexing and frustrating observation that faith communities tend to be disproportionately concerned with the bodies of their individual members in terms of dress, diet and sexual practice: they stand for something greater. In his letters Paul offers a highly sophisticated account of the relationship between the body of the community and the individual,[3] and in 1 Corinthians he extends this to the body of the Eucharistic bread. All three are understood in some way to be the body of Christ.

---

1 T. Scheck (tr.), 2008, *St. Jerome Commentary on Matthew*, Washington DC: Catholic University of America Press, p. 323.

2 M. Douglas, 2007, *Natural Symbols*, London: Routledge, p. 72.

3 For a helpful analysis see M. Croasmun, 2017, *The Emergence of Sin: The cosmic tyrant in Romans*, New York: Oxford University Press.

The readings in this chapter are therefore arranged under three modes of concern with the embodied Christ: care for the corporate community of faith; devotion to the Eucharistic bread – the *Corpus Christi*; and the body of the individual believer as identified with Christ's body. In each of these areas there is a recognition that the body in question is *both* really Christ's body *and* not really Christ's body (the dialectic of the present and the absent Jesus of Chapter 1), and that this impossibility is made possible by the Holy Spirit in his capacity as Comforter.

5.1 The body of the community

The concern with martyrdom in the previous chapter combines the themes of witness and community solidarity. The Letter to the Hebrews talks of a 'great cloud of witnesses' (many of whom were also martyrs), emphasizing its corporate nature. If the body of the community of the faithful represents Christ, then solidarity, harmony and unity amongst its members become important because Christ must not be dismembered. This is a key principle in the emergence of monasticism as a corporate rather than individual endeavour.

Life of Pachomius (c.292–c.348) (extract)
Anonymous (third century)

Author Unknown. Details of Pachomius' life are almost exclusively drawn from this biography. He was born in upper Egypt to pagan parents but converted to Christianity after an encounter with some Christians in Thebes while a military conscript. After a period of studying the faith, he began to pursue the life of a solitary ascetic hermit in the Egyptian desert in the tradition of Antony (see Chapter 9), but then felt called to establish a community of hermits in a more agrarian setting. Pachomius can thus be understood as the father of 'cenobite' monasticism, where the communal aspects of the religious life are emphasized (as opposed to 'eremitic' monasticism in which individual withdrawal is key). Many were attracted to this life (there were separate communities for both men and women with which Pachomius' brother and sister were involved), and it was necessary to develop regulations to manage them. Apart from the *Life* (which exists in several versions), there are various free-floating anecdotes, several versions of a written rule (probably codified after Pachomius' death) and references to Pachomius in general histories of the desert communities.

Language The manuscript history of the *Life* is very complicated. The earliest manuscripts are in Greek, Coptic and Arabic; it is likely, though not certain, that the original language was Coptic. An early Greek version was translated into Latin in the sixth century and that manuscript still exists. The translation of that edition below is by Benedict Baker.

Date The earliest versions probably date from shortly after Pachomius' death.

Genre and context The *Life* is said be based on Athanasius' *Life of Antony* in form, but some of the early prologues assert that Pachomius' model is Paul. Paul's letters are concerned with building Christian communities to which he stands in a quasi-parental relationship, and it is said that the habit of referring to Pachomius as 'Abba' (and hence the term 'abbot') is derived from this.

Life of Pachomius

Chapter XXI

And as Pachomius was thus watching in prayer, an Angel of the Lord appeared to him. 'The will of the Lord, Pachomius,' said the Angel, 'is that you serve him with a pure mind, and gather together a great number of monks, who may strive to serve God by keeping all the rules in the book which has been shown to you'. For he had already recently been given tablets on which the following words were inscribed:

Chapter XXII

Let each one eat and drink according to their strength, and let them work according to what they eat. Don't forbid them either to fast or to eat in moderation, but give harder work to those who are strong and eat more, lighter work to the weak and those who fast. Build a number of different cells, and put them three to a cell. Let all the food be prepared and eaten in the one place. At night let them wear linen lebitons,* girded about the loins, and let them each have a melote, that is a goat skin dyed white, without which they should neither eat nor sleep. When they come to the Communion of the Sacraments of Christ let them loosen their belts and take off their melotes, and wear only their cowls …

The Angel who spoke with Pachomius also laid down that there should be twelve prayers for the daytime, twelve for the evening and twelve for the night. When Pachomius remarked at how few that was, the Angel replied: 'It has been set at that number so that the weaker won't find the task too difficult. But the perfect need not feel deprived by this rule, for in the privacy of their own cells they can go on praying if they are being nourished by divine contemplation in purity of mind.'

After saying all this the heavenly messenger departed, and Pachomius gave thanks to God, for it was now by a threefold revelation that his vision was confirmed. He began to receive all who offered themselves to the mercy of God through penitence, and after a long trial of the life, they were enrolled into the family of monks. He urged them to flee from the immorality of the world, and to cleave always to the holy rules. He warned them that the overall rule according to the Gospel was that the monk renounces first the whole world, then his family, and lastly denies himself, so that he may take up his cross and follow in the footsteps of Christ (Luke 14.26–7). Instructed in that sort of teaching by the blessed old man, they soon brought forth most worthy fruits of penitence. Although he was now of advanced age he pursued the purpose of the spiritual life with undiminished zeal. He not only committed himself to a stricter rule but took upon himself the control and care of the whole monastery, aiming to be a servant of all even if it were beyond his strength. He punctually prepared the common meal for the brothers and performed the usual offices. He gathered the vegetables from the garden which he had watered with his own hands. When anyone knocked at the monastery door he would be the one who went to open it and give a ready response. He nursed the sick day and night. In all these things he gave a most excellent example to his disciples. Newcomers to the service of the Lord were thus more readily drawn into the duties of devotion.

* A sleeveless tunic. *Ed.*

Rule (extract)
Benedict of Nursia (traditionally 480–547, possibly somewhat later)

Author Benedict was born in what is now called Norcia in northern Italy, reputedly to a family from the nobility. As a young man he studied in Rome, then ruled by the Goths. The city was at peace, but social and religious structures were fragile. Benedict was repelled by the decadence he encountered there and withdrew to the surrounding countryside, eventually pursuing the life of a hermit. His continuing quest for solitude was interrupted first by a short-lived and unsuccessful period as the abbot of a nearby monastery and then by would-be disciples flocking to find him. After setting up twelve monastic communities in that region, each of twelve monks and an abbot, in 530 Benedict finally established the monastery for which he is known at Monte Cassino.

Language Latin. Earliest manuscripts date from the eighth century. The version below is a twentieth-century translation by Abbot Parry OSB.

Date c.520.

Genre and context In the cenobite tradition of Pachomius, and drawing on an earlier work, *The Rule of the Master*, and also probably on *The Rule of Basil* (see Chapter 12), Benedict composed a manual for a balanced and well-ordered Christian life in community. While rigorous, it is not ascetic by the standards of the time, and it shows a care for both the physical body of individuals and, influenced by Romans 12, the healthy functioning of the body of the community and its visitors. The reference to children in this extract concerns child oblates who were given to the community by their parents as a form of divine sacrifice based on Hannah's gift of Samuel to God (1 Samuel 1.24).

Rule of Benedict
Chapters XXXI and LXIII: 1–7, 10–19

XXXI What kind of man the Cellarer of the Monastery should be

As cellarer of the monastery should be chosen from the community one who is sound in judgement, mature in character, sober, not a great eater, not self-important, not turbulent, not harshly spoken, not an off-putter, not wasteful, but a God-fearing man who will be a father to the whole community. He is to have charge of all affairs, but he is not to act without the Abbot's approval, and he must carry out his orders. He must not sadden the brethren. If any brother happens to make an unreasonable demand of him, he should not upset him by showing contempt, but refuse the ill-advised petitioner with reasons modestly presented. He must keep guard over his own soul, always bearing in mind that saying of the Apostle that he who ministers well gains a good reputation for himself (1 Timothy 3:13). With all compassion he is to have care for the sick, the children, the guests and the poor, knowing for certain that in the day of judgement he will have to render account for his treatment of them all. He must regard the chattels of the monastery and its whole property as if they were the sacred vessels of the altar. He should neglect nothing. He must neither succumb to avarice nor be a wasteful squanderer of the monastery's goods; but he should conduct all his affairs with prudence and in accordance with the Abbot's instructions.

It is essential that he should have humility and if he has nothing material to give, he should at least offer kind words of reply, as it is written, 'A good word surpasses the best gift' (Sirach 18:17). He must keep under his own care whatever the Abbot has entrusted to him, but he should not undertake anything the Abbot has forbidden.

He must provide the brethren with their regular allowance of food, without fuss or keeping them waiting, so as not to make for them an occasion for sin, keeping in mind the divine saying about retribution of him 'who causes one of the little ones to sin' (Matthew 18:6). If the community is rather large, helpers should be given him, so that with their aid he may himself tranquilly perform the office entrusted to him.

Whatever has to be asked for or given should be asked for or given at suitable times, so that no one may be upset or saddened in the household of God.

LXIII: The order of the Community

The time of their entering monastic life, their personal merits, and the decision of the Abbot, shall decide the order which they keep in the monastery. Yet the Abbot must not upset the flock entrusted to him, nor should he make any unjust arrangement as though he were free to give orders as he pleases, for he must always bear in mind that he is going to have to render an account of all his decisions and actions. In the order, then, which he has laid down, or which they otherwise have among themselves, shall the brethren come to the kiss of peace, or to Communion, or intone a Psalm or occupy their place in choir. In no circumstances or places is age to decide order or have any bearing upon it, for the youthful Samuel and Daniel acted as judges over their elders. Therefore, with the exception of those whom, as we have said, the Abbot has promoted or degraded for definite reasons, the rest are to take their places according to the time of their coming into the monastery; for example, one who has entered the monastery at the second hour is to know that he is junior to him who entered at the first, whatever his age or dignity …

Juniors, therefore, must show respect for their seniors, and seniors must love their juniors. In calling one another by name it is not allowed to anyone to use the name alone. Seniors should address their juniors by the name brother; juniors should address their seniors as *Nonnus*, by which is signified the reverence due to a father. The Abbot, however, as he is believed to act in the place of Christ, should be called Lord and Abbot, not because he demands these titles, but for the honour and love of Christ. He himself must bear this in mind, and show himself worthy of such honour.

Whenever the brethren meet one another, the junior should seek a blessing of the elder. A younger monk should rise and offer his meat to an older one if he passes by, nor should he venture to sit down again, unless the older one tells him to, so that it may be as it is written, 'Forestall one another in paying honour' (Romans 12:10).

Children and youths are to keep their places, in good order, in the oratory and at table. Out of doors also and anywhere at all they should be under supervision and discipline, until they reach an age that can understand.

Sermon on the Day of Pentecost
Augustine of Hippo (354–430)

Author Aurelius Augustinus was born in what is now eastern Algeria. His mother, Monica, was a devout Christian but his early adult life was devoted to pursuing secular academic and political advancement. During this time he had a longstanding relationship with a girl of modest background by whom he had a son, Adeodatus. Augustine had a deep interest in questions of philosophy and theology, and for a while was involved in Manicheism, an ascetic faith which incorporated some elements of Christian teaching, but which understood the universe to be subject to an eternal battle between the forces of good and evil. As his career advanced, Augustine moved from Carthage to Rome and finally Milan, where he came under the influence of its bishop, Ambrose. He converted to Christianity in 386. Following his conversion, he became a well-known preacher and then returned to his birthplace to set up a Christian monastic community. Here, while visiting the coastal town of Hippo, he was (unexpectedly and reluctantly) ordained priest and then, in 395, bishop. He began work on the *Confessions* almost immediately. He continued with his episcopal ministry and writing until his death. Augustine was a prolific writer and, apart from the *Confessions* and several biblical commentaries, his best known works include *The City of God*, *On the Trinity* and *On Christian Doctrine*.

Language Latin. The translation below is by Edmund Hill OP.

Date c.405–411.

Genre and context This is the text of a short sermon to the newly baptized (*ad infantes*) which explains the nature of the sacrament of Holy Communion as 'one thing seen and another understood', emphasizing the fact that the baptized community is itself the sacrament. Augustine had a deeply corporate understanding of the life of faith, drawing heavily on 1 Corinthians and expressed in the societal metaphor of his crowning work *The City of God*.

Sermon 272

What you see on God's altar, you've already observed during the night that has now ended. But you've heard nothing about just what it might be, or what it might mean, or what great thing it might be said to symbolize. For what you see is simply bread and a cup – this is the information your eyes report. But your faith demands far subtler insight: the bread is Christ's body, the cup is Christ's blood. Faith can grasp the fundamentals quickly, succinctly, yet it hungers for a fuller account of the matter. As the prophet says, 'Unless you believe, you will not understand' (Isaiah 7:9). So you can say to me, 'You urged us to believe; now explain, so we can understand.' Inside each of you, thoughts like these are rising: 'Our Lord Jesus Christ, we know the source of his flesh; he took it from the virgin Mary. Like any infant, he was nursed and nourished; he grew; became a youngster; suffered persecution from his own people. To the wood he was nailed; on the wood he died; from the wood, his body was taken down and buried. On the third day (as he willed) he rose; he ascended bodily into heaven whence he will come to judge the living and the dead. There he dwells even now, seated at God's right.

So how can bread be his body? And what about the cup? How can it (or what it contains) be his blood?' My friends, these realities are called sacraments because in them one thing is seen, while another is grasped. What is seen is a mere physical likeness; what is grasped bears spiritual fruit. So now, if you want to understand the body of Christ, listen to the Apostle Paul speaking to the faithful: 'You are the body of Christ, member for member' (1 Corinthians 12:27). If you, therefore, are Christ's body and members, it is your own mystery that is placed on the Lord's table! It is your own mystery that you are receiving! You are saying 'Amen' to what you are: your response is a personal signature, affirming your faith. When you hear 'The body of Christ', you reply 'Amen.' Be a member of Christ's body, then, so that your 'Amen' may ring true! But what role does the bread play? We have no theory of our own to propose here; listen, instead, to what Paul says about this sacrament: 'The bread is one, and we, though many, are one body' (1 Corinthians 10:17). Understand and rejoice: unity, truth, faithfulness, love. 'One bread,' he says. What is this one bread? Is it not the 'one body,' formed from many? Remember: bread doesn't come from a single grain, but from many. When you received exorcism, you were 'ground.' When you were baptized, you were 'leavened.' When you received the fire of the Holy Spirit, you were 'baked.' Be what you see; receive what you are. This is what Paul is saying about the bread. So too, what we are to understand about the cup is similar and requires little explanation. In the visible object of bread, many grains are gathered into one just as the faithful (so Scripture says) form 'a single heart and mind in God' (Acts 4:32). And thus it is with the wine. Remember, friends, how wine is made. Individual grapes hang together in a bunch, but the juice from them all is mingled to become a single brew. This is the image chosen by Christ our Lord to show how, at his own table, the mystery of our unity and peace is solemnly consecrated. All who fail to keep the bond of peace after entering this mystery receive not a sacrament that benefits them, but an indictment that condemns them. So let us give God our sincere and deepest gratitude, and, as far as human weakness will permit, let us turn to the Lord with pure hearts. With all our strength, let us seek God's singular mercy, for then the Divine Goodness will surely hear our prayers. God's power will drive the Evil One from our acts and thoughts; it will deepen our faith, govern our minds, grant us holy thoughts, and lead us, finally, to share the divine happiness through God's own son Jesus Christ. Amen!

5.2 The body of the Eucharistic bread

Augustine's sermon (above) makes a very close connection between Christ embodied in the community of faith and the body of Christ as Eucharistic bread. Nowhere is the issue of the 'dialectic of the present and the absent Jesus' more obviously expressed than in the church's historical debates about the 'real presence' of Christ in the bread of Communion. These post-date Augustine by many centuries and are a feature of the medieval period, when the rediscovery of Aristotelian approaches to the material world raised questions as to how the transformation of bread into human flesh might actually be possible. These theological debates were lent added passion by the lived experience of those many believers who had developed an intense spiritual devotion to the Eucharistic bread, treating it as if it were the physical body of Christ. The most prominent of the these was a Belgian religious community gathered round Juliana of Liège (c.1192–1258).

For many years Juliana petitioned for the establishment of a feast in honour of the Eucharist. Her biography (based on what was a nearly contemporaneous account by her friend Eve of St-Martin) recounts that this was in part motivated by a series of visions of Christ. Juliana was successful and the feast was kept locally in her own diocese. It appears that she composed many aspects of the liturgy (both words and music) which began with the antiphon *Animarum Cibus* ('Food of Souls'). The practice spread, with liturgical variants, until the feast of Corpus Christi was officially established across the church in 1264 by Pope Urban IV.

Pange Lingua
Thomas Aquinas (1225–1274)

Author Thomas Aquinas came from an aristocratic Italian family with connections to the Benedictine order. Thomas, however, insisted on becoming a Dominican friar despite violent family opposition. This was a period when universities were emerging, and the more scholastic religious orders were strongly identified with them. Thomas' work, in a number of centres across Europe, was therefore largely academic, and he was well suited to this. He is best known for his systematic approach to theology which deeply engaged with the thought of Aristotle, expressed most fully in his work the *Summa Theologica* (see Chapter 11); but his theological writing is always situated in the religious life of private devotion, service and corporate worship, exemplified in the *Pange Lingua*.

Language Latin. The version below is a nineteenth-century metric translation by John Mason Neale.

Date 1260s.

Genre and context This is a liturgical hymn written under the supervision of the Roman Catholic magisterium and with a more developed sacramental theology than the earlier devotional emphasis of Juliana's work. Thomas was charged with writing a liturgy for the first celebration of Corpus Christi in the early 1260s while he was temporarily based in Orvieto, having responsibility for the formation of the Dominican community there. It is likely that he drew on existing material including Juliana's liturgy. He is thought to have revised the overall liturgy for a final version under Pope Clement V, but the hymn itself probably remained unchanged from the earlier version.

Tell, Oh Tongue

Of the glorious body telling,
O my tongue, its mysteries sing;
And the blood, all price excelling,
Which for this world's ransoming
In a generous womb once dwelling,
He shed forth, the gentiles' king.

Given for us, for us descending
Of a virgin to proceed,
Man with man in converse blending
Scattered he the gospel seed:
Till his sojourn drew to ending,
Which he closed in wondrous deed.

At the last great supper seated,
Circled by his brethren's band,
All the law required, completed
In the feast its statutes planned,
To the Twelve himself he meted
For their food with his own hand.

Word made flesh, by word he maketh
Very bread his flesh to be;
Man in wine Christ's blood partaketh,
And if senses fail to see,
Faith alone the true heart waketh
To behold the Mystery.

Therefore we, before it bending,
This great sacrament adore:
Types and shadows have their ending
In the new rite evermore:
Faith, our outward sense amending,
Maketh good defects before.

Honour, laud, and praise addressing
To the Father and the Son,
Might ascribe we, virtue, blessing,
And eternal benison:
Holy Ghost, from both progressing,
Equal laud to Thee be done! Amen.

The Imitation of Christ (extracts)
Thomas Kempis (1380–1471)

Author Although the work is anonymous, the attribution to Thomas Kempis is certain. He was born in Kemper in the Rhineland but spent much of his life as a member of an Augustinian monastic community in Zwolle in the Netherlands, where he twice served as subprior. Like Thomas Aquinas, but in a more modest capacity, he had responsibility for the teaching and formation of the community. He was a scholar of the Bible, and his writings are strongly grounded in the New Testament. Apart from the *Imitation*, his most famous work, he also wrote sermons and meditations for the novices in his charge and biographies of some key figures in the *Devotio Moderna* movement (see below).

Language Latin. An original manuscript by Thomas himself from 1441 is still preserved. The translation below is by Leo Sherley-Price.

Date 1418–1427.

Genre and context The *Imitation* is written in a monastic context but appears to be directed towards any Christian who wishes to advance in the Christian life. Its most distinctive feature is the way that it is presented as a conversation between the believer and Christ. Thomas writes in the tradition of the *Devotio Moderna*, a Dutch/German reform movement originating with Geert Grote (1340–1384), who founded the 'Brothers and Sisters of the Common Life'. In many ways it anticipated the Protestant Reformation of the following century: it was a reaction against the perceived decadence and clericalism of the established church; it emphasized personal piety and a return to the teaching of the New Testament. However, it also had a distinctive mystical element (see section on Jan Van Ruysbroeck in Chapter 8). In the extracts below, devotion to Christ's body is presented as a means of enduring the wait for ultimate communion with God.

The Imitation of Christ
Book 4: On the Blessed Sacrament, Chapters III:1 and XI:1–3

III On the Value of Frequent Communion

The Disciple: Lord, I come to You to receive the benefit of Your gift, and to enjoy the Feast that You have graciously prepared for the poor. In You I find all that I can or should desire; You are my Saviour and my Redeemer, my hopes and my strength, my honour and my glory. Therefore, Lord Jesus, gladden the soul of Your servant today, for to You I raise my soul. I desire to receive You with reverence and devotion: I long to invite You into my house, that, like Zaccheus, I may win Your blessing and be numbered among Your chosen. My soul longs to receive Your Body; my heart yearns to be united with You.

XI How the Body of Christ and the Holy Scripture are most Necessary to the Faithful Soul

The Disciple: Dearest Lord Jesus, how great is the joy of the devout soul who feasts at Your banquet, where the food set before it is none other than Your very Self, its only-Beloved, desirable above all the heart's desire! How deeply I long to pour my heartfelt tears in Your presence, and like the devoted Magdalen, bathe Your feet with my tears. But where is my devotion? And where this flood of holy tears? Surely, in Your presence and that of Your holy Angels my whole heart should burn and melt for joy! For here You are truly present with me in Your Sacrament, though veiled beneath another form.

I could not endure to gaze on You in the full glory of Your Divinity, nor could the whole world bear the splendour and glory of Your Majesty. Therefore You bear with my frailty, and conceal Yourself in this holy Sacrament. Here I truly possess and adore Him whom the Angels adore in Heaven; I, as yet, by faith alone, but they by sight and unconcealed. I must rest content with the light of true faith, and so remain until the day of endless glory dawn, and the shadow of figures pass away. When that which is perfect is come, the use of Sacraments will come to an end, for the Blessed in glory need no sacramental healing. They enjoy

---

the presence of God for ever, and view his unveiled glory; transformed from glory into glory of His own unsearchable divinity, they taste the Word of God made man, as He was from the beginning, and as He abides eternally.

When I consider these wonders, even spiritual consolations become wearisome; for so long as I cannot see my Lord in his unveiled glory, I value as nothing all that I can see or hear in this world. Lord, You are my witness that nothing can comfort me, nor can I rest content in anything created, but in You alone, O my God, on whom I long to gaze for ever. But this is not possible for me in this mortal life, so I must cultivate true patience, and submit all my desires to You. Your holy Saints, who now share Your joy in the Kingdom of Heaven, during their lives waited the coming of Your glory with great faith and patience. What they believed, I also believe; what they hoped to enjoy, I hope to enjoy; and whither they have arrived by Your grace, I hope to arrive also. Meanwhile I will walk in faith, strengthened by the example of the Saints; the holy scriptures shall be the comfort and mirror of my life, and above all Your most holy Body shall be my especial remedy and refuge.

5.3 The body of the believer

A concern with the transformation of the body of the believer is found in both Western and Eastern Christian spirituality, as the readings below illustrate. They all emphasize the incarnation, and understand it as conferring divinity on humanity in a kind of interchange. The Western readings are from the Franciscan tradition which understands devotion to the person of Christ to be most fully expressed in the physical medium of the believer's body.

Hymn of Divine Love 2 (extract)
Symeon the New Theologian (949–1022)

Author Symeon came from a wealthy aristocratic Byzantine family and was raised in preparation for a career as a court official in the imperial palace in Constantinople. It is therefore very likely that he was a eunuch, which makes his concern with the transformation of the body particularly poignant. During what was, by his own account, a colourful early career at court, he came under the influence of Symeon Eulabes, a monk from the local Stoudios Monastery, who is said to have shown great reverence for individual human bodies as manifestations of Christ himself. In 969 Symeon experienced a mystical vision (see p. 166), but it was not until 976, having taken refuge in the monastery following a palace coup, that he seriously pursued the religious life. This decision was marked by a vision of Christ in radiance. He moved to the monastery of St Mamas, where he was soon elected abbot and wrote several works of instruction for novices (*Discourses*). Following the death of his mentor around 986, Symeon faced increasing opposition from the imperial and ecclesiastical hierarchy; his *Treatises* on theology and ethics are in response to their charges of heresy. In 1009 he was banished to Paloukiton on the other side of the Bosphorus. He established a new monastery and remained there until his death. The *Hymns* date from this period. The title 'New Theologian' is thought to distinguish him from John the Evangelist and Gregory of Nazianzus (see Chapter 11), indicating the high regard in which he came to be held in a tradition which sees theology as the exclusive province of those who have seen the divine light.

Language Greek. The hymns circulated individually during Symeon's life. His disciple, Nicetas Stethatos, collected existing manuscripts and edited them into a definitive version in 1035. The translation below is by John Anthony McGuckin.

Date 1009–1022.

Genre and context Symeon wrote 58 hymns while in exile. They were composed as an adjunct to the formal liturgies of the church, aimed at supporting individual and communal spiritual advancement, and their personal and intimate tone are unprecedented in Eastern Christianity. They begin with an invocation of the Holy Spirit, who descends and then works on the individual to achieve *theosis*, drawing her into the godhead. In this extract Symeon alludes to a past marked by shame and sexual violation, but scholars have been cautious about taking this as a simple autobiographical statement. In contrast to Thomas Kempis, Symeon insists that Christ can be known directly now (see his entry in Chapter 9). For him the Eucharist is not so much something on account for the future as an expression of a present reality.

Hymn of Divine Love 2:1–19

By what boundless mercy, my Saviour,
Have you allowed me to become a member of your body?
Me, the unclean, the defiled, the prodigal.
How is it that you have clothed me
With the brilliant garment,
Radiant with the splendour of immortality,
That turns all my members into light?
Your body, immaculate and divine,
Is all radiant with the fire of your divinity,
With which it is ineffably joined and combined.
This is the gift you have given me, my God:
That this mortal and shabby frame
Has become One with your immaculate body
And that my blood has been mingled with your blood.
I sense too that here I have been made one with your divinity,
And have even become your own most pure body:
A brilliant member lucidly transparent,
Luminous and holy.
I see the beauty of it all, I can gaze upon your radiance.
I have become a reflection of the light of your grace.

The Life of Francis and The Mystical Vine (extracts)
Bonaventure (c.1217–1274)

Author Giovanni di Fidanza was born in Bagnoregio in central Italy, the son of a physician. During his childhood he suffered a near-fatal illness from which he dramatically recovered; he attributed this to divine action in response to his mother's invocation of Francis of Assisi (who by then was probably already dead). When Giovanni was 17, he went to study at the University of

Paris and came directly under the influence of Franciscans, and he entered the Order in 1243, taking on the name Bonaventure. He worked first as an academic theologian and in 1257 became the Minister General of the Franciscan Order. In 1273 he was appointed Cardinal Bishop of Albano, taking on wider responsibilities across the church as a whole. He seems to have combined personal holiness, intellectual prowess and political skill. Bonaventure wrote many works of theology and spirituality, the most famous being *The Tree of Life* and *The Soul's Journey into God* (see Chapter 10).

Language Latin. The translation of *The Life of Francis* is by Ewart Cousins and *The Mystical Vine* is by an anonymous Franciscan.

Date *The Life* was commissioned in 1260 by the Franciscan Chapter of Narbonne. The authorship and date of *The Mystical Vine* is much less certain, but most scholars agree that it is, at least in large part, the work of Bonaventure.

Genre and context *The Life* is a formal sacred biography but it is also deeply personal. Bonaventure spent time meditating on Mount Verna, where Francis had received the wounds of Christ on his own body in September 1224. *The Mystical Vine* is thought to be based on a sermon that explores the metaphor of the Church as the vine. The section below presents Christ's bodily wounds as a point of entry to a process of transformation in the believer.

The (Longer) Life of Francis
Chapter XIII: On his Sacred Stigmata

5. When the true love of Christ
had transformed his lover into his image
and the forty days were over
that he had planned to spend in solitude,
and the feast of St. Michael the Archangel
had also arrived,
the angelic man Francis
came down from the mountain,
bearing with him
the image of the Crucified,
which was depicted not on tablets of stone
or on panels of wood
by the hands of a craftsman,
but engraved in the members of his body
by the finger of the living God.

The Mystical Vine
Chapter XXIV: An Exhortation to the Contemplation
of the Passion and Charity of Christ

… Therefore, O soul, meditate with affection on all these things, for that is the only possible way by which you can enter that Paradise which is better than all paradises. Later you will become worthy enough to enter it in body as well as in soul.

Nor should you curtail your embrace of this Paradise, but you should like a bee fly into each flower and lick each petal. As the streams of his blood are sprinkled now on his right hand, and now on his left, he draws closer to us, and our approach to him becomes more intimate. Everywhere we may cull devotion, and the grace of a tearful compunction. From either side we may ponder the rough way in which those nails were driven in, the sensitiveness of his nerves, and how painful must have been the rupture of the bones in his hands, those hands that made heaven and earth.

See how he has wrought 'salvation in the midst of the earth.' You should often meditate on these things. 'Restore unto me the joy of thy salvation' in the manner of the little bee, who while flying makes a continual buzz and is only silent when he enters a flower, where he gathers and sucks the sweet honey for which he has longed so much. Oh, how happy will you be if, after you have entered these sanguinary flowers, the wounds of Christ, which belong to our garden so blooming, a garden sweeter than all other, you are found worthy of a complete release from the din of this world and from all bouts of temptation, and be free to attend to Jesus alone.

Then when you have come to him, you will 'taste and see how gracious the Lord is.' In the same way you must also look upon his feet, for there was just as much blood on them, and as much pain in them as in his hands. They, too, were pierced and perforated; they, too, were dripping and besprinkled with sanguinary streams and drops of blood.

Finally, through the door of his lanced side, we enter that humblest of all hearts, the heart of Jesus the most high. Here without any doubt lies that ineffable treasure, the love for which we have ever longed. There, too, we shall find that devotion whence the grace of tears is drawn, and from which we may learn gentleness and patience in adversity and sympathy with all who are afflicted. In particular we shall find there a humble and contrite heart. So great a love longs for and craves for your heart; such love longs to embrace you.

That head, so full of blossom, pierced with so many pricks, inclines towards you. It offers you the kiss of peace, and says, as it were: 'See how transfixed, how pierced, how immolated I am.' I suffer all this that I may place you, my wandering sheep, upon my shoulders, and bring you back to my garden of heavenly pastures. I bid you, in your turn, to yield yourself to me. Allow yourself to be moved with pity at my wounds, and 'set me' just as you see me 'as a seal upon thy heart, as a seal upon thine arm,' so that my image may be impressed upon you, and that in all the thoughts of your heart and in all the works of your hands you may be found such as you see me to be.

I will have you formed to the image of my deity, in which I created you. It was in order that I might fashion you that I myself was fashioned in the image of your humanity. Do you, then, who failed to preserve the likeness of my deity impressed upon you in your creation, at least preserve that humanity of yours, which was impressed upon me at your recreation. If you no longer preserve the form in which I created you, preserve at least the form in which I have recreated you …

The Memorial of Angela of Foligno (extract)
Brother A (late thirteenth century)

Author An anonymous friar. Very little is reliably known of Angela Foligno/ de Foligna herself. She was born in the mid-thirteenth century, died in 1309, and presumably came from Foligno in the Umbrian province of Perugia. Around 1285, deeply aware of her own sinfulness, she took up a life of poverty and humility and undertook a pilgrimage to Assisi, where she underwent a dramatic experience of spiritual abandonment at the entrance to the Basilica, with her distress very evident to onlookers. This was the beginning of her relationship with Brother A who later became her biographer. She was not a member of the Franciscan order and is usually described as a 'lay penitent'. However, she followed a rule of life rather like that of present-day Third Order Franciscans, and she had many associates who were members of the order. She was well-known for her piety, her mystical spirituality and her teaching ministry. She had a large following, who wrote up her collected teachings under the title of *The Instructions*.

Language Dictated in vernacular Italian and translated into Latin. The original manuscripts are lost and surviving earliest copies, from at least 20 years after the original, show a good deal of variation. The translation below is by Paul LaChance OFM.

Date 1292–1296.

Genre and context Sacred biography. Angela's 'writings' cover a wide range of theological topics, and give detailed accounts of her mystical experiences. This passage (not for the squeamish) is focused on divine knowledge received 'through the ears of the body'.

The Memorial
Chapter V: Third supplementary step

Imagine a man who has many friends and invites all of them to a banquet. And he sets a place aside for those who accept his invitation – for not all do – at his banquet table. This man is grief-stricken over those who do not come, for the banquet he had prepared was very lavish. All those who do come he places at his banquet table. But even though he loves all his guests and treats them all to his banquet, there are some he loves more, and these are placed at a special table near him. And those whom he loves even more intimately get to eat from the same plate and drink from the same cup as he does.

[Brother A] I ... challenged what she had said to me concerning the aforementioned teachings ... how the special sons ... even if they initially experience this eating and drinking as bitter, it nonetheless becomes sweet for them, and indeed most delectable – I insisted that their experience was a bitter one. In response, Christ's faithful one related a story to me through which she tried to show me that it was not bitter but sweet.

This is what she told me: On Maundy Thursday I suggested to my companion that we go out to find Christ: 'Let's go', I told her, 'to the hospital and perhaps we will be able to find Christ there among the poor, the suffering, and the afflicted.' We brought with us all the head veils we could carry, for we had nothing else. We told Giliola, the servant at the hospital, to sell them and from the sale to buy some food for those in that hospital to eat. And, although initially she strongly resisted our request, and said we were trying to shame her, nonetheless, because of our repeated insistence, she went ahead and sold our small head veils and from the sale bought some fish. We had also brought with us all the bread which had been given us to live on.

And after we had distributed all that we had, we washed the feet of the women and the hands of the men, and especially those of one of the lepers which were festering in an advanced stage of decomposition. Then we drank the very water with which we had washed him. And the drink was so sweet that, all the way home, we tasted its sweetness and it was if we had received Holy Communion. As a small scale of the leper's sores was stuck in my throat, I tried to swallow it. My conscience would not let me spit it out, just as if I had received Holy Communion. I really did not want to spit it out but simply to detach it from my throat.

Further reading

Augustine's Preached Theology: Living as the body of Christ by J. Patout Burns Jr. Grand Rapids, MI: Eerdmans, 2022.

The Book of Mystical Chapters: Meditations on the soul's ascent, from the Desert Fathers and other early Christian contemplatives by John Anthony McGuckin. Boulder, CO: Shambala Publications, 2003.

A Gift of Presence: The theology and poetry of the Eucharist in Thomas Aquinas by Jan-Heiner Tük. Washington DC: Catholic University of America Press, 2018.

Illness and Authority: Disability in the life and Lives of Francis of Assisi by Donna Trembinski. Toronto: University of Toronto Press, 2020.

Pachomius: The making of a community in fourth-century Egypt by Philip Rousseau. Berkeley, CA: University of California Press, 1999.

Pillars of Community: Four rules of pre-Benedictine monastic life by Terence Kardong OSB. Collegeville, MN: Liturgical Press, 2010.

Seeking God: The way of St Benedict by Esther de Waal. Norwich: Canterbury Press, 1999.

6

(re-)Attaching Imaginatively

Abide in me as I abide in you. Just as the branch cannot bear fruit by itself unless it abides in the vine, neither can you unless you abide in me. I am the vine, you are the branches. Those who abide in me and I in them bear much fruit, because apart from me you can do nothing.
(John 15.4–5)

'Jerusalem, Jerusalem, the city that kills the prophets and stones those who are sent to it! How often have I desired to gather your children together as a hen gathers her brood under her wings, and you were not willing!'
(Matthew 23.37)

'"For this reason a man shall leave his father and mother and be joined to his wife, and the two shall become one flesh." So they are no longer two, but one flesh. Therefore what God has joined together, let no one separate.'
(Mark 10.7–9)

For I am convinced that neither death, nor life, nor angels, nor rulers, nor things present, nor things to come, nor powers, nor height, nor depth, nor anything else in all creation, will be able to separate us from the love of God in Christ Jesus our Lord.
(Romans 8 38–39)

I want to know Christ and the power of his resurrection and the sharing of his sufferings by becoming like him in his death, if somehow I may attain the resurrection from the dead. Not that I have already obtained this or have already reached the goal; but I press on to make it my own, because Christ Jesus has made me his own.
(Philippians 3.10–12)

Bonaventure's exploration of Christ the mystical vine draws on John 15, part of Jesus' farewell discourse in which he impresses on his followers the need to remain attached to him in the future, even though he will not be physically present with them. Attachment-separation is a strong theme in bereavement. Back in the 1940s when the psychiatrist John Bowlby was beginning the work that he would eventually build into attachment theory, he was already reflecting on the resonances between the reactions of young children to parental separation and the response of adults to bereavement: they share a continuing, often desperate, desire to remain connected to the one who has been lost with strikingly similar emotional and behavioural features. The final volume of his famous trilogy *Attachment and Loss* is devoted almost entirely to this theme.[1]

When a child is separated from a parent for an extended period it is necessary for her to loosen her attachment to the absent parent and find alternative attachment figures. Bowlby pointed out that this is also an aspect of bereavement, but it is now understood that maintaining some sort of continuing bond with the deceased is also important.[2]

The use of the imagination plays a big part in this. My parents died over ten years ago but I still talk to them fairly often. I am not deluding myself that they are physically present with me, but neither does it feel like total fantasy. One way of understanding this is to invoke the psychological concept of 'transitional space'.[3] This is a mental mode characterized by 'As if' thinking: when I talk to my parents it can be 'as if' they were present with me in the room. Now, this is absolutely not what is going on in the New Testament reports of encounters with the risen Christ; but it *is* what much of Christian spirituality through the ages has explicitly encouraged as a means of staying connected to the ascended Christ. The imagination is seen as a vital part of prayer, a potentially sacred faculty which is to be cultivated under the guidance of the community of faith, all the while trusting to the help of the Holy Spirit to lead it aright.[4]

This chapter presents readings that engender a sense of attachment to and intimacy with Christ in a number of different ways. The first draws on the most primal human feelings by presenting Christ as the mother who nurtures and protects the believer. The second presents Christ as the believer's lover, offering something more like erotic union. (Incidentally, Bowlby's theory notes that the affectional bonds between lovers are in many respects a re-working of the parental attachment bonds of infancy, so the two are quite closely connected.) The third frames suffering in this life as a means of coming closer to the Christ who suffered for us. Finally, there are readings which understand immersion in the written word as a means of attaching to the eternal Word (John 1.1).

---

1 J. Bowlby, 1980, *Loss: Sadness and depression*, London: Hogarth Press.

2 M. Stroebe, H. Shut and K. Boerner, 2010, 'Continuing bonds in adaptation to bereavement: Towards theoretical integration', *Clinical Psychology Review*, 30, pp. 259–68.

3 See J. Collicutt, 2015, *The Psychology of Christian Character Formation*, London: SCM Press, pp. 170–3 for a full discussion.

4 See T. Luhrman, 2012, *When God Talks Back*, New York: Alfred A. Knopf for a detailed exploration in a contemporary charismatic evangelical context.

6.1 Parental attachment

Prayer to St Paul (extract)
Anselm of Canterbury (1033–1109)

Author (see p. 38).

Language Latin. This translation is by Benedicta Ward SLG from contemporary manuscripts.

Date c.1070.

Genre and context (see p. 38). This prayer may have been written specifically for Princess Adelaide (daughter of William the Conqueror). The maternal imagery is juxtaposed with the vocabulary of atonement, and the connection with Paul is evident in the language of justification.

Prayer to St Paul
(final stanza)

Christ, my mother,
you gather your chickens under your wings;
this dead chicken of yours puts himself under those wings.
For by your gentleness the badly frightened are comforted,
by your sweet smell the despairing revived,
your warmth gives life to the dead,
your touch justifies sinners.
Mother, know again your dead son,
both by the sign of your cross and the voice of his confession.
Warm your chicken, give life to your dead man,
justify your sinner.
Let your terrified one be consoled by you;
despairing of himself let him be comforted by you;
and in your whole and unceasing grace
let him be refashioned by you.
For from you flows consolation for sinners;
to you be blessing for ages and ages. Amen.

The Way of Perfection (extract)
Teresa of Avila (1515–1582)

Author Teresa de Cepeda y Ahumada was born in Avila in central Spain into a family of Jewish heritage. Her grandfather had converted to Christianity under the Inquisition in Toledo and had used his wealth to establish a new life and Christian identity in Avila. When Teresa was twelve her mother died, and this loss appears to have played an important part in the subsequent development of her spirituality. She entered the Carmelite Convent of the Incarnation in 1536 but almost immediately fell very seriously ill. During her recovery she began to read more deeply in theology and spirituality. She was particularly influenced by Francisco de Osuna's *The Third Spiritual Alphabet*, which introduced her to contemplative prayer. After several years of apparent stability, she experienced a deep intensification of her faith, including frequent mystical experiences. She felt called to form a new Carmelite community, aspiring to a simpler and more solitary life in keeping with that of Elijah, the original inspiration for the Carmelite order. This initially met with strong resistance from the Avila city authorities, and the rest of Teresa's life was marked by periods of ecclesiastical and political opposition to the extent of persecution, and factional in-fighting as she, together with John of the Cross (see Chapter 8), pursued a much wider programme of reform of the order across Europe. This ended with the formal separation of its two arms into the Ancient Observance and Teresian communities in 1581. Teresa was a prolific writer; her most famous works are *The Way of Perfection*, *The Interior Castle* and her autobiography.

Language Spanish. Two original manuscripts still exist, though Teresa's final version had undergone some editing by a Dominican friar, García de Toledo. The translation below is by E. Allison Peers.

Date 1560s, probably 1566.

Genre and context Teresa had written her spiritual autobiography between 1562 and 1565 during her time in her first independent community in Avila. Her sisters were eager to read the work as a source of spiritual instruction, but Teresa's confessor, the Dominican theologian Domingo Bànñez, was concerned that the vivid description of mystical experiences would not be suitable for nuns who had a more modest experience of prayer. It was therefore agreed that she write a manual on the life of prayer. She partly modelled it on Thomas Kempis' *Imitation* (see Chapter 6), and it was checked for doctrinal orthodoxy by de Toledo. In this extract she describes the 'prayer of quiet', a phase between discursive meditation and wordless contemplation in which the believer lets go and, as it were, rests in God as if they were an infant at the breast.

The Way of Perfection
Chapter XXXI

Now, daughters, I still want to describe this Prayer of Quiet to you, in the way I have heard it talked about, and as the Lord has been pleased to teach it to me, perhaps in order that I might describe it to you. It is in this kind of prayer, as I have said, that the Lord seems to me to begin to show us that He is hearing our petition: He begins to give us His Kingdom on earth so that we may truly praise Him and hallow His name and strive to make others do so likewise.

This is a supernatural state, and, however hard we try, we cannot reach it for ourselves; for it is a state in which the soul enters into peace, or rather in which the Lord gives it peace through His presence, as He did to that just man Simeon ... Just so, though less clearly, does the soul know Who He is. It cannot understand how it knows Him, yet it sees that it is in the Kingdom (or at least is near to the King Who will give it the Kingdom), and it feels such reverence that it dares to ask nothing. It is, as it were, in a swoon, both inwardly and outwardly, so that the outward man (let me call it the 'body', and then you will understand me better) does not wish to move, but rests, like one who has almost reached the end of his journey, so that it may the better start again upon its way, with redoubled strength for its task ...

Pay great attention to the following comparison, which *the Lord suggested to me when I was in this state of prayer, and which* seems to me very appropriate. The soul is like an infant still at its mother's breast: such is the mother's care for it that she gives it its milk without its having to ask for it so much as by moving its lips. That is what happens here. The will simply loves, and no effort needs to be made by the understanding, for it is the Lord's pleasure that, without exercising its thought, the soul should realize that it is in His company, and should merely drink the milk which His Majesty puts into its mouth and enjoy its sweetness. The Lord desires it to know that it is He Who is granting it that favour and that in its enjoyment of it He too rejoices. But it is not His will that the soul should try to understand how it is enjoying it, or what it is enjoying; it should lose all thought of itself, and He Who is at its side will not fail to see what is best for it. If it begins to strive with its mind so that the mind may be apprised of what is happening and thus induced to share in it, it will be quite unable to do so, and the soul will perforce lose the milk and forgo that Divine sustenance.

This state of prayer is different from that in which the soul is wholly united with God, for in the latter state it does not even swallow its nourishment: the Lord places this within it, and it has no idea how. But in this state it even seems to be His will that the soul should work a little, though so quietly that it is hardly conscious of doing so. What disturbs it is the understanding and this is not the case when there is union of all the three faculties, since He Who created them suspends them: He keeps them occupied with the enjoyment that He has given them, without their knowing, or being able to understand, the reason. *Anyone who has had experience of this kind of prayer will understand quite well what I am saying if, after reading this, she considers it carefully, and thinks out its meaning: otherwise it will be Greek to her.*

Letter to Sister Françoise-Thérèse III (extract)
Thérèse of Lisieux (1873–1897)

Author Marie Françoise-Thérèse Martin was born in Alençon in Normandy, the youngest of five surviving daughters, to extremely devout Roman Catholic parents. Like Teresa of Avila, she lost her mother in childhood, but at the earlier age of four, after which the family moved the few miles to Lisieux. Her mother's death affected her greatly and the loss was compounded from the age of nine by the sequential departure of her older sisters to the religious life, three as Carmelites in Lisieux and one as a Visitandine in Caen. These women had effectively acted as surrogate mothers for Thérèse, and a desire for reunion seems to have contributed to her sense of calling to enter the local Carmelite convent herself, which she did at the exceptionally early age of 15. Much of her spirituality was focused on the process of maturing in the Christian life, both in relation to her struggles of being the baby in a motherless family and then as a teenage religious. Despite being widely read in theology and spirituality, she embraced a way of life that treasured childlike simplicity, emphasized love and repeatedly returned to the words and actions of Jesus in the Gospels. When her oldest sister, Pauline, was elected prioress in 1893, Thérèse became her assistant and mistress of novices, and much of her teaching on spirituality was delivered in this context. Apart from her spiritual autobiography, *Story of a Soul*, and her personal letters, her thought is known only through the report of others, mainly Pauline (Mother Agnes). She died of tuberculosis at the age of 24.

Language French. The translation below is by T. N. Taylor.

Date 12 July 1896

Genre and context A letter from Thérèse to her sister Léonie (Sister Françoise-

Thérèse) at the convent at Caen, when she knew that her condition was terminal. Here she uses a favourite image of the Christian life as that of a toddler stumbling along within the holding environment provided by a warm and indulgent mother.

Letter to Sister Françoise-Thérèse III

My Dear little Léonie,

… You are right – Jesus is content with a tender look or a sigh of love. For my part, I find it quite easy to practise perfection, now that I realise it only means making Jesus captive through His Heart. Look at a little child who has just vexed its mother, either by giving way to temper or by disobedience. If it hides in a corner and is sulky, or if it cries for fear of being punished, its mother will certainly not forgive the fault. But should it run to her with its little arms outstretched, and say; 'Kiss me, Mother; I will not do it again!' what mother would not straightway clasp her child lovingly to her heart, and forget all it had done? … She knows quite well that her little one will repeat the fault – no matter, her darling will escape all punishment so long as it makes appeal to her heart.

Even when the law of fear was in force, before Our Lord's coming, the prophet Isaias said – speaking in the name of the King of Heaven: 'Can a woman forget her babe? … And if she should forget, yet will I not forget thee.' What a touching promise! We who live under the law of Love, shall we not profit by the loving advances made by our Spouse? How can anybody fear Him Who allows Himself to be made captive 'with one hair of our neck'?

Let us learn to keep Him prisoner – this God, the Divine Beggar of love. By telling us that a single hair can work this wonder, He shows us that the smallest actions done for His Love are those which charm His Heart. If it were necessary to do great things, we should be deserving of pity, but we are happy beyond measure, because Jesus lets Himself be led captive by the smallest action. … With you, dear Léonie, little sacrifices are never lacking. Is not your life made up of them? I rejoice to see you in presence of such wealth, especially when I remember that you know how to make profit thereby, not only for yourself but likewise for poor sinners. It is so sweet to help Jesus to save the souls which He has ransomed at the price of His Precious Blood, and which only await our help to keep them from the abyss.

It seems to me that if our sacrifices take Jesus captive, our joys make Him prisoner too. All that is needful to attain this end is, that instead of giving ourselves over to selfish happiness, we offer to our Spouse the little joys He scatters in our path, to charm our hearts and draw them towards Him.

You ask for news of my health. Well, my cough has quite disappeared. Does that please you? It will not prevent Our Lord from taking me to Himself whensoever He wishes. And I need not prepare for that journey, since my whole endeavour is to remain as a little child. Jesus Himself must pay all its expenses, as well as the price of my admission to Heaven.

Good-bye, dearest one, pray to Him without fail for the last and least of your sisters.

6.2 Erotic union

The language of marriage, the sexual imagery of penetration and with-drawal, and framing yearning for God in terms of erotic desire are common among Christian spiritual writers (including Angela of Foligno, Bonaventure, Teresa and Thérèse whom we have already encountered). Beginning with the third-century church father Origen, many early Christian writers focused on the Song of Songs as an allegory of the believer's relationship with Christ. Writing in the fourth century, Gregory of Nyssa (see Chapter 7) was one of the first to note the way the interplay of presence and absence in this book intensifies a sense of longing, describing the spiritual progress of the soul as 'constantly going on with her quest and never ceasing in her ascent, now seeing that every fulfilment of her desire continually generates a further desire for the Transcendent'.[5]

***Commentary on the Song of Songs* (extracts)**
Bernard of Clairvaux (1090–1153)

Author Bernard de Fontaine was born in Burgundy, the son of the knight keeper of the local castle, and therefore of noble heritage. At the age of 19, following the death of his mother, to whom he appears to have been close, he joined the Benedictine community at the nearby abbey at Cîteaux (from which the name 'Cistercian' derives), taking many young men with him. This community had been founded in 1098 with the goal of returning to the ascetic and eremitic spirit of early monasticism (whose literature was being redis-covered) and following the rule of Benedict more rigorously. In 1115 Bernard was sent by the Abbot, Stephen Harding, to establish a new community at Clairvaux, which became hugely successful, coming both to dominate Euro-pean monasticism and to generate new movements including the Knights Templar (for which Bernard wrote the rule) and the Canons Regular of St Augustine. Bernard travelled widely in Europe, effectively acting as an authoritative peacemaker in several ecclesiastical and political disputes. He was also an enthusiastic and inspirational supporter of the Second Crusade. He wrote a good deal; his most famous works include the *Book of Consider-ations*, *Homilies in Praise of the Blessed Virgin Mary*, *On Loving God*, *On the Steps of Humility and Pride* and *Sermons on the Song of Songs*.

Language Latin. Many manuscripts circulated almost immediately through-out Cistercian abbeys and many of these remain in existence. The translation below is by Kilian Walsh OCSO.

Date 1130s.

---

5 Gregory of Nyssa, *Commentary on the Song of Songs*, tr. C. McCauley, Brookline: Hellenic College Press.

Genre and context Bernard wrote this series of 86 'sermons' during a period of relative calm in his life 'at home' in Clairvaux Abbey. He presents them as substantial teachings on the life of faith directed at experienced monks. There has been much scholarly debate as to whether these were orally delivered sermons written down at the time by a scribe or Bernard's written reflections in sermonic form, with more recent scholarship tending to favour the former. On the face of it this is a text about the believer's personal relationship with Christ but, as noted on p. 25, it is also embedding key theological ideas; notice also the very practical turn at the end of the extract.

Commentary on the Song of Songs
Sermons I.8, II.3, III.6

I.8 On the title of the book

We must conclude then it was a special divine impulse that inspired these songs of his that now celebrate the praises of Christ and his Church, the gift of holy love, the sacrament of endless union with God. Here too are expressed the mounting desires of the soul, its marriage song, an exultation of spirit poured forth in figurative language pregnant with delight.

II.3. On the various meanings of the kiss

I must ask you to try to give your whole attention here. The mouth that kisses signifies the Word who assumes human nature; the nature assumed receives the kiss; the kiss however, that takes its being both from the giver and the receiver, is a person that is formed by both, none other than 'the one mediator between God and mankind, himself a man, Christ Jesus.' It is for this reason that none of the saints dared say: 'let him kiss me with his mouth,' but rather, 'with the kiss of his mouth.' In this way they paid tribute to that prerogative of Christ, on whom uniquely and in one sole instance the mouth of the word was pressed, that moment when the fullness of the divinity yielded itself to him as the life of his body. A fertile kiss therefore, a marvel of stupendous self-abasement that is not a mere pressing of mouth upon mouth; it is the uniting of God with man. Normally the touch of lip on lip is the sign of the loving embrace of hearts, but this conjoining of natures brings together the human and divine, shows God reconciling 'to himself all things, whether on earth or in heaven.' 'For he is the peace between us, and has made the two into one.' This was the kiss for which just men yearned under the old dispensation, foreseeing as they did that in him they would 'find happiness and a crown of rejoicing,' because in him

---

were hidden 'all the jewels of wisdom and knowledge.' Hence their longing to taste that fullness of his.

III.6. The kiss of the Lord's feet, hands, and mouth

To you, Lord Jesus, how truly my heart has said: 'My face looks to you. Lord, I do seek your face.' In the dawn you brought me proof of your love, in my first approach to kiss your revered feet you forgave my evil ways as I lay in the dust. With the advancement of the day you gave your servant reason to rejoice' when, in the kiss of the hand, you imparted the grace to live rightly. And now what remains, O good Jesus, except that suffused as I am with the fullness of your light, and while my spirit is fervent, you would graciously bestow on me the kiss of your mouth, and give me unbounded joy in your presence. Serenely lovable above all others, tell me where will you lead your flock to graze, where will you rest it at noon?' Dear brothers, surely it is wonderful for us to be here, but the burden of the day calls us elsewhere. These guests, whose arrival has just now been announced to us, compel me to break off rather than to conclude a talk that I enjoy so much. So I go to meet the guests, to make sure that the duty of charity, of which we have been speaking, may not suffer neglect, that we may not hear it said of us: 'They do not practise what they preach.' Do you pray in the meantime that God may accept the homage of my lips for your spiritual welfare, and for the praise and glory of his name.

Letter IX
Hadewijch (thirteenth century)

Author Almost nothing is known of Hadewijch's life. Her writings indicate that she was well educated: in addition to vernacular Dutch, she was proficient in Latin and French. This, together with the courtly themes in her writing, suggests that she was from an upper-class family, probably from Antwerp. She indicates that she was for a time the head of a Beguine community. The Beguines were part of a lay 'pious woman' movement inspired by the itinerant Breton preacher Robert D'Arbrissel that arose in the Low Countries in the thirteenth century. They pursued a life modelled on the early church as described in Acts. Later, Hadewijch seems to have adopted an itinerant form of life that was in keeping with the romantic quest for true love characteristic of the contemporary troubadour ballads that influenced her writings. These writings include poems, letters and a *Book of Visions*.

Language Middle Dutch, Brabant dialect. Her work was disseminated among

Beguine communities but there is only one surviving manuscript of her letters dating from the fourteenth century. The translation below is by Paul Mommaers.

Date Possibly 1230s.

Genre and context The 31 letters may have been written as a form of spiritual instruction to a community of pious women, either local or dispersed. Hadewijch's writing is influenced by Bernard of Clairvaux and some of his successors, and is pervaded with the language of love, exploring its complex ramifications in the believer's relationship with God and other human beings. The letters are poetic in form, perhaps crafted for reading aloud.

Letter IX
I in him and he in me

May God make known to you, dear child,
who He is
and how He deals
with his servants,
and especially with His handmaids;
and devour you in Him:

where the depth of His wisdom is,
there He will teach you
what He is,
and how wondrously sweetly
one beloved indwells the other,
and so through and through indwells the other
that neither of them recognises himself,
but they mutually enjoy each other
mouth in mouth,
and heart in heart,
and body in body,
and soul in soul,
and one sweet divine nature flowing through them both,
and both of them one through each other
and also both remain,
yes, so they remain.

Fourth letter to Agnes of Prague (extract)
Clare of Assisi (1194–1253)

Author Chiara Offreduccio was born to a wealthy aristocratic family in Assisi. Her mother was a devout Christian and Clare is said to have been a prayerful child. In 1212, having heard Francis preach and with his help, she embraced a life of poverty initially under the protection of local Benedictine convents. Eventually she was provided with a house and established her own community at San Damiano, living according to a rule provided by Francis. In 1216 she officially became abbess of the order (later to be known as the Poor Clares). Although the women led a largely enclosed life, they became well-known across Europe through their more mobile Franciscan brothers. Throughout her life, Clare strongly resisted repeated attempts to impose a less austere Benedictine form of rule on her community and fiercely guarded its independent identity. Francis and Clare were close spiritual and intellectual companions, and his death in 1226 was a great personal loss to her. Her writing is in part a means of keeping his teaching alive. She wrote *The Form of Life* (a rule for her order), several letters to leaders of female Franciscan and Beguine communities, *The Blessing*, and possibly *The Testament*.

Language Latin. The manuscript history is complex and there are early translations in several languages, but an existing manuscript appears to be a copy of the original letter made in 1332. The translation below is by Regis Armstrong OFMCap.

Date 1253.

Genre and context This is the last of four letters, all exhibiting the formal epistolary and rhetorical conventions of the time but nevertheless also reflecting a strong personal bond forged over a number of years engaged in the same mission. Clare's education is said to have been limited and it is likely that she was assisted in the composition by an unknown male scribe as the literary style is elaborate and sophisticated. Agnes, another aristocratic woman, had heard of Clare via Francis and, having established a monastery and hospital in Prague, requested that some women be sent from the Assisi community to help her set up her own community of Poor Clares in 1234. All four letters make heavy use of the mirror as an image for the soul, with the fourth letter, written shortly before Clare's death, having a strong emphasis on contemplation.

Fourth letter to Agnes of Prague

Now, however, as I write to your love, I rejoice and exult with you in the joy of the Spirit, O spouse of Christ, because, since you have totally abandoned the vanities of this world, like the other most holy virgin, Saint Agnes, you have been marvellously espoused to the spotless Lamb, Who takes away the sins of the world.

Happy, indeed, is she
to whom it is given to drink at this sacred banquet
so that she might cling with her whole heart
to Him
Whose beauty all the blessed hosts of heaven
unceasingly admire,
Whose tenderness touches,
Whose contemplation refreshes,
Whose kindness overflows,
Whose delight overwhelms,
Whose remembrance delightfully dawns,
Whose fragrance brings the dead to life again,
Whose glorious vision will bring happiness
to all the citizens of the heavenly Jerusalem,
which vision
since He is the radiance of eternal glory
is the brightness of eternal light and
the mirror without blemish.

Gaze upon that mirror each day,
O Queen and Spouse of Jesus Christ,
and continually study your face in it,
that you may adorn yourself completely,
within and without,
covered and arrayed in needlework
and similarly adorned
with the flowers and garments of all the virtues,
as is becoming, the daughter and dearest bride
of the Most High King.

Indeed,
in that mirror,
blessed poverty,
holy humility,
and inexpressible charity shine forth
as, with the grace of God,
you will be able to contemplate them throughout
the entire mirror.

Look, I say, at the border of this mirror, that is, the poverty of Him
Who was placed in a manger and wrapped in swaddling clothes.

O marvellous humility! O astonishing poverty!
The King of angels,
the Lord of heaven and earth,
is laid in a manger!

Then reflect upon, at the surface of the mirror, the holy humility, at
least the blessed poverty,
the untold labours and punishments
that He endured for the redemption of the whole human race.
Finally contemplate, in the depth of this same mirror,
the ineffable charity that He chose
to suffer on the tree of the Cross
and to die there the most shameful kind of death.

Therefore,
that Mirror, suspended on the wood of the Cross, warned those passing
by that here are things to be
considered, saying:
'All you who pass by the way, look and see if there is any suffering like
my suffering!'
'Let us respond to Him,' It says,
crying out and lamenting, in one voice, in one spirit:
'Remembering this over and over
leaves my soul sinking within me!'

O Queen of our heavenly King, may you, therefore, be inflamed ever
more strongly with the fire of love! As you further contemplate His
ineffable delights, riches and perpetual honors, and, sighing, may you
cry out from the great desire and love of your heart:

'Draw me after you,
let us run in the fragrance of your perfumes,
O heavenly Spouse!
I will run and not tire,
until You bring me into the wine-cellar,
until Your left hand is under my head
and Your right hand will embrace me happily,
You will kiss me with the happiest kiss of Your mouth.'

Resting in this contemplation, may you remember your poor little mother,
knowing that I have inscribed the happy memory of you indelibly on the
tablets of my heart, holding you dearer than all others.

Sermon on Isaiah 54.5 (extract)
George Whitefield (1714–1770)

Author George Whitefield was born in Gloucester, the son of innkeepers. Though poor, he gained entry to Oxford University where he met the Wesleys (see later in this chapter). Notwithstanding his Calvinist (as to opposed to their Arminian) stance on predestination, he became part of their 'Holy Club', and later president of the Methodist Conference. Following an intensification of his faith through a 'born again' experience, he offered himself for ordination in the Church of England and was ordained deacon in 1736 and priest in 1739. Like the Wesleys, his ministry had an emphasis on the evangelism of working people, and a good deal of it was conducted in the open air. Also like them, he spent a part of his ministerial life in the USA, and he devoted time, money and energy to the establishment of orphanages in Georgia and in Pennsylvania. His attitude to slavery and the rights of African Americans was complex: he was a plantation owner and used proceeds from slave labour for some of his philanthropic projects, but these in their turn were often directed at the emancipation, education and evangelization of enslaved people, and he was famously eulogized by the enslaved African American poet, Phillis Wheatley. Whitefield is best known for his involvement with revivals from about 1740, first in the USA and then Britain, in which he preached to huge crowds, said to number tens of thousands. This unorthodox, populist and emotional approach placed him in conflict with the conventional churches in both countries. He died in Massachusetts aged 55 and, despite their theological differences, John Wesley preached at his funeral.

Language English.

Date Delivered in July 1742 from notes and written up later.

Genre and context Whitefield was by all accounts an inspirational and charismatic preacher and his sermons were 'events'. But he was also eager to disseminate his message as widely as possible and so, with the help of his publicist William Seward, he produced written versions of his sermons for publication in newspapers and books, and it seems that he moderated their tone in the process. The text below is based on a sermon on Isaiah 54.5 that was first preached in the village of Cambuslang near Glasgow at an open-air service of Holy Communion with 1,700 communicants and many more attendees. The sermon is said to have electrified the crowd. It is different from the previous readings in this section as it is addressed to lay people, both men and women, married and single, yet it invokes the same imagery of attachment and separation from the beloved to communicate spiritual and theological truths.

'For thy Maker is thy husband.'

… But, though the words were originally spoken to the Jews, yet they are undoubtedly applicable to all believers in all ages, and, when enlarged on in a proper manner, will afford us suitable matter of discourse both for sinners and for saints; for such as know God, as well as for such who know him not; and likewise for those, who once walked in the light of his blessed countenance, but are now backslidden from him, have their harps hung upon the willows, and are afraid that their beloved is gone, and will return to their souls no more…

And indeed it is not so very material, though no doubt it is very satis-factory, if we cannot relate all the minute and particular circumstances, that attended our conversion; if so be we are truly converted now, and can say, the work is done, and that, 'our Maker is our husband.' And I question, whether there is one single adult believer, now on earth, who lived before conversion, either in a course of secret or open sin, but can, in a good degree, give an account of the beginning and progress of a work of grace in his heart …

And if you are adult, and are indeed married to Jesus Christ, though you may be unlearned, and what the world terms illiterate men, cannot you tell me the rise and progress, and consummation of the spiritual marriage, between Jesus Christ and your souls? Know you not the time, when you were first under the drawings of the Father, and Jesus began to woo you for himself? Tell me, O man, tell me, O woman, knowest thou not the time, or at least, knowest thou not, that there was a time, when the blessed Spirit of God stripped thee of the fig-leaves of thy own righteousness, hunted thee out of the trees of the garden of thy perform-ances, forced thee from the embraces of thy old husband the law, and made thee to abhor thy own righteousness, as so many filthy rags? Canst thou not remember, when, after a long struggle with unbelief, Jesus appeared to thee, as altogether lovely, mighty and willing to save? And canst thou not reflect upon a season, when thy own stubborn heart was made to bend; and thou was made willing to embrace him, as freely offered to thee in the everlasting gospel? And canst thou not, with pleasure unspeakable, reflect on some happy period, some certain point of time, in which a sacred something (perhaps thou could it not then well tell what) did captivate, and fill thy heart, so that thou could say, in a rapture of holy surprise, and ecstasy of divine love, 'My Lord and my God! My beloved is mine, and I am his; I know that my Redeemer liveth;' or, to keep to the words of our text, 'My Maker is my husband.' Surely, amidst this great and solemn assembly, there are many that can answer these questions in the affirmative. For these are transactions, not easily to be forgotten; and the day of our espousals is, generally, a very remarkable day; a day to be had in everlasting remembrance.

6.3 Solidarity through suffering-with

Revelations of Divine Love (extract)
Julian of Norwich (1343–c.1416)

Author Almost nothing is known about the anonymous woman called 'Julian' (possibly after the church to which she was attached) other than that she was (at least in later life) an anchorite living in Norwich, known and valued for her wise counsel. Autobiographical aspects of her writings indicate that, while critically ill at the age of 30, she experienced a series of visions or 'shewings', which she recounted in detail following her recovery.

Language Middle English. The translation below is by Clifton Wolters. The earliest manuscript dates from the fifteenth century.

Date The shewings occurred in May 1373 over a period of seven days, and the 'shorter text' was probably written soon after.

Genre and context The shorter text, from which the extract below is taken, appears to be a near contemporaneous first-person account of a series of visions, either written by Julian or dictated to a scribe. A longer account which is thought to date from about 20 years later is a more leisured theological reflection on the visions, with editorial contributions from others. The setting in which Julian lived was one dominated by the sufferings of plagues, which swept through Norwich three times in her lifetime, the civil conflict of the Peasants' Revolt and the Hundred Years War in Europe. The need to find meaning in suffering was never far away.

Revelations of Divine Love
Chapter III

When I was half way through my thirty-first year God sent me an illness which prostrated me for three days and nights. On the fourth night I received the last rites of Holy Church as it was thought I could not survive till day. After this I lingered two more days and nights, and on the third night I was quite convinced that I was passing away – as indeed were those about me.

Since I was still young I thought it a great pity to die – not that there was anything on earth I wanted to live for, or on the other hand any pain that I was afraid of, for I trusted God and his mercy. But were I to live I might come to love God more and better, and so ultimately to know and love him more in the bliss of heaven. Yet compared with that eternal bliss the length of my earthly life was so insignificant and short that it

---

seemed to me to be nothing. And so I thought, 'Good Lord, let my ceasing to live be to your glory!' Reason and suffering alike told me I was going to die, so I surrendered my will wholeheartedly to the will of God.

Thus I endured till day. By then my body was dead from the waist downwards, so far as I could tell. I asked if I might be helped and supported to sit up, so that my heart could be more freely at God's disposal, and that I might think of him while my life still lasted.

My parish priest was sent for to be at my end, and by the time he came my eyes were fixed, and I could not longer speak. He set the cross before my face and said, 'I have brought you the image of your Maker and Saviour. Look at it, and be strengthened.'

I thought indeed that what I was doing was good enough, for my eyes were fixed heavenwards where by the mercy of God I trusted to go. But I agreed none the less to fix my eyes on the face of the crucifix if I could. And this I was able to do. I thought that perhaps I could look straight ahead longer than I could look up.

Then my sight began to fail, and the room became dark about me, as if it were night, except for the image of the cross which somehow was lighted up; but how was beyond my comprehension. Apart from the cross everything else seemed horrible as if it were occupied by fiends.

Then the rest of my body began to die, I could hardly feel a thing. As my breathing became shorter and shorter I knew for certain that I was passing away.

Suddenly all my pain was taken away, and I was as fit and well as I had ever been; and this was especially true of the lower part of my body. I was amazed at this sudden change, for I thought it must have been a special miracle of God, and not something natural. And though I felt so much more comfortable I still did not think I was going to survive. Not that this experience was any real comfort to me, for I was thinking I would much rather have been delivered from the world!

Then it came suddenly to mind that I should ask for the second wound of our Lord's gracious gift, that I might in my own body fully experience and understand his blessed passion. I wanted his pain to be my pain; a true compassion producing a longing for God. I was not wanting a physical vision or revelation of God, but such compassion as a soul would naturally have for our Lord Jesus, who for love became a mortal man. Therefore I desired to suffer with him.

Was you there?
Anonymous African American Spiritual (nineteenth century)

Author Anonymous.

Language American English.

Date The first published version is in *Jubilee Songs as Sung by Slayton's Jubilee Singers* of 1884–5.

Genre On the face of it this is a simple lament for Christ in the tradition of some of the texts in Chapter 4 but, like all spirituals, it carries other meanings. There is a strong sense of solidarity between the crucified Christ and the singer, whose first-person voice stands, like that of the Psalmist, for the whole community. The reference to execution on a tree draws out the connection with lynchings that were common in that period; to be lynched is to be identified with Christ in his suffering.

Was you there?

Was you there when they crucified my Lord?
Was you there when they crucified my Lord?
O sometimes it causes me to tremble! tremble! tremble!
Was you there when they crucified my Lord?

Was you there when they nailed him to the tree?
Was you there when they nailed him to the tree?
O sometimes it causes me to tremble! tremble! tremble!
Was you there when they nailed him to the tree?

Was you there when they pierced him in the side?
Was you there when they pierced him in the side?
O sometimes it causes me to tremble! tremble! tremble!
Was you there when they pierced him in the side?

Was you there when the sun refused to shine?
Was you there when the sun refused to shine?
O sometimes it causes me to tremble! tremble! tremble!
Was you there when the sun refused to shine?

6.4 'Holding fast to the word of life'[6]

Commentary on the Twelve Psalms (extracts)
Ambrose of Milan (c.339–397)

Author Ambrose was born in Trier, then part of the Roman province of Gaul. His father was a senior Roman administrator who died when Ambrose was young, and the family then moved to Rome where he received a classical education. Ambrose entered public service and in 373 was appointed Governor of Upper Italy by Emperor Valentinian. He was appointed Bishop of Milan as a recently baptized Christian for largely political reasons (his capacity to keep the peace between different factions in the aftermath of the Arian controversy) and he was always politically as well as ecclesiastically active. Following his consecration, he began a lifelong deep study of the Bible, and it remained central to his theology. From the beginning of the fourth century, the eastern and western parts of the Roman Empire had been splitting and there was increasing pressure from Germanic forces. This, together with the continuing, often violent, conflict between Christians holding Arian or Nicene beliefs about the person of Christ, resulted in volatile switches between periods when Ambrose exercised great influence through imperial patronage and others when he underwent strong opposition and persecution. Despite his administrative duties Ambrose wrote a good deal of biblical, dogmatic and spiritual theology. He is also known for his hymnody, possibly including the *Exsultet* (the long hymn traditionally sung on Holy Saturday).

Language Latin. The translation below is by Íde Ní Riain.

Date c.390–397. The earliest manuscripts are medieval.

Genre and context These are from sermons preached in church, which were later polished by Ambrose and dictated to his secretary, Paulinus. Ambrose not only interpreted the Old Testament as pointing forward to Christ, but as a place where Christ is encountered sacramentally, and the psalms as the prayers of Christ in which the believer can participate (Romans 8.34).

---

6 Philippians 2.16.

Commentary on the Twelve Psalms

Psalm 1:2 But his delight is in the law of the Lᴏʀᴅ; and in his law doth he meditate day and night.

… Drink the cup[7] of Old or New Testament. In both you are drinking Christ. Drink Christ, for he is the vine. Drink Christ, for he is the rock from which the water gushes and the very fountain of life. Drink Christ for he is the river that flows through the city of God and gives it joy. Drink Christ, for he is our peace. Drink Christ, for 'from his breast shall fountains of living water flow'. Drink Christ, that you may drink the blood that redeemed you; drink Christ, that you may drink his words; his word is the Old Testament, his word is the New Testament. Divine scripture is imbibed, divine scripture is eaten, when the juice of the word eternal runs through the veins of the mind and enters into the vital parts of the soul. 'Man lives not by bread alone, but by every word of God.' Drink this word, but do so in proper order. 'First drink this,' meaning the Old Testament, and then drink the New…

Psalm 41:4[8] I said, Lᴏʀᴅ, be merciful unto me: heal my soul; for I have sinned against thee.

This could be spoken in person of King David. In spirit he saw Christ's glorious victory and he begs him for grace. He asks Christ to forgive him all his sins and to have mercy on him, As king, he was above all human laws, and yet he had to answer to God for those sins, and David knew that. He confesses his fault so that he might win forgiveness and gain a general indulgence as God's free gift.

The verse could also be said in the person of the Saviour, praying to God for mercy on us and saying that he had sinned – because for our sakes he was made sin. He is teaching us at the same time that when we find ourselves really hard put to it in battle with the enemy, we should pray to God for help. We should tell him our sins, all the more so when under terrible stress, laid low by grief and prostrate with sorrow. On these occasions do not appear silent, for by confessing you will find that the healing remedy reaches you sooner. Then, when we are feeling better, we can resist our agonist. For how can a wounded person enter the fight again? Let us learn from this that we are wounded by the stings of our own sins. A wound requires the doctor. The doctor insists on being told all.

---

7 Psalm 23.5 (also set for the day).
8 Psalm 40.5 in the Vulgate numbering system used by Ambrose.

Sermons on Several Occasions (extracts)
John Wesley (1703–1791)

Author John Wesley was born in Epworth, Lincolnshire, the son of a Church of England parish priest, Samuel, and his wife, Susanna (see Chapter 10). He studied at Oxford University, was ordained as a priest himself and became a Fellow of Lincoln College, Oxford. His younger brother Charles, while a student at Oxford, formed the 'Holy Club', a daily prayer and Bible study group aimed at deepening faith and personal holiness, and John joined in 1729. Group members received daily Holy Communion and practised good works, which would now be understood as social justice initiatives. Their disciplined and systematic approach to virtuous Christian living earned them the pejorative nickname 'Methodists'. Following a bruising period as a minister in Savannah, Georgia, from 1735 to 1737, during which time he came under the influence of Arminian teaching on the place of free will in salvation, John returned to England and became involved in the Moravian Church. It was at one of their meetings in London in 1738 that he famously underwent a 'conversion' experience. He began to develop his own distinct theological approach, which was influenced not only by Western Protestantism but by aspects of Eastern Orthodoxy, some of whose literature was becoming available at that time. He eventually joined George Whitefield in the practice of open-air preaching, largely because he was by then banned from many Anglican churches. However, he was more committed to indoor liturgical worship, and quickly developed both a network of accredited lay preachers (and later ordained ministers) and chapel buildings devoted to worship. He was a talented hymn writer and translator, highly progressive in his social views (for example on slavery and the status of women), and wrote widely in the areas of biblical theology, liturgy and spirituality including *Explanatory Notes on the New Testament* and *The Christian Library*.

Language English.

Date 'The Means of Grace' is from the period 1747; 'On God's Vineyard' is from the period between 1747 and 1788.

Genre and context These are extracts from a four-volume collection covering a period of nearly 50 years. Wesley explains in the preface that they are 'plain truth for plain people', setting out 'what I find in the Bible concerning the way to heaven'; and that they are not verbatim records of his sermons but sermon-like summaries of the substance of his teaching. For Wesley the Bible is the key to the virtuous life that enables us to wait well for the return of Jesus and to be drawn heavenwards ready for that day.

Sermons on Several Occasions

Preface to Volume I

… I want to know one thing, – the way to heaven; how to land safe on that happy shore. God himself has condescended to teach the way: For this very end he came from heaven. He hath written it down in a book. O give me that book! At any price, give me the book of God! I have it: Here is knowledge enough for me. Let me be *homo unius libri.* Here then I am, far from the busy ways of men. I sit down alone: Only God is here. In his presence I open, I read his book; for this end, to find the way to heaven …

The Means of Grace

'Ye are gone away from mine ordinances, and have not kept them.' (Malachi 3:7)

7. All who desire the grace of God are to wait for it in searching the Scriptures.
Our Lord's direction, with regard to the use of this means, is likewise plain and clear. 'Search the Scriptures,' saith he to the unbelieving Jews, 'for they testify of me.' (John 5:39.) And for this very end did he direct them to search the Scriptures, that they might believe in him …

10. Nor is this profitable only for the men of God, for those who walk already in the light of his countenance; but also for those who are yet in darkness, seeking him whom they know not. Thus St. Peter, 'We have also a more sure word of prophecy:' Literally, 'And we have the prophetic word more sure;' confirmed by our being 'eye-witnesses of his Majesty,' and 'hearing the voice which came from the excellent glory;' unto which – prophetic word; so he styles the Holy Scriptures – 'ye do well that ye take heed, as unto a light that shineth in a dark place, until the day dawn, and the Daystar arise in your hearts.' (2 Peter 1:19.) Let all, therefore, who desire that day to dawn upon their hearts, wait for it in searching the Scriptures.

On God's Vineyard

'What could have been done more to my vineyard, that I have not done in it wherefore, when I looked that it should bring forth grapes, brought it forth wild grapes.' (Isaiah. 5:4)

… From the very beginning, from the time that four young men united together, each of them was *homo unius libri* – a man of one book. God taught them all to make his 'Word a lantern unto their feet, and a light in all their paths.' (Psalm 119:105). They had one, and only one rule of judgment in regard to all their tempers, words, and actions, namely, the oracles of God. They were one and all determined to be 'Bible-Christians.' They were continually reproached for this very thing, some terming them in derision 'Bible bigots'; others 'Bible moths' – feeding they said upon the Bible as moths do upon cloth. And indeed unto this day it is their constant endeavour to think and speak as the oracles of God …

Further reading

At the Foot of the Cross with Julian of Norwich by Emma Pennington. Abingdon: Bible Reading Fellowship, 2020.

A Joyful Noise: Praying the psalms with the early church by Mike Aquilina. Steubenville, OH: Emmaus Road Publishing, 2018.

Plenty Good Room: A Lenten Bible study based on African American spirituals by Marilyn E. Thornton. Nashville, TN: Abingdon Press, 2016.

The Privilege of Poverty: Clare of Assisi, Agnes of Prague and the struggle for a Franciscan rule for women by Joan Mueller. University Park, PA: Pennsylvania State University Press, 2006.

The Song of Songs: A contemplative guide by Graeme Watson. London: SPCK, 2014.

Teresa of Avila: Doctor of the soul by Peter Tyler. London: Bloomsbury, 2014.

Thérèse of Lisieux: God's gentle warrior by Thomas Nevin. Oxford: Oxford University Press, 2006.

Wesley and the People Called Methodists by Richard Heitzenrater. Nashville, TN: Abingdon Press, 2013.

7

Returning

Jesus answered … 'Very truly, I tell you, no one can see the kingdom of God without being born from above.' Nicodemus said to him, 'How can anyone be born after having grown old? Can one enter a second time into the mother's womb and be born?'
(John 3.3–4)

After these things Jesus showed himself again to the disciples by the Sea of Tiberias; and he showed himself in this way. Gathered there together were Simon Peter, Thomas called the Twin, Nathanael of Cana in Galilee, the sons of Zebedee, and two others of his disciples. Simon Peter said to them, 'I am going fishing.' They said to him, 'We will go with you.'
(John 21.1–3)

The women who had come with him from Galilee … were terrified and bowed their faces to the ground, but the men said to them, 'Why do you look for the living among the dead? He is not here, but has risen. Remember how he told you, while he was still in Galilee, that the Son of Man must be handed over to sinners, and be crucified, and on the third day rise again.' Then they remembered his words …
(Luke 23.55; 24.5–8)

… our ancestors were all under the cloud, and all passed through the sea, and all were baptized into Moses in the cloud and in the sea, and all ate the same spiritual food, and all drank the same spiritual drink. For they drank from the spiritual rock that followed them, and the rock was Christ.
(1 Corinthians 10.1b–4)

Thinkers as far apart as the ancient Greek philosopher Heraclitus and the Lancashire comedian Peter Kay have, like Nicodemus, observed that, 'You can't go back.' Their point is that the past to which so many of us long to return ultimately eludes us. Nevertheless, the desire to go back remains a deep human instinct; and it is a particular feature of grief. We see it in Peter's return to the place, activity and identity he had when he first met Jesus, where hope first stirred and before the brutal reality of the cross all but wiped it out.

Mourning often involves a psychological journey (or repeated journeys) back; back to the place it all started when things were fresh and vibrant, perhaps innocent, and the years had not yet taken their toll. Funeral orders of service are increasingly adorned with photographs of the deceased in happier times when they were young and fit. This attempt to reclaim or recover the person's 'true identity' feels particularly important if the death has been preceded by an extended period of mental or physical decline.

Sometimes a physical journey is involved. Then the practicalities of travelling can feel very helpful, even more so if the destination enables one to fill in gaps, make memories more vivid, and see old contexts in new ways.

There is a kind of deep nostalgia at work here; with the recovery of memories come smiles and a sense of reconnection. It is even possible to be nostalgic for a time one hasn't personally experienced; Hogwarts is a school from a vicariously recalled past, but no less delightful for that. Yet, this desire to return has often been frowned upon: philosophers like Heraclitus assert that it is simply impossible; bereavement counsellors have tended to see it as an illusory form of escape from the reality of a loss that must be faced; and in the history of the church there has been an ambivalence about forms of spirituality that aim to (re)connect with the Jesus who walked this earth but has now departed.

In 2 Corinthians, Paul famously insists 'even though we once knew Christ from a human point of view [literally 'according to the flesh'], we know him no longer in that way' (5.16). Of course, Paul would have had a personal agenda here as he never met this human Jesus himself, but he is making a broader theological point: with the resurrection and ascension, the new age has arrived, and it makes no sense to live in the past (v.17).

The early church father John Cassian took a similar view; he held that imaginative contemplation of Jesus in his 'humble human flesh' was an inferior form of prayer when compared to contemplation of Jesus glorified and coming in his kingdom.[1] The practice of pilgrimage (journeying back) has also proved deeply controversial in both in the early and medieval church.

It appears then that the habit of returning, while clearly a strong human instinct, can, as in so much else, be embraced in a more or less healthy manner. While it is impossible to wipe out the reality of the intervening years, and misguided to try and do so, it is possible to travel back to the old in the light of the new and enter it afresh. This is, in effect, what is required when reading historical texts like the ones in this book, something referred to by the philosopher Paul Ricoeur as 'second naïveté'.

This chapter presents readings that return: travelling back to the source of it all; going back to the womb; and looking back with hindsight, as Paul does when he sees that the rock from which the people of Israel drank in their exodus wanderings had been Christ all along.

---

1 Cassian, *Conferences of the Desert Fathers* X.6.

7.1 *Ad fontes* (to the source)

The instinct to go back literally to where it all started is first seen in the development of pilgrimage to the Holy Land in the fourth century. Perhaps the most famous of these early pilgrims is Helena, the mother of the Emperor Constantine, who visited the Holy Land around 326–328. In the period when it was still relatively safe to travel there (before the seventh century) pilgrimages, and indeed the search for relics, became popular, especially for women. This period was soon enough after the time of Jesus for people to have some hope that traces of him still lingered (clearly evident in accounts of Helena's discovery of the 'true cross').

In Jewish tradition, pilgrimage essentially meant going up to the Jerusalem Temple. The first Christians rejected this idea because they understood themselves to be living stones built into a temple inhabited by the Holy Spirit (1 Peter 2.5), and anyway the Jerusalem Temple had been destroyed in AD 70. So, when Christian pilgrimage emerged it was not a journey to find God on his holy hill, but instead appears to have developed out of contemporary mourning rituals for departed saints and martyrs, which involved paying respects at the places they had ministered and been buried and communing with them there (the site of Cyprian's martyrdom is one of the earliest examples of this). If this could be done for the saints, why not for Jesus himself? The origins of Christian pilgrimage are thus, perhaps unexpectedly, to be found in bereavement.

The Pilgrimage of Egeria (extract)
Egeria (fourth century)

Author Nothing is known about Egeria other than what can be reconstructed from the text. She is believed to have come from northern Spain and was reasonably well educated, with a good knowledge of the Bible. She was wealthy enough to travel and to determine her own itinerary. She may have been a member of a religious order, but it is more likely that she was a devout laywoman.

Language Latin. The earliest surviving manuscript fragments are from the ninth century. The translation below is by Anne McGowan.

Date Most scholars believe the journey took place in the 380s but some place it up to two centuries later.

Genre and context A travel narrative in the form of letters home to a community of faith. Egeria's journey took several years, and she seems to have spent a good deal of time in Jerusalem. Her route went via Constantinople, through Asia Minor south to Antioch, then through Syria to Jerusalem, and culminated in a visit to Mount Sinai via Egypt. She took great care to describe liturgical practice at the sites she visited. In the extracts below the *Lazarium* is the tomb of Lazarus, the *Anastasis* is part of what is now the Church of the Holy Sepulchre on the site of Christ's tomb, the *Eleona* is the church on the Mount of Olives, the *Martyrium* the main church, and the *Imbomon* is the traditional site of the Ascension.

The Pilgrimage of Egeria
The Great Week in Jerusalem

The Eve of Palm Sunday in Bethany

When the Sabbath morning begins to grow light, the bishop offers and makes the oblation on the Sabbath morning. As the dismissal is being done, the archdeacon raises his voice and says: 'Let all be ready today at the seventh hour in the Lazarium.' Thus, when the seventh hour begins to approach, everyone comes to the Lazarium. The Lazarium, that is Bethany, is about two miles from the city. Going from Jerusalem to the Lazarium, about five hundred paces from that place there is a church on the road in that place where Mary, the sister of Lazarus, met the Lord. So, when the bishop comes there, all the monks meet him and the people enter there; one hymn is recited and one antiphon and that passage from the gospel is read where the sister of Lazarus meets the Lord. And then when prayer has been made and all have been blessed, they go from there to the Lazarium with hymns …

The Fifth Day (Thursday) on the Mount of Olives

… At the eighth hour all the people gather at the Martyrium according to custom, but earlier than on other days because it is necessary for the dismissal to be done sooner. Thus, when all the people have gathered, they do what is to be done; that day the oblation is made at the Martyrium and the dismissal is done there about the tenth hour. But before the dismissal is done, the archdeacon raises his voice and says, 'At the first hour of the night let us all come together at the church that is on Eleona, because the greatest labour awaits us today, this very night.' When the dismissal has been done at the Martyrium, they come behind the Cross, one hymn only is recited there, prayer is made, and the bishop offers the oblation there and all receive Communion. For except on that one day it is never offered behind the Cross throughout the whole year except on that one day only. So the dismissal having been done there, they go to the Anastasis, prayer is made, the catechumens are blessed according to the custom and then the faithful, and the dismissal is done.

And then everyone returns to their homes to eat, because as soon as they have eaten, they all go to Eleona, to the church in which there is the cave in which on this day the Lord was with the apostles. And there until about the fifth hour of the night hymns and antiphons appropriate to the day and place are continually recited, similarly also readings; prayers are interspersed; those passages also from the gospel are read in which the Lord addressed the disciples that very day, sitting in the same cave that is in that church. And from there at about the sixth hour of the night they go up with hymns to the Imbomon, to that place where the Lord ascended into heaven. And there again similarly readings and hymns and antiphons appropriate to the day are recited; also whatever prayer there are that the bishop says are always appropriate both to the day and to the place.

Thus, when the cocks begin to crow, they come down from the Imbomon with hymns and come to that place where the Lord prayed, as it is written in the gospel: 'And he approached a stone's throw and prayed,' and the rest. For in that place there is a fine church. The bishop and all the people enter, a prayer appropriate to the place and day is recited there, an appropriate hymn is also recited and that passage from the gospel read where he said to his disciples, 'Watch, lest you enter into temptation.' And the whole of that passage is read through there and then prayer is made. And from there with hymns, even down to the smallest child, they come down on foot with the bishop to Gethsemane, where on account of the large size of the crowd both wearied from the vigil and weak from daily fasting, because they have to come down such a large mountain, they come very slowly with hymns to Gethsemane. More than two hundred church candles are prepared to give light to all the people.

So, when they have arrived at Gethsemane, first the appropriate prayer is made, then a hymn is recited; then is read that passage from the gospel where the Lord was arrested. When that passage has been read, there is such groaning and moaning from all the people, with weeping, that the lamentation of all the people is heard about as far away as the city …

The Pilgrimage of Holy Paula (extract)
Jerome (c.342–420)

Author Jerome was a scholar and priest of the church in Rome, best known for his translation of the Bible into Latin, his biblical commentaries and his ascetic approach to spirituality, which was in sharp contrast to the hedonistic culture of contemporary Roman society. This reading is about Paula, one of several well-born Roman women with whom he had close friendships and who acted as his patrons. He was eventually accused of impropriety in his relationship with Paula, and this compromised his position in the papal circle. More seriously, his insistence on extreme ascetic practices for consecrated virgins and widows may have contributed to the early death of her daughter, Blaesilla, in 384, causing public outrage in Rome. Paula and Jerome judiciously departed on a pilgrimage to the Holy Land, where Paula settled, dying there in 404 at the age of 57. Paula and Jerome effectively acted as partners: as a wealthy widow, she almost certainly funded his translation of the Bible and the building of the monastery they established together for men and women in Bethlehem. She was also said to be a formidable scholar in her own right, perhaps rivalling Jerome himself.

Language Latin. The extract below is translated by W. H. Fremantle, G. Lewis and W. G. Martley.

Date 404.

Genre and context Unlike Egeria's record, this is not a first-hand account, but a carefully crafted sacred biography, written very shortly after Paula's death, partly as a eulogy. It is in the form of a letter written to comfort Paula's surviving daughter, Eustochium, to whom Jerome was also close; but some scholars have argued that its primary aim was achieving Roman ecclesiastical recognition of both Paula and Bethlehem-centred devotion (Jerome also ended his days in Bethlehem). It appears to have succeeded, as Paula was declared a saint the following year. This extract, dense with biblical allusions, reflects the belief that being in the place 'where it all happened' and looking at it with the eyes of faith somehow makes Jesus present again.

The Pilgrimage of Holy Paula
Letter 108 to Eustochium

... Then, after distributing money to the poor and her fellow-servants so far as her means allowed, she proceeded to Bethlehem ... and entered into the cave where the Saviour was born. Here, when she looked upon the inn made sacred by the virgin and the stall where the 'ox knew his owner and the ass his master's crib' (Isaiah 1.3), and where the words of the same prophet had been fulfilled. 'Blessed is he that sows beside the waters where the ox and the ass trample the seed under their feet' (Isaiah 32.20): when she looked upon these things I say, she protested in my hearing that she could behold with the eyes of faith the infant Lord wrapped in swaddling clothes and crying in the manger, the wise men worshipping Him, the star shining overhead, the virgin mother, the attentive foster-father, the shepherds coming by night to see the word that had come to pass and thus even then to consecrate those opening phrases of the evangelist John 'In the beginning was the word and the word was made flesh' (John 1:1, 14). She declared that she could see the slaughtered innocents, the raging Herod, Joseph and Mary fleeing into Egypt; and with a mixture of tears and joy she cried: 'Hail Bethlehem, house of bread, wherein was born that Bread that came down from heaven. (John 6:51) ... Well did David swear, well did he make a vow saying: Surely I will not come into the tabernacle of my house nor go up into my bed: I will not give sleep to my eyes, or slumber to my eyelids, or rest to the temples of my head, until I find out a place for the Lord, an habitation for the God of Jacob (Psalm 142:4–5). And immediately he explained the object of his desire, seeing with prophetic eyes that He would come whom we now believe to have come. Lo we heard of Him at Ephratah: we found Him in the fields of the wood (Psalm 132:6). The Hebrew word *Zo* as you have learned from your lessons means not *her*, that is Mary the Lord's mother, but *him* that is the Lord Himself. Therefore he says boldly: We will go into His tabernacle: we will worship at His footstool (Psalm 132:7). I too, miserable sinner though I am, have been accounted worthy to kiss the manger in which the Lord cried as a babe, and to pray in the cave in which the travailing virgin gave birth to the infant Lord. This is my rest for it is my Lord's native place; here will I dwell for this spot has my Saviour chosen. I have prepared a lamp for my Christ. My soul shall live unto Him and my seed shall serve Him.

The Spiritual Exercises (extract)
Ignatius of Loyola (c.1491–1556)

Author Iñigo López was born in Loyola in the Basque region of Spain to a respected and wealthy family. His mother died soon after his birth, and at a young age he entered the service of a relative who held an administrative post in the kingdom of Castile. He enjoyed courtly life and, following the death of his patron, he joined the army at the age of 17, though his duties were largely diplomatic. In 1521 he was famously injured in the leg by a cannonball during the Siege of Pamplona. It was during his long and painful recovery from surgery that he underwent a gradual conversion experience, out of which arose his concepts of spiritual 'consolation' and 'desolation'. He then moved to Manresa, where he embraced a life of solitary asceticism and had a number of significant mystical experiences. This was followed by a pilgrimage to the Holy Land and a period of university study, first in Spain (where he was thrice interrogated by the Inquisition) and finally in Paris. Here he gathered some like-minded companions around him. In 1534 the group took vows dedicating themselves to their new form of life in St Peter's Church, Montmartre. Ignatius (as he had then come to be known) spent the next years in negotiation with the papal authorities, and in 1540 the Society of Jesus was officially founded. Following Ignatius' example, the Jesuits are an active and outward facing religious order, focused on a living relationship with Jesus, scholarship, evangelism, support of the spiritual life of all Christians based on structured self-examination, social justice and public theology. Apart from the *Exercises*, Ignatius dictated an autobiography, wrote a spiritual diary, many letters and the Jesuit *Constitutions*.

Language Spanish. The translation below is by Joseph Munitiz SJ and Philip Endean SJ.

Date The final work is based on notes made by Ignatius from 1524 onwards. A manuscript, annotated but not written by him, dates from around 1550. A Latin translation was published during Ignatius' lifetime.

Genre and context The *Exercises* is a manual for spiritual direction covering four weeks, with the opportunity to use the material flexibly. There is an emphasis on increasing understanding of the self as a vital part of achieving a deepened and more authentic encounter with God. One way into this is imaginative engagement with the Bible, especially the Gospel narratives, together with reflecting on an appropriate personal response. In the extract below the phrase 'newly incarnate' indicates that Ignatius sees this sort of imaginative contemplation, like that of Paula's many centuries earlier, as in some sense bringing Christ to life again for the believer here and now.

The Spiritual Exercises
Second week, Second Contemplation on the Nativity
The call of the earthly king will help us to contemplate
the life of the Eternal King

The preparatory prayer is to ask God Our Lord for grace that all my intentions, actions and operations may be directed purely to the service and praise of His Divine Majesty.

Preamble 1 The narrative here will be how Our Lady, almost nine months pregnant (as we may devoutly think of her) and seated on a donkey, with Joseph and a servant girl, taking with them an ox, out from Nazareth for Bethlehem to pay the tribute which Caesar had imposed on all those lands.

Preamble 2 Composition, seeing the place. Here it will be to see with the eyes of the imagination the road from Nazareth to Bethlehem, considering the length and breadth of it, whether it is a flat road or goes through valleys or over hills; and similarly to look at the place or grotto of the Nativity, to see how big or small it was, how low or high, and what was in it.

Preamble 3 I ask for what I want: here for interior knowledge of the Lord who became human for me so that I may better love and follow Him.

Point 1 This is to see the people, i.e. Our Lady, and Joseph, and the servant girl, and the child Jesus after his birth. Making myself into a poor and unworthy little servant, I watch them, and contemplate them, and serve them in their needs as if I were present, with all possible submission and reverence; and afterwards I reflect within myself to derive some profit.

Point 2 I watch, notice and contemplate what they are saying and reflect within myself to derive some profit.

Point 3 I watch and consider what they are doing, e.g. their travel and efforts, so that Christ comes to be born in extreme poverty and, after so many labours, after hunger, thirst, heat and cold, outrages and affronts, he dies on the cross, and all of this for me; then I reflect within myself to derive some spiritual profit.

Colloquy At the end a colloquy is to be made. I think about what I ought to be saying to the Eternal Word incarnate, or to his mother, Our Lady, and I make a request, according to my inner feelings, so that I may better follow and imitate our Lord, thus newly incarnate, saying an Our Father.

A Life of Jesus (extract)
Ernest Renan (1823–1892)

Author Ernest Renan was born in Brittany to a middle-class Roman Catholic family. He excelled at school, and at the age of 16 was sent to Paris to study philosophy but later specialized in the study of languages of the Ancient Near East. This naturally led him to critical biblical scholarship (for example by observing that a single book in the Old Testament appeared to be the work of more than one author). He had originally planned to become a priest, but his studies raised many doubts about the church and its teaching, and he instead became a teacher. Renan was attracted by the rapid developments in empirical science at the time, seeing it as a way to discovering objective truth. He was highly engaged with politics throughout his life, though his views changed in response to the Franco-Prussian War of 1870–71. He wrote widely on historical approaches to the Bible, the origins of Christianity, and his theories on race that arose in part from his studies of language and ancient cultures. Apart from *A Life of Jesus*, his best-known work was *Souvenirs D'enfance et de Jeunesse* (memories of childhood and youth). This was written towards the end of his life and (interestingly in view of the next section in this chapter) was essentially a return to his childhood experiences in Brittany.

Language French. This translation is by John Haynes Holmes.

Date 1863.

Genre and context Renan's book is part of the early phase of what has become known as the 'quest for the historical Jesus'. It is a biography informed by his knowledge of ancient cultures based on textual study and archaeological findings, which presents Jesus as a human figure, liberated from what Renan viewed as the unwarranted mythical overlay of the Gospels and subsequent Christian tradition. At the time this was a deeply shocking approach in the eyes of the church; but its sympathetic and accessible portrayal of Jesus meant that it was a popular success and enriched the spiritual lives of many, supported by the work of visual artists including James Tissot (1836–1902) and William Holman Hunt (1827–1910). As well as breaking the link between Jesus and the supernatural, Renan also attempted to extricate him from some aspects of his Jewish ethnic and cultural heritage by foregrounding the distinction between northern Galilee and southern Judea and locating him firmly in the former. This move was reversed in the third phase of the quest, in which Jesus' roots in Palestinian Judaism are re-emphasized. (Theissen's *Shadow of the Galilean* discussed in Chapter 1 is a product of this third phase.) The quest for the historical Jesus is essentially an attempt to get back to the 'real' Jesus through the systematic use of human sciences. The extract below returns to Jesus' earliest days (rejecting the tradition that he was born in Bethlehem).

A Life of Jesus
Chapter II. Infancy and Youth of Jesus: His First Impressions

Jesus was born at Nazareth, a small town of Galilee, which before his time had no celebrity. All his life he was designated by the name of 'the Nazarene,' and it is only by a rather embarrassed and round-about way, that, in the legends respecting him, he is made to be born at Bethlehem …

He proceeded from the ranks of the people. His father, Joseph, and his mother, Mary, were people in humble circumstances, artisans living by their labour, in the state so common in the East, which is neither ease nor poverty … the town of Nazareth, in the time of Jesus, did not perhaps much differ from what it is to-day. We see the streets where he played when a child, in the stony paths or little crossways which separate the dwellings. The house of Joseph doubtless much resembled those poor shops, lighted by the door, serving at once for shop, kitchen, and bedroom, having for furniture a mat, some cushions on the ground, one or two clay pots, and a painted chest.

Even in our times Nazareth is still a delightful abode, the only place, perhaps, in Palestine in which the mind feels itself relieved from the burden which oppresses it in this unequalled desolation. The people are amiable and cheerful; the gardens fresh and green …

The horizon from the town is limited. But if we ascend a little the plateau, swept by a perpetual breeze, which overlooks the highest houses, the prospect is splendid. On the west are seen the fine outlines of Carmel, terminated by an abrupt point which seems to plunge into the sea. Before us are spread out the double summit which towers above Megiddo; the mountains of the country of Shechem, with their holy places of the patriarchal age; the hills of Gilboa, the small, picturesque group to which are attached the graceful or terrible recollections of Shunem and of Endor; and Tabor, with its beautiful rounded form, which antiquity compared to a bosom. Through a depression between the mountains of Shunem and Tabor are seen the valley of the Jordan and the high plains of Peræa, which form a continuous line from the eastern side. On the north, the mountains of Safed, in inclining toward the sea conceal St. Jean d'Acre, but permit the Gulf of Khaïfa to be distinguished. Such was the horizon of Jesus. This enchanted circle, cradle of the kingdom of God, was for years his world. Even in his later life he departed but little beyond the familial limits of his childhood. For yonder, northward, a glimpse is caught, almost on the flank of Hermon, of Cæsarea-Philippi, his furthest point of advance into the Gentile world; and here southward, the more sombre aspect of these Samaritan hills foreshadows the dreariness of Judea beyond, parched as by a scorching wind of desolation and death.

If the world, remaining Christian, but attaining to a better idea of the esteem in which the origin of its religion should be held, should ever wish to replace by authentic holy places the mean and apocryphal sanctuaries to which the piety of dark ages attached itself, it is upon this height of Nazareth that it will rebuild its temple. There, at the birthplace of Christianity, and in the centre of the actions of its Founder, the great church ought to be raised in which all Christians may worship. There, also, on this spot where sleep Joseph, the carpenter, and thousands of forgotten Nazarenes who never passed beyond the horizon of their valley, would be a better station than any in the world beside for the philosopher to contemplate the course of human affairs, to console himself for their uncertainty, and to reassure himself as to the Divine end which the world pursues through countless falterings, and in spite of the universal vanity.

7.2 Back to the womb

Renan's quest to find Jesus in history is mirrored by his own return to his Breton childhood in *Souvenirs*. Many spiritual writers bring these two returns together, finding Jesus in something that is rather like a journey back to the womb. This is a desire we all experience, especially at times of stress or loss; to be back in a place where things were safe, where nothing was required of us beyond simply being, and where we were intimately connected to one who cares for and nurtures us. Sigmund Freud referred to this as the 'oceanic' feeling, where the sense of a separate self dissolves, recalling a time in the womb or early infancy before the individual ego emerges and conceptual thought has developed.

The Philokalia (extracts)
The Hesychasts (thirteenth–fourteenth century)

Author Extract 1: Attributed to Symeon the New Theologian (see Chapter 5) but likely to be a later author, possibly the thirteenth-century monk Nikiphoros the Hesychast; Extract 2: Gregory of Sinai (1260s–1346). Following an eventful young adulthood, when he was kidnapped by Turks and then ransomed back to Greece, Gregory entered Saint Catherine's Monastery on Mount Sinai. He is then likely to have learnt to practise hesychasm during a period in Crete, after which he joined the monastic community of Mount Athos, where he remained for 25 years. The final years of his life were spent in Bulgaria where he and some companions had fled from the danger of further Turkish and Arab raids.

Language Greek. The translation below is by G. E. H. Palmer, Philip Sherrard and Kallistos Ware.

Date The original versions probably dated from the thirteenth or early fourteenth century. However, as noted in Chapter 2, the *Philokalia* was published in 1782, and the degree of editorial changes made at this time remains unknown.

Genre and contexts The texts instruct monks in the art of prayer and meditation. Hesychasm may have emerged as early as the eighth century, though the texts describing the practice date from a later period. It is the combined practice of *nepsis* (watchfulness, see Chapter 12), *hesychia* (stillness) and *kardia* (heart prayer) aimed at a transformative participation in the divine nature (2 Peter 1.4). This is an explicitly Trinitarian practice, centred on repeating the words of the Jesus Prayer (variants of 'Lord Jesus Christ, Son of God, have mercy on me, a sinner') and openness to the Spirit achieved by careful attention paid to breathing and body posture. It was highly radical in a culture in which prayer involved active discursive thought and took place standing; it adopts what is essentially a foetal position seated on a low stool, and it aims to quiet the rational intellect through breathing and a focus on the 'heart', which is understood as the centre of gravity of the whole person. Some of what is known about the practice comes from the vitriolic parodies written by opponents of the Hesychasts who described them as 'navel-gazers' because of this foetal posture.

Philokalia IV [69]
The Third Method of Prayer

Let us now begin to speak about the third method of prayer, which is truly astonishing and hard to explain. For those ignorant of it, it is not only difficult to understand but virtually incredible, and there are very few to be found who practise it ...

The starting-point of this third method of prayer is not to gaze upwards, to raise one's hands aloft, to concentrate one's thoughts and to call down help from heaven ...

Having cleared the ground and indicated in a preliminary way the true character of attentiveness, let us now speak clearly and concisely about its characteristics. True and unerring attentiveness and prayer mean that the intellect keeps watch over the heart while it prays; it should always be on patrol within the heart, and from within – from the depths of the heart – it should offer up its prayers to God. Once it has tasted within the heart that the Lord is bountiful, then the intellect will have no desire to leave the heart, and it will repeat the words of the Apostle Peter, 'It is good for us to be here.' It will keep watch always within the heart, repulsing and expelling all thoughts sown there by the enemy. To those who have no knowledge of this practice it appears extremely harsh and arduous; and indeed it is oppressive and laborious, not only to the uninitiated, but also to those who, although genuinely experienced, have not yet felt the delight to be found in the depths of the heart. But those who have savoured this delight proclaim with St Paul, 'Who will separate us from the love of Christ?' ...

Now if you would like to learn also about the method of prayer, with God's help I will tell you about this too, in so far as I can. Above all else you should strive to acquire three things, and so begin to attain what you seek. The first is freedom from anxiety with respect to everything, whether reasonable or senseless – in other words, you should be dead to everything. Secondly, you should strive to preserve a pure conscience, so that it has nothing to reproach you with. Thirdly, you should be completely detached, so that your thoughts incline towards nothing worldly, not even your own body. Then sit down in a quiet cell, in a corner by yourself, and do what I tell you. Close the door and withdraw your intellect from everything worthless and transient. Rest your beard on your chest, and focus your physical gaze, together with the whole of your intellect, upon the centre of your belly or your navel. Restrain the drawing-in of breath through your nostrils, so as not to breathe easily, and search inside yourself with your intellect so as to find the place of the heart, where all the powers of the soul reside. To start with you will find there darkness and an impenetrable density. Later, when you persist and practise this task day and night, you will find, as though miraculously, an unceasing joy. For as soon as the intellect attains the place of the heart, at once it sees things of which it previously knew nothing. It sees the open space within the heart and it beholds itself entirely luminous and full of discrimination. From then on, from whatever side a distractive thought may appear, before it has come to completion and assumed a form, the intellect immediately drives it away and destroys it with the invocation of Jesus Christ. From this point onwards the intellect begins to be full of rancour against the demons and, rousing its natural anger against its noetic enemies, it pursues them and strikes them down. The rest you will learn for yourself, with God's help, by keeping guard over your intellect and by retaining Jesus in your heart. As the saying goes, 'Sit in your cell and it will teach you everything.'

Philokalia IV [276]
On Prayer: Seven Texts
How the Hesychast Should Sit for Prayer and
Not Rise Again Too Quickly

Sometimes – and most often – you should sit on a stool, because it is more arduous; but sometimes, for a break, you should sit for a while on a mattress. As you sit be patient and assiduous, in accordance with St Paul's precept, 'Cleave patiently to prayer'. Do not grow discouraged and quickly rise up again because of the strain and effort needed to keep your intellect concentrated on its inner invocation. It is as the prophet says: 'The birth-pangs are upon me, like those of a woman in travail'. You must bend down and gather your intellect into your heart – provided it has been opened – and call on the Lord Jesus to help you. Should you feel pain in your shoulders or in your head – as you often will – endure it patiently and fervently, seeking the Lord in your heart. For 'the kingdom of God is entered forcibly, and those who force themselves take possession of it'. With these words the Lord truly indicated the persistence and labour needed in this task. Patience and endurance in all things involve hardship in both body and soul.

Some of the fathers advise us to say the whole prayer, 'Lord Jesus Christ, Son of God, have mercy', while others specify that we say it in two parts – 'Lord Jesus Christ, have mercy', and then 'Son of God, help me' – because this is easier, given the immaturity and feebleness of our intellect. For no one on his own account and without the help of the Spirit can mystically invoke the Lord Jesus, for this can be done with purity and in its fullness only with the help of the Holy Spirit. Like children who can still speak only falteringly, we are unable by ourselves to articulate the prayer properly.

Sermon on Ephesians 4.23 (extract)
Meister Eckhart (c.1260–1328)

Author Eckhart von Hochheim was born in Thuringia, Germany, probably to a wealthy family. Little is known of his early life. At the age of 18 he entered the Dominican community at Erfurt where he eventually became Prior. In 1303 he became Dominican Provincial Superior for Saxony, and in 1307 Vicar General of Bohemia with responsibility for 56 monastic communities. He was a gifted scholar, having a teaching role within his order, and spending extended periods at the University of Paris and later Strasbourg, and around 1322 was appointed to the most senior teaching position of his order in Cologne. Between 1325 and 1327 he faced a number of accusations of heresy by the local archbishop. At least some of this centred on his habit of presenting nuanced ideas to ordinary people who might lack the intellectual subtlety to receive them. In response he pointed to the prologue to John's Gospel that was written for all people. He travelled to Avignon (the papal seat at the time) to appeal to the pope but died either there or en route before he could be condemned officially. Always admired as a writer on both theology and spirituality (and with many works erroneously attributed to him), in recent years he has been largely rehabilitated in the Roman Catholic Church.

Language Middle High German. The translation below is by Maurice O'C. Walshe.

Date Probably from Eckhart's period in Strasbourg in the 1310s.

Genre and context This is a transcript of an oral sermon, very possibly made by one of the nuns who formed Eckhart's regular audience. This passage interprets the renewal of mind promised in Ephesians as the setting aside of conceptual thought about and imaginative reflection on God. It invokes apophatic language – saying what God is *not* – as a step towards oceanic union with the divine.

Sermon 96 (Q83*)
Ephesians 4.23 'You shall be renewed in the spirit of your minds'

... So be silent and do not chatter about God, because by chattering about Him you are lying and so committing a sin. So, if you want to be without sin and perfect, don't chatter about God. Nor should you (seek to) understand anything about God, for God is above all understanding. One master says, 'If I had a God I could understand, I would no longer consider him God.' So, if you understand any thing of Him, that is not He, and by understanding anything of Him you fall into misunderstanding, and from this misunderstanding you fall into brutishness, for whatever in creatures is uncomprehending is brutish. So, if you don't want to become brutish, understand nothing of God the unutterable ...

–'Oh, but what should I do then?' You should wholly sink away from your youness and dissolve into His Hisness, and your 'yours' and His 'His' should become so completely one 'Mine' that with Him you understand His uncreated self-identity and His nameless Nothingness ...

You should love God apart from loveworthiness: that is, not because He is worthy of love, for God is not loveworthy, He is above all love and loveworthiness. –'Then how should I love God?' You should love God nonspiritually: that is to say the soul should be de-spirited, stripped of spiritual dress. For as long as the soul is in spirit form, she has images; as long as she has images, she has means; as long as she has means, she has not unity or simplicity, and as long as she has not simplicity she has never rightly loved God, for true love lies in simplicity. Therefore your soul should be de-spirited of all spirit, she should be spiritless, for if you love God as He is God, as He is spirit, as He is person and as He is image – all that must go! –'Well, how should I love Him then?' –You should love Him as He is: a non-God, a non-spirit, a non-person, a non-image; rather, as He is a sheer pure limpid One, detached from all duality. And in that One may we eternally sink from nothingness to nothingness. So help us God. Amen.

*Q refers to Josef Quint's system of numbering. *Ed.*

Centuries of Meditations (extract) and *The Return*
Thomas Traherne (c.1636–1674)

Author Traherne was born in Hereford, where his father was a master cobbler, and it seems likely that he lost his mother at an early age. He studied at Brasenose College, Oxford, and from 1657 served as Rector of St Mary's, Credenhill, Herefordshire, being ordained priest in 1660 after the restoration of the monarchy. He had close connections with Hereford Cathedral. At some point after 1667 he was appointed chaplain to Sir Orlando Bridgeman, an eminent royalist politician, and died in his London home of smallpox while still in his thirties.

Language English (modern spelling).

Date Unknown. Most of Traherne's writing, which spanned a number of genres, remained unpublished until manuscripts of his work were rediscovered in 1896. More manuscripts have gradually been coming to light since then.

Genre and context *Centuries of Meditations* is a spiritual autobiography loosely modelled on Augustine's *Confessions*. *The Return* is from a collection entitled *Poems of Felicity*. The extracts below both concern infancy and early childhood, a favourite theme of Traherne and other poets of the day, most famously Henry Vaughan (1621–1695). Traherne saw this period of life as a theological metaphor for humanity's state before the Fall, but also as a spiritual metaphor for the individual's journey of faith. Scholars disagree as to whether Traherne is writing about his own early experience or using his imagination to paint an idealized picture. He appears to have read widely, and many influences, both classic and contemporary, can be traced in his writing. In another of his poems, 'Silence', he, like Eckhart, describes the state of union with God as like being in an ocean where the boundaries of self dissolve.

Centuries of Meditations
The Third Century

1. Will you see the infancy of this sublime and celestial greatness? Those pure and virgin apprehensions I had from the womb, and that divine light wherewith I was born are the best unto this day, wherein I can see the Universe. By the Gift of God they attended me into the world, and by His special favour I remember them till now.

The Return

To Infancy, O Lord, again I come,
That I my Manhood may improve:
My early Tutor is the Womb;
I still my Cradle love.
'Tis strange that I should Wisest be,
When least I could an Error see.
Till I gain strength against Temptation, I
Perceive it safest to abide
An Infant still; and therfore fly
(A lowly State may hide
A man from Danger) to the Womb,
That I may yet New-born become.
My God, thy Bounty then did ravish me!
Before I learned to be poor,
I always did thy Riches see,
And thankfully adore:
Thy Glory and thy Goodness were
My sweet Companions all the Year.

7.3 The gift of hindsight

In his poem 'The Approach', also taken from *Poems of Felicity*, Traherne writes about the way an adult can look right back to childhood with hindsight and see the hand of God there all along, much as we may do at the end of our or a loved one's life. This way of making sense of the past in the light of the present is also key to typological readings the Bible, which find Christ present from the very beginning of the story of the people of God, walking with them, and repeatedly approaching in love.

The Approach
Thomas Traherne (c.1636–1674)

The Approach

That childish thoughts such joys inspire,
Doth make my wonder, and His glory higher,
His bounty, and my wealth more great
It shews His Kingdom, and His work complete.
In which there is not anything,
Not meet to be the joy of Cherubim.

He in our childhood with us walks,
And with our thoughts mysteriously He talks;
He often visiteth our minds,
But cold acceptance in us ever finds:
We send Him often grieved away,
Who else would show us all His Kingdom's joy.

O Lord, I wonder at Thy Love,
Which did my infancy so early move:
But more at that which did forbear
And move so long, though slighted many a year:
But most of all, at last that Thou
Thyself shouldst me convert, I scarce know how.

Thy gracious motions oft in vain
Assaulted me: my heart did hard remain
Longtime! I sent my God away
Grieved much, that He could not give me His joy.
I careless was, nor did regard
The End for which He all those thoughts prepared.

But now, with new and open eyes,
I see beneath, as if above the skies,
And as I backward look again
See all His thoughts and mine most clear arid plain.
He did approach, He me did woo;
I wonder that my God this thing would do,

From nothing taken first, I was;
What wondrous things His glory brought to pass!
Now in the World I Him behold,
And me, enveloped in precious gold;
In deep abysses of delights,
In present hidden glorious benefits.

These thoughts His goodness long before
Prepared as precious and celestial store
With curious art in me inlaid,
That childhood might itself alone be said
My Tutor, Teacher, Guide to be,
Instructed then even by the Deitie.

The Life of Moses (extract)
Gregory of Nyssa (c.335–c.395)

Author Gregory was one of those who have come to be known as the 'Cappadocian Fathers', the other two being his older brother Basil and their friend, Gregory of Nazianzus (see Chapter 12). He was born to a noble and respected Christian family from Caesarea Mazaca in what is now Turkey but was then part of the old kingdom of Cappadocia under Roman-Byzantine rule. He had a more extensive education than his older brother and, unusually, was married. After an early career as a secular rhetorician, he was elected bishop of the new province of Nyssa in 372 under Basil, who was bishop of the overall province. Gregory experienced a politically and ecclesiastically troubled time as Bishop of Nyssa, interrupted for a short period when he became Bishop of Sebaste in Armenia. In his later years he travelled more widely, participating in the first Council of Constantinople in 381, and later went to Syria and Jerusalem to settle ecclesiastical and theological disputes. Gregory was a prolific author, robustly defending teaching on the nature of Christ agreed by the Council of Nicaea in 325. His works include *On Perfection, On Virginity, The Life of Macrina* and *Homilies on the Song of Songs*.

Language Greek. The work was soon translated into Latin and there are many variants. The translation below is by Herbert Musurillo SJ.

Date Late 390s.

Genre and context This is a treatise possibly designed to be read aloud. After paraphrasing the biblical story of Moses and the Exodus in Book I, it presents a spiritual interpretation described as the fruit of contemplation. The aim is to use the story of Moses as an allegory for the spiritual progress of the believer. This approach to interpreting the Bible was common at the time, but here Gregory goes beyond saying that Exodus offers a picture of the Christian life and develops a typological reading (see p. 19), asserting that Christ was actually present to Moses at the time. At points Moses himself seems to function as a type for Christ.

The Life of Moses
Book II: Contemplation

240. But what is that place which is seen next to God? What is the rock? And what again is the hole in the rock? What is the hand of God that covers the mouth of the rock? What is the passing by of God? What is his back which God promised to Moses when he asked to see him face to face?

248. We say, then, that Moses' entrance into the rock has [this] significance … For, since Christ is understood by Paul as the rock, all hope of good things is believed to be in Christ, in whom we have learned all the treasures of good things to be. He who finds any good finds it in Christ who contains all good.

249. He who attained to this and was shadowed by the hand of God, as the text promised (for the hand of God would be the creative power of what exists, the only begotten God, by whom all things were made, who is also 'place' for those who run, who is, according to his own words, the 'way' of the course, and who is 'rock' to those who are well established and 'house' to those who are resting), he it is who will hear the One who summons and will see the back of the One who calls, which means he will follow Yahweh your God, as the Law commands.

250. When the great David heard and understood this, he said to him who dwells in the shelter of the most High; He will overshadow you with his shoulders, which is the same as being behind God (for the shoulder is on the back of the body). Concerning himself David says,

---

My soul clings close to you, your right hand supports me. You see how the Psalms agree with the history. For as the one says that the right hand is a help to the person who has joined himself close behind God, so the other says that the hand touches the person who waits in the rock upon the divine voice and prays that he might follow behind.

251. But when the Lord who spoke to Moses came to fulfil his own law, he likewise gave a clear explanation to his disciples, laying bare the meaning of what had previously been said in a figure when he said, If anyone wants to be a follower of mine and not 'If any man will go before me.' And to the one asking about eternal life he proposes the same thing, for he says Come, follow me. Now, he who follows sees the back.

252. So Moses, who eagerly seeks to behold God, is now taught how he can behold Him: to follow God wherever he might lead is to behold God. His passing by signifies his guiding the one who follows, for someone who does not know the way cannot complete his journey safely in any other way than by following behind his guide. He who leads, then, by his guidance shows the way to the one following. He who follows will not turn aside from the right way if he always keeps the back of his leader in view.

Modern Painters II (extract)
John Ruskin (1819–1900)

Author John Ruskin was a geologist, artist, art critic and socio-political commentator, and the first Slade Professor of Fine Art at Oxford University. He was also a keen amateur biblical scholar and meteorologist. He was of Scottish heritage and was raised as an evangelical by a devout Presbyterian mother. He was a highly influential figure in his day, making effective use of the new genre of the public lecture. Troubled by physical and mental ill health for much of his later life, he eventually lived as a near recluse in his home in the English Lake District. He wrote an enormous amount, most famously the five-volume *Modern Painters*, *The Stones of Venice*, *Elements of Drawing* and *Unto this Last*.

Language English.

Date 1846.

Genre and context Nineteenth-century Evangelicals were uncomfortable with allegorical readings of the Bible because there seemed to be no limits on the meaning that could be made from it, but they also recognized that the

Bible was full of symbolism. They solved this dilemma through the rediscovery of typological readings. In *Modern Painters II* Ruskin applied this to the visual arts through the use of 'typological symbolism'. In the passage below, whose crucial phrase is 'there is more meant than this', he argues that a painting of the Annunciation by the Venetian artist Tintoretto (1518–1594)[2] presents Christ as the ever-present cornerstone of the household of God, now fully recognized with hindsight (Acts 4.11; Ephesians 2.20; 1 Peter 2.4). As was typical of the time, Ruskin contrasts Judaism with Christianity in a way that may trouble the present-day reader; nonetheless, he emphasizes God's continued presence in both traditions.

Modern Painters II
Part II, Chapter III: Of Imagination Penetrative

17. The Annunciation

Let us take another instance. No subject has been more frequently or exquisitely treated by the religious painters than that of the Annunciation; though, as usual, the most perfect type of its pure ideal has been given by Angelico … Severe would be the shock and painful the contrast, if we could pass in an instant from that pure vision to the wild thought of Tintoret. For not in meek reception of the adoring messenger, but startled by the rush of his horizontal and rattling wings, the Virgin sits, not in the quiet loggia, not by the green pasture of the restored soul, but houseless, under the shelter of a palace vestibule ruined and abandoned, with the noise of the axe and the hammer in her ears, and the tumult of a city round about her desolation. The spectator turns away at first, revolted, from the central object of the picture forced painfully and coarsely forward, a mass of shattered brickwork, with the plaster mildewed away from it, and the mortar mouldering from its seams; and if he look again, either at this or at the carpenter's tools beneath it, will perhaps see, in the one and the other, nothing more than such a study of scene as Tintoret could but too easily obtain among the ruins of his own Venice, chosen to give a coarse explanation of the calling and the condition of the husband of Mary. But there is more meant than this. When he looks at the composition of the picture, he will find the whole symmetry of it depending on a narrow line of light, the edge of a carpenter's square, which connects these unused tools with an object at the top of the brickwork, a white stone, four square, the corner-stone of the

---

2 'The Annunciation. Tintoretto', *Wikiart*, https://www.wikiart.org/en/tintoretto/the-annunciation-1587, accessed 17.01.2024.

old edifice, the base of its supporting column. This, I think, sufficiently explains the typical character of the whole. The ruined house is the Jewish dispensation; that obscurely arising in the dawning of the sky is the Christian; but the corner-stone of the old building remains, though the builders' tools lie idle beside it, and the stone which the builders refused is become the Headstone of the Corner.

Further reading

Dangerous Mystic: Meister Eckhart's path to the God within by Joel F. Harrington. London: Penguin, 2022.

Echoes of Scripture in the Gospels by Richard Hays. Waco, TX: Baylor University Press, 2018.

The Jesus Prayer by Simon Barrington-Ward. Abingdon: Bible Reading Fellowship, 2022.

Living the Story: The Ignatian way of prayer and scripture reading by Joe Cassidy. Norwich: Canterbury Press, 2020.

Travel Writing: Discovering the New Testament story through icons and pilgrimage by J. Richard Smith. Durham: Sacristy Press, 2022.

Wanting like a God: Desire and freedom in the works of Thomas Traherne by Denise Inge. London: SCM Press, 2009.

The Way of a Pilgrim, anonymous nineteenth-century (several editions available in hard copy and on the internet).

8

Engaging with Absence

My God, my God, why have you forsaken me? Why are you so far from helping me, from the words of my groaning?
(Psalm 22.1)

As a deer longs for flowing streams, so my soul longs for you, O God. My soul thirsts for God, for the living God. When shall I come and behold the face of God? My tears have been my food day and night, while people say to me continually, 'Where is your God?'
(Psalm 42.1–3)

If I go forward, he is not there; or backward, I cannot perceive him; on the left he hides, and I cannot behold him; I turn to the right, but I cannot see him.
(Job 23.8–9)

Who among you fears the LORD and obeys the voice of his servant, who walks in darkness and has no light, yet trusts in the name of the LORD and relies upon his God?
(Isaiah 50.10)

And the Spirit immediately drove him out into the wilderness.
(Mark 1.12)

Mary said to them, 'They have taken away my Lord, and I do not know where they have laid him.'
(John 20.13b)

One day we were playing a game of opposites with our five-year-old grandson. 'What is the opposite of tall? Of big? Of light?' we asked. He was quick to give the correct single-word answers. Then somebody asked him, 'What is the opposite of friendly?' He thought for a moment and came up with a compound word, 'All-by-yourself.' It was a deeply touching moment. 'All-by-yourself'.

At some point after a bereavement most people reach a point of feeling all-by-yourself. Perhaps it is after the last guest departs from the wake. Perhaps it is much later, as the reality of the loved one's absence begins to make itself felt. Many manage to keep this sense of absence at bay through the processes of imaginative attachment and return described in the previous two chapters; but for some the sense of absence and separation can be almost overwhelming. When I told a close friend who had recently lost her mother that I talk to my deceased parents most days, she looked at me with horrified incomprehension. 'Don't you understand?' she said, 'She has gone – there is nothing but darkness and emptiness.' Her feeling of being alone, indeed abandoned, stayed with her for over a year.

This theme comes up again and again in stories of bereavement: a sense of being separated from the loved one who has died and from the broader community, feeling lonely, being alone. For many this goes deeper, and becomes a sense of separation from the self, an existential as well as a social aloneness. It reflects the fact that our identity is bound up with the one we have lost, that we feel less ourselves when they have gone. So, there is then also a sense of being lost, of not knowing the way forward. This must have been especially true of Jesus' first disciples, whose lives, vocations and sense of self had been transformed by him, and above all for Mary Magdalene, a person who had been deeply broken in unspecified and unspeakable ways until she met Jesus.[1]

Research on bereavement has shown that not everyone has to negotiate deep darkness to come through it well.[2] In this respect it diverges from the Christian tradition which, beginning with Jesus himself (Mark 8.34), insists that the spiritual life will involve such periods (though they seem to be darker for some than others). But in both cases if the disorientation is fully inhabited and the darkness faced, unexpected treasures may be yielded.[3] John Ruskin, who appeared in Chapter 7, put it this way:

> Now, as far as I have watched the main powers of human mind, they have risen first from the resolution to see fearlessly, pitifully, and to its very worst, what these deep colours mean, wheresoever they fall ... all great and beautiful work has come of first gazing without shrinking into the darkness.[4]

The readings in this chapter are arranged in three groups. The first is on enduring and making sense of affliction; the second on the discipline of detachment from everyday life in order to enter purposefully into a place of disorientation; and the third on facing up to the absence of God.

---

1 For a full discussion, see J. Collicutt, 2009, *Jesus and the Gospel Women*, London: SPCK, chapter 6.

2 For example, G. Bonanno, C. Wortman, D. Lehman, et al., 2002, 'Resilience to loss and chronic grief: A prospective study from pre-loss to 18 months post-loss', *Journal of Personality and Social Psychology*, 83, pp. 1150–64.

3 S. Joseph, 2011, *What Doesn't Kill Us: A guide to overcoming adversity and moving forward*, New York: Basic Books.

4 J. Ruskin, 1860, *Modern Painters V*, London: George Allen, p. 271.

8.1 Enduring suffering and separation

As in the Bible, the writers in this section offer several ways of making sense of adversity in this life and a feeling of being alienated from or abandoned by God. Their works are meant to offer encouragement to the faithful by showing that 'nothing happens without a reason' for God is still in charge; that they are not on their own in their difficulties; and by reminding them of the spiritual resources that will enable them to navigate their situations well.

Pastoral Rule Book and *Moralia on Job* (extracts)
Gregory the Great (c.540–604)

Author Gregory was born in Rome to a wealthy noble family with close connections to the church. After his father's death in 574 he converted the family villa to a monastery dedicated to St Andrew and lived a simple monastic existence, eventually being ordained as a deacon. In 579 the Pope appointed him ambassador to the imperial court in Constantinople with the (unsuccessful) objective of securing military aid for Rome. The city had declined from the height of its powers four centuries earlier and had been laid waste by previous wars and plague. It was no longer the capital of the empire (which was now split between Ravenna and Constantinople) and was facing increasing new threats from Germanic tribes. In 590, following his return to Rome, Gregory was elected pope, remaining in office until his death. Rome was by then in an even worse state and, as no aid was forthcoming from Constantinople, Gregory took control of a relief effort in which charitable giving from wealthy families was efficiently distributed to those in need, supported by a clear and effective system of accounting. Even though he seems to have been a contemplative at heart, he had an acute sense of the need for evangelism and sent groups of missionaries into northern Europe. The most famous of these forays was the mission to Britain in 595 under Augustine, the prior of the original monastery founded by Gregory, who has come to be known as Augustine of Canterbury. Gregory wrote several sacred biographies, many works of biblical exegesis, and countless official and personal letters.

Language Latin. The earliest manuscripts of both works date from the seventh century. They were translated into many languages, and the *Pastoral Rule Book* was particularly influential, even being translated into English by Alfred the Great. The translation below is by Henry Davis SJ. The nineteenth-century translation of *Moralia on Job* is by John Henry Parker.

Date *Moralia on Job* was based on talks given during Gregory's time in Constantinople in the 580s but written up during his papacy. The *Pastoral Rule Book* dates from c.590.

Genre and context The very difficult social context of the time, in which it seemed as if civilization was breaking down completely, led many Christians to believe that they were living in the last days. This was perhaps behind the urgency of Gregory's missional programme: if the final judgement was imminent, then the need to help people avoid sin also became more pressing. The *Pastoral Rule Book* is a treatise on pastoral ministry written for clergy, and in the extract below Gregory makes sense of affliction by arguing that it can have a beneficial cleansing effect, readying the Christian for judgement. In this extract he picks up the image of the people of God as living stones, arguing that suffering essentially knocks them into shape. Gregory himself suffered terribly from gout from his middle years onward, and he viewed his pain as a form of penance.

Moralia on Job is a systematic commentary on the book of Job that offers three readings of each passage: first a historical reading (as in a present-day biblical commentary); then an allegorical reading which treats the text as a metaphor for aspects of the Christian story;[5] and finally a moral interpretation offering practical implications. The extracts below are allegorical, and here the focus is not on physical suffering but the sense of being separated from God. Gregory identifies 'the dialectic of the present and absent Jesus' (p. 7) as something that increases love for God through the experience of longing, instilling the virtue of patience and opening up a space for wisdom to grow.

Pastoral Rule Book Part Three
Chapter XII How to admonish the hale and the sick

Admonition 13

… On the other hand, the sick are to be admonished to realise that they are sons of God by the very fact that the scourge of discipline chastises them. For unless it were in His plan to give them an inheritance after their chastisements, He would not trouble to school them in affliction. For this reason the Lord says by the angel to John: 'Such as I love, I rebuke and chastise'. It is for the same reason that Scripture says: 'My son, neglect not the discipline of the Lord, neither be thou wearied whilst thou art rebuked by Him. For whom the Lord loveth He chastiseth', and 'He scourgeth every son whom He receiveth'. So, the Psalmist says: 'Many are the afflictions of the just, but out of them all will the Lord deliver them.' So, too, holy Job, crying out in his sorrow says: 'If I be just, I shall not lift up my head, being filled with affliction and misery.'

---

5 This is not the same as the typological readings in the previous chapter. Those readings understand texts from the Old Testament to be historically true in their own right, but also to anticipate the Christian story. An allegorical reading treats the text primarily as a way of telling the Christian story through metaphor.

The sick should be told that if they believe that the heavenly country is for them, they must needs endure labours in this country, as if it were an alien one. Hence it is that the stones for building the Temple of God were hammered outside, that they might be set in the building without the sound of hammer; so we are now smitten with scourges outside, that afterwards we may be set into the Temple of God without the stroke of discipline, and that the strokes may now cut away whatever is inordinate in us, and that then only the concord of charity may bind us together in the building...

The sick are to be admonished to consider how great a gift is bodily affliction, in that it both cleanses sins committed and restrains such as could be committed, and that a troubled mind suffers the wounds of penitence inflicted by outward stripes. Hence Scripture says: 'The blueness of a wound cleanses evils, and stripes in the more inward parts of the belly.' The blueness of a wound cleanses evil, that is, the pain of chastisements cleanses wickedness, whether meditated or perpetrated. The mind is commonly signified by the term 'belly' because, as the belly consumes food, so the mind assimilates cares by brooding over them. We are taught that the mind is called the belly by that sentence in which it is written: 'The spirit of a man is the lamp of the Lord, which searcheth all the hidden things of the bowels.' This is as if it had been said that the illumination of divine inspiration, entering the mind of man, shows them into itself by enlightening it, for before the coming of the Holy Spirit it could, indeed, entertain evil things, but did not know how to weigh them.

So, the blueness of a wound cleanses evils, and stripes in the more inward parts of the belly. That is, when we are outwardly smitten, we are recalled, silent and afflicted, to the memory of our sins, and we bring before our eyes all the evil we have done, and in proportion as we suffer outwardly, the more do we grieve inwardly for our deeds. Wherefore, it happens that together with the open wounds of the body, the secret blow in the belly cleanses us the more completely, in that a hidden wound of sorrow heals the wickedness of evil-doing.

Moralia on Job
Comment on Job 23:8 'O that one would grant me that I might know and find Him, that I might come even to His seat!'

Allegorical interpretation:

33. An elect person if he did not know God, assuredly would not love Him. But it is one thing to 'know' by faith, and another to know by His own Form, one thing to find by trustfulness, another to find Him by

contemplation. In consequence whereof it is brought to pass that Him Whom they know by faith, all of the Elect long to see by His own Form as well. With the love of Whom they burn and glow because the honey of His sweetness they already taste of in the mere certainty of their faith. Which that person in the country of the Gerasenes cured of the devils well represents, who wishes to depart with Jesus; but by the Master of health it is, told him, *Return to thine own house, and shew what great things God hath done unto thee* (Luke 8:39). For on him that loves delay is still imposed, that by the longing of love delayed the title to rewarding may be heightened. And so to us Almighty God is made sweet in miracles, and yet in His own loftiness remains hidden from our eyes, that both by shewing something of Himself, He may by secret inspiration set us on fire in the love of Him, and yet by hiding the gloriousness of His Majesty may increase the force of that love of Him by the heat of longing desire. For except the holy man sought to see This Being in His Majesty, surely he would not bring in the words, *that I might come even to His seat*? For what is the 'seat' of God but those angelical Spirits, who as Scripture testifies are called 'Thrones?' He then that desires to 'come to the seat of God,' what else does he long for but to be among the Angelic spirits, that no failing moments of the periods of time he henceforth be liable to, but rise up to abiding glory in the contemplation of eternity.

Comment on Job 30:20 'I will cry unto Thee, but Thou wilt not hear me; I stand, and Thou regardest me not.'

Allegorical interpretation:
1. Since Holy Church in the time of her persecution 'stands' by faith, and 'cries' by longings. But she is grieved that she is 'not regarded' as it were, when she sees her wishes under tribulations delayed. For by a high counsel, Almighty God, when His Saints are wrung tightly by the persecutions of adversaries, and when they cry with never ceasing entreaties that they may be set free, is wont to put off their voices in entreating Him, that their merits in suffering may be increased, in order that they may be the more heard in answer to merit, the more they are not heard quickly in answer to wishing. Whence it is elsewhere written, *O my God, I cry in the day time, but Thou hearest not, and in the night season* (Psalm 22:2). And the very usefulness itself resulting from the delay of hearing is immediately added, when it is there brought in directly, *And not for foolishness to me*. Since for redoubling the wisdom of the Saints it is beneficial, that what is prayed for they receive slowly, that by delay

desire may increase, and by desire the understanding may be aug-mented. But when the understanding is stretched to the full, there is opened a more ardent affection thereof towards God. And the affec-tion is made large for obtaining the things of heaven, in proportion as it was long suffering in expecting. Yet in the midst of these things grief prompts the patience of the Saints to utterance, and whilst being delayed they gain ground, they dread lest their powers failing they should being despised be rejected.

The Pilgrim's Progress (extract)
John Bunyan (1628–1688)

Author John Bunyan grew up in Bunyan's End, Elstow near Bedford. He received only a basic education and took up the family trade as a tinker. As a youth he joined the Parliamentarian army during the Civil War and, by his own account, lived a dissipated life at that time. During the late 1640s he underwent an intensification of his Puritan faith and was drawn to the Bedford Free Church, eventually becoming a regular preacher there and in the surrounding area. With the restoration of the monarchy in 1660, this practice became illegal, and he was imprisoned, initially for three months. However, due to his refusal to desist from preaching, this eventually extended to twelve years. On his release in 1672 he returned to preaching in Bedford and beyond, becoming increasingly well-known for his writing. Apart from *The Pilgrim's Progress*, his best-known work is the autobiographical *Grace Abounding*.

Language English.

Date Published by Nathaniel Ponder in 1678.

Genre and context *The Pilgrim's Progress* is an allegorical work influenced by both secular and Christian genres including romantic heroism, confessional autobiographies, Puritan tracts, and travelogues. Yet it was something entirely new, combining skilful imaginative word painting, theological argu-ment, and engagement with the psychology of the individual. Bunyan is thought to have begun work on it during his long imprisonment; it appears to be written from a place of adversity and suffering and is addressed to a general readership. The extract below comes towards the end of the Pilgrim's journey to the Celestial City and describes a place of darkness and abandon-ment that is the consequence of earlier having wandered from the way on to an apparently easier route.

The Pilgrim's Progress from this World, to that which is to Come
XXV: Christian and Hopeful are captured by Giant Despair

… Now there was, not far from the place where they lay, a castle called Doubting Castle, the owner whereof was Giant Despair; and it was in his grounds they now were sleeping: wherefore he, getting up in the morning early, and walking up and down in his fields, caught Christian and Hopeful asleep in his grounds. Then, with a grim and surly voice, he bid them awake; and asked them whence they were, and what they did in his grounds. They told him they were pilgrims, and that they had lost their way. Then said the Giant, You have this night trespassed on me, by trampling in and lying on my grounds, and therefore you must go along with me. So they were forced to go, because he was stronger than they. They also had but little to say, for they knew themselves in a fault. The Giant, therefore, drove them before him, and put them into his castle, into a very dark dungeon, nasty and stinking to the spirits of these two men. Here, then, they lay from Wednesday morning till Saturday night, without one bit of bread, or drop of drink, or light, or any to ask how they did; they were, therefore, here in evil case, and were far from friends and acquaintance. Now in this place Christian had double sorrow, because it was through his unadvised counsel that they were brought into this distress …

CHRISTIAN. Brother, said Christian, what shall we do? The life that we now live is miserable. For my part I know not whether is best, to live thus, or to die out of hand. 'My soul chooseth strangling rather than life', and the grave is more easy for me than this dungeon. Shall we be ruled by the Giant?
HOPEFUL. Indeed, our present condition is dreadful, and death would be far more welcome to me than thus for ever to abide; but yet, let us consider, the Lord of the country to which we are going hath said, Thou shalt do no murder: no, not to another man's person; much more, then, are we forbidden to take [the Giant's] counsel to kill ourselves. Besides, he that kills another, can but commit murder upon his body; but for one to kill himself is to kill body and soul at once. And, moreover, my brother, thou talkest of ease in the grave; but hast thou forgotten the hell, for certain the murderers go? 'For no murderer hath eternal life,' &c. And let us consider, again, that all the law is not in the hand of Giant Despair. Others, so far as I can understand, have been taken by him, as well as we; and yet have escaped out of his hand. Who knows, but the God that made the world may cause that Giant Despair may die? or that,

at some time or other, he may forget to lock us in? or that he may, in a short time, have another of his fits before us, and may lose the use of his limbs? and if ever that should come to pass again, for my part, I am resolved to pluck up the heart of a man, and to try my utmost to get from under his hand. I was a fool that I did not try to do it before; but, however, my brother, let us be patient, and endure a while. The time may come that may give us a happy release; but let us not be our own murderers.

With these words Hopeful at present did moderate the mind of his brother; so they continued together (in the dark) that day, in their sad and doleful condition. Well, towards evening, the Giant goes down into the dungeon again, to see if his prisoners had taken his counsel; but when he came there he found them alive; and truly, alive was all; for now, what for want of bread and water, and by reason of the wounds they received when he beat them, they could do little but breathe. But, I say, he found them alive; at which he fell into a grievous rage, and told them that, seeing they had disobeyed his counsel, it should be worse with them than if they had never been born …

Well, on Saturday, about midnight, they began to pray, and continued in prayer till almost break of day. Now a little before it was day, good Christian, as one half amazed, brake out in passionate speech: What a fool, quoth he, am I, thus to lie in a stinking Dungeon, when I may as well walk at liberty. I have a Key in my bosom called Promise, that will, I am persuaded, open any Lock in Doubting Castle. Then said Hopeful, That's good news; good Brother pluck it out of thy bosom and try.

Then Christian pulled it out of his bosom, and began to try at the Dungeon door, whose bolt (as he turned the Key) gave back, and the door flew open with ease, and Christian and Hopeful both came out. Then he went to the outward door that leads into the Castle-yard, and with his Key opened that door also. After he went to the iron Gate, for that must be opened too, but that Lock went damnable hard, yet the Key did open it. Then they thrust open the Gate to make their escape with speed; but that Gate as it opened made such a creaking, that it waked Giant Despair, who hastily rising to pursue his Prisoners, felt his limbs to fail, for his Fits took him again, so that he could by no means go after them. Then they went on, and came to the King's High-way again, and so were safe, because they were out of his jurisdiction.

8.2 Purposeful detachment

These readings go beyond making sense of suffering and loss, asserting that it is only through loosening ties to the people, habits, and things that normally give comfort that the believer can come to a deeper knowledge of God. The imagery is profoundly paradoxical and based on Christ's assertion that it is through losing one's life that one finds it.

The Spiritual Espousals (extract)
John Van Ruysbroeck (1293–1381)

Author Jan (later John) was born in Ruusbroec near Brussels. He had an early vocation to the priesthood, and was ordained in 1318, remaining a parish priest in Brussels for the next 25 years. He lived a life of austerity and scholarship and found himself in conflict with a populist movement called the Brethren of the Free Spirit, whose ideas he strongly resisted as heterodox. Finally, he withdrew with some companions to a hermitage in Groenendael in the neighbouring Brabant area,[6] where they formed an Augustinian religious community. Van Ruysbroeck was well-known as a spiritual director visited by many including Geert Grote, the founder of the *Devotio Moderna* (see Chapter 5), and he wrote many letters. His works include *The Sparkling Stone* and *The Spiritual Tabernacle*. He was aware that *The Espousals*, though widely read, was a challenging work, and so he produced simpler versions aimed at a more general readership and with a more transparent theology, *The Little Book* and *The Twelve Beguines*.

Language Middle Dutch. Many early manuscripts survive, both in the original language and translation. The translation below is by Eric Colledge.

Date 1350s.

Genre and context Van Ruysbroeck's spiritual writings are both practical and deeply theological. He took a highly systematic approach to the life of faith. (Evelyn Underhill's quote on p. 4 is referring directly to his system.) In *The Spiritual Espousals* he divides this life into three parts: the active life of virtue, the life of yearning for God, and the life of contemplation of God This final part is described in negative language very similar to that of Meister Eckhart (see last reading in this chapter), but it is located in an overall system in which other ways of knowing God are acknowledged as valid, if perhaps lesser steps along the way. The extract below is from the section on the life of yearning for God; it is based on the story of the wise and foolish bridesmaids, and offers reassurance and counsel to the believer who feels the absence

---

6 It is possible that he knew Hadewijch and he quotes her at one point in *The Spiritual Espousals*.

of Christ. It is presented as an opportunity for self-abandonment and the loosening of attachments to the things of this world in readiness for the way of contemplation.

The Spiritual Espousals Book II 'The Life of Yearning for God'
Part 2: 'The Bridegroom comes, go out':
The Threefold Coming of Christ

The fourfold manner of the first coming in a man's heart

… The fourth manner: man's forsakenness
Now let us go on to speak of the fourth manner of the coming of Christ, which exalts and perfects man in inward exercise in the lowest part of his humanity …

2. How Christ conceals Himself
The first work and the new coming of Christ in this manner is that He thus hides Himself and withdraws the radiance of His light and His heat. Now to such a man Christ says spiritually: Go out in the manner which I now show to you.

4. Our response
Here a man should observe with a humble heart that he of himself has nothing but want: and in patience and in abandonment of himself he shall say the words which Job, that holy man, spoke: 'God gave, God took away: as it was pleasing to the Lord, so did it happen; blessed be the name of the Lord.' And he shall abandon himself in all things, and say and intend in his heart: 'Lord, I will as gladly be poor in the lack of all this of which I have been robbed, as I would be rich, Lord, if Thou wilt have it so and it be to Thine honour. Lord, not my will according to nature, but Thy will and my will according to Thy Spirit, let that be done, Lord, for I am Thine, and I would as gladly be in hell as in heaven, if it may do Thee honour. Lord, in all virtuous things do with me that it be to Thine excelling.' And out of all his desolation a man shall make an inward joy, and offer himself into the hands of God, and rejoice that he may suffer to the glory of God …

5. The obstacles to this way
… And particularly in this abandonment man has need of great forti-tude, and of exercise in the manner in which I have already instructed you: and if he does so he will never be deceived. But the unwise man

---

who governs himself ill falls easily into such sickness, because in him the season has grown cold. This is why man s nature grows weary of virtues and good works, and longs for bodily ease and comfort, sometimes immoderately and more than there is need of. And such men would gladly accept consolation from God, if He would bring it to them without their effort and labour; and such men seek solace in His creatures, from which many a time great harm comes to them.

The Scale of Perfection Book Two (extract)
Walter Hilton (c.1340–1396)

Author There is no direct information about Hilton's background and youth, but it is possible that he came from the north of England, probable that he studied at Cambridge University and certain that he trained in canon law. Following a period in the service of the Bishop of Ely, Thomas Arundel, Hilton joined the Augustinian community at Thurgarton Priory in Nottinghamshire at some point in the 1380s, where he remained for the rest of his life. *The Scale of Perfection* is by far his most famous work; other published writings include *Treatise to the Devout Man* and *Song of Angels*.

Language Middle English. Early copies of the original manuscript have survived, as has a contemporary Latin translation. The translation below is by John P. H. Clark and Rosemary Dorward.

Date 1390s.

Genre and context Although presented as two volumes of the same work, the two books of *The Scale* are distinct in style and content and may be separated by some years. The first is addressed to an individual female anchorite. The second seems aimed at a broader readership and is concerned to elucidate points that have attracted criticism (for example from the author of *The Cloud of Unknowing*). Hilton here presents the Christian life as a pilgrimage to Jerusalem, emphasizing that, just as a pilgrim setting out on such a journey has to detach himself from the comforts of home and family if he is to travel light and reach his destination, so must the seeker after Christ detach herself from worldly concerns. There is a great emphasis on attaining a depth of subjective awareness of the truths of faith that goes beyond intellectual assent, as part of the journey towards divine contemplation. Love is a fundamental theme. As with Van Ruysbroeck, there is a good deal of substantial theological content in both volumes.

The Scale of Perfection Book Two
Chapter XXIV

An evil day and a good night: What it means, and how the love of the world is compared to an evil day, and the love of God to a good night.

If you then want to know what this desire is, it is in truth Jesus, for he makes this desire in you, and he gives it you, and it is that is desired: ...

The prophet [Isaiah] speaks thus about this desire: *Memoriale tuum Domine ...'* Lord Jesus, the remembrance of you is impressed on the desire of my soul, for my soul has desired you in the night, and my spirit has longed for you in all my thoughts. And why the prophet says he has desired God all in the night, and what he means by it I shall tell you.

You know well that a night is a space of time between two days, for when one day is ended another comes not at once, but night comes first to divide the days – sometimes long and sometimes short – and then after that there comes another day. The prophet meant not only this kind of night but he meant by it also a night of the spirit. You shall understand that there are two days or two lights. The first is a false light; the second is a true light. The false light is the love of this world that a man has in himself from the corruption of his flesh; the true light is the perfect love of Jesus felt in a man's soul through grace ...

But the everlasting love of Jesus is a true day and a blessed light, for God is both love and light; and he is everlasting; and therefore the man who loves him is in everlasting light, as St. John says: *Qui diligit Deum manet in lumine.* He who loves God stays wholly in light. Then whoever perceives and sees the love of this world to be false and failing, and is therefore ready to forsake it and seek the love of God, cannot at once feel the love of him but has to abide awhile in the night. For he cannot suddenly come from the one light to the other, that is, from the love of the world to perfect love of God.

This night is nothing but a separation and withdrawal of the thought of the soul from earthly things, by great desire and yearning to love, see and feel Jesus and the things of the spirit. This is the night. For just as the night is dark, a hiding place for all bodily creatures, and a rest from all bodily works, so someone who fully intends to think of Jesus and to desire only the love of him takes care to hide his thought from vain regarding, and his affection from carnal pleasure in all bodily creatures, so that his thought may be set free – not fixed – and his affection neither bound, pained nor troubled with anything lower or worse than he is himself. And if he can do so, then it is night for him; for then he is in darkness.

But this is a good night and luminous darkness, for it is a shutting out of the false love of this world, and it is a drawing near to the true day.

And certainly the darker this night is, the nearer is the true day of the love of Jesus, since the more the soul can be hidden from the noise and din of carnal affections and unclean thoughts, through longing for God, the nearer it is to feeling the light of the love of him, for it is almost there. This, it seems is what the prophet [Micah] meant when he said *Cum in tenebris sedeo, Dominus lux mea est*. That is: When I sit in the darkness, our Lord is my light, that is, When my soul is hidden from all stirrings of sin – as it were in sleep – then our Lord is my light. For then he draws near by his grace to show me something of his light.

Nevertheless this night is sometimes painful … if it should be like this with you, do not be too heavyhearted and do not strive too hard … but wait for grace, bear this quietly, and do not break yourself too much … in due course it will become easier and more restful for you through the feeling of grace. That is when your soul is made so free, so powerful and so gathered into itself through grace that it has no desire to think of anything at all, and it can think of nothing, without hindrance from any bodily thing: then it is in a good darkness…

And indeed it is not all dark or negative when it thinks like this, for although it is dark from false light it is not all dark from true light, since Jesus, who is both love and light, is in this darkness. Whether it is painful or restful he is in the soul.

The Cloud of Unknowing (extract)
Anonymous (late fourteenth century)

Author Unknown, but evidence suggests that he was a priest from the English east midlands. He wrote several other works including *The Mystical Theology of St Denys* and *The Book of Privy Counselling*.

Language Middle English. The translation below is by A. C. Spearing.

Date Late fourteenth century. The earliest surviving manuscript dates from the early fifteenth century.

Genre and context This is a work of spiritual direction written for a novice in the religious life, not intended for wider consumption (see p. 21). It is written as if based on personal experience and is highly influenced by the apophatic theology of Pseudo-Dionysius (see Chapter 9), presenting the spiritual life as an ascent through virtuous acts and imaginative meditation to pure contemplation in which the usual framework provided by discursive thought is left behind. The image of the cloud is drawn from Exodus 24 in which Moses ascends Mount Sinai and encounters God. The author appears to know Hilton's *Scale* and is appreciative of it, but also expresses some reservations about that work's inward focus. The language itself is subversive: theological writing in the vernacular was radical at this time but, more than that, as with Eckhart, the use of verbal paradox is designed to move the reader beyond words.

The Cloud of Unknowing
Chapters III and IV

III

Lift up your heart towards God with a humble stirring of love; and think of himself, not of any good to be gained from him. See, too, that you refuse to think of anything but him, so that nothing acts in your intellect or will but God himself. And do what you can to forget all of God's creations and all their actions, so that your thoughts and desires are not directed and do not reach out to any of them, in general or in particular. But leave them alone, and pay no heed to them …

Do not give up, then, but labour at it till you feel desire. For the first time you do it, you will find only a darkness, and as it were a cloud of unknowing, you do not know what, except that you feel in your will a naked purpose towards God. Whatever you do, this darkness and this cloud are between you and your God, and hold you back from seeing him clearly by the light of the understanding in your reason, and from experiencing him in the sweetness of love in your feelings. And so prepare to remain in this darkness as long as you can, always begging for him you love; for if you are ever to feel or see him, so far as is possible in this life, it must always be in this cloud and in this darkness. And if you are willing to labour eagerly as I tell you, I trust in his mercy that you will reach your goal.

IV

… Do not suppose, because I call it a darkness or a cloud, that it is a cloud condensed out of the vapours that float in the air, or a darkness like that in your house at night when your candle is out. By intellectual ingenuity you can imagine such a darkness or cloud brought before your eyes on the brightest day of summer, just as, conversely, in the darkest night of winter you can imagine a clear shining light. Give up such errors; that is not what I mean. For when I say 'darkness' I mean an absence of knowing, in the sense that everything you do not know, or have forgotten, is dark to you, because you cannot see it with your mind's eye. And for this reason it is not called a cloud in the air but a cloud of unknowing that is between you and your God.

8.3 Treasures of darkness[7]

Each of the readings in this section 'gazes without shrinking into the darkness' but makes sense of it in a slightly different way. Nevertheless they have in common an emphasis on the need to let go of conceptual thought, ideas about God, and attachment to the objects of this life. Each in its own way uses paradox to convey the otherness of God.

Commentary on the First Twenty-two Psalms (extract)
Martin Luther (1483–1546)

Author Martin Luther was born near Mansfeld in Germany (then part of the Holy Roman Empire) to middle-class parents, who wanted him to become a lawyer. Martin was not amenable to this and at university in Erfurt he studied theology and philosophy, but in 1505 he left and entered St Augustine's monastery in the same city, much to his family's displeasure. He was ordained priest in 1507 and deployed as a lecturer in the University of Wittenberg. He excelled in this academic environment and in 1512 was appointed to the chair in theology, a position he held until his death. He also had oversight of the eleven Augustinian communities in the province of Saxony. During this time Luther's studies of the Bible led him to develop the beginnings of his understanding of justification by faith, and from 1516 onwards he issued a series of challenges to contemporary practice in the church, initially focused on the sale of papal indulgences to exempt souls from purgatory, but fundamentally about the relative authority of the pope and the Bible. He was excommunicated from the church and then outlawed by the Holy Roman Emperor in 1521, but came under the protection of the Emperor of Saxony and found refuge in Wartburg Castle, where he undertook a translation of the New Testament into German. The development of the printing press meant that Luther's ideas spread rapidly; combined with social and political factors, they were taken up by others in more radical form and expressed in direct action and social unrest in Wittenberg and beyond. Massive social change was under way. In the midst of this, Luther, who was by now married to Katharine von Bora, was central to the establishment of a new church – its ordering, doctrine and liturgical practice. He was a gifted musician and hymn writer, and by 1534 had translated the whole Bible into German. His last years were limited by ill health, though he remained highly engaged with church and state. Luther's literary output was massive; his most well-known work is probably his commentary on Paul's letter to the Romans based on lectures given in 1515–16.

Language Latin in manuscript form, being published later as parts of compilations. The translation below is by Alister McGrath.

---

7 Isaiah 45.3.

Date 1519.

Genre and context Luther had lectured on the psalms early in his academic career. He appears to have envisaged writing a more devotional commentary on the whole book but, due to other demands on his time, and to his frustration, he had by 1519 only managed to get as far as Psalm 22 and stopped there. Luther's approach to a sense of abandonment by God is much less 'optimistic' than those in the previous section. He does not see it as a step towards greater intimacy but as an expression of the fact that God cannot be known in this life other than by the action of the Spirit; the gulf between the human and divine is simply too great. God is revealed in Jesus but the paradoxical glory of this revelation is not so much the crucified Jesus as the *empty* cross and the *absent* Jesus, who is not simply suffering and dying but dead and gone (descended into hell). This idea is sometimes referred to as *Deus absconditus* (Isaiah 45.15). While the Spirit may at times make Christ present experientially, the Bible is the most reliable way to connect with him (see section 6.4).

Commentary on the First Twenty-two Psalms
Psalm 3.4

… For surely even Christ on the cross cried out with a physical voice and taught us that we should cry out in distress, so that we may call upon the Lord with all our strength, within and without.

He spoke about his 'holy mountain.' I see that this mountain is understood in various ways … Yet it is unnameable, having neither appearance nor name. I take this to mean that we should all be taught that in times of temptation we must indeed hope for divine help from above, but that the manner, time, and kind of this help are unknown to us, so that there is room for faith and hope, which rest on those things which are neither seen or heard, and have not entered the human heart. And so the eye of faith looks into the inner shadows and the darkness of the mountain, looking up on high and waiting for help to come. It sees and expects a helper from on high, but it does not know what this 'on high' is or what kind of help it will be …

For since God is ineffable, incomprehensible, inaccessible, so is his will and help, especially in times of abandonment. Therefore, no words can convey what this 'holy mountain' of God is, apart from someone who has experienced it by faith, and tested it in times of temptation. It is therefore the same as if he had said: 'He heard me from his holy mountain' … He heard me in an ineffable and incomprehensible way, which I had never thought of. I know that I am heard, but not in what way. He rescued me from above and took me on high … but I do not know what this 'above', this 'on high', this 'mountain,' is. And it is the same when God leaves us and does not hear us: for we do not know where the Spirit comes from, even though we hear his voice when he breathes, as Christ says. If he comes to me, I will not see him, if he goes away, I will not understand him. So it is, Christ says, with 'everyone that is born of the Spirit.' He departs when the Spirit departs; that is, he is left alone when the Spirit leaves him: and he 'comes when the Spirit comes;' that is, he is heard when the Spirit hears: and yet he knows neither the one nor the other, nor how this takes place.

This is what the term 'holy' means. As was said above, it signifies 'separate' and 'secret', and is clearly that which cannot be reached either by sense or by the mind, into which someone is taken into the invisible God and is most perfectly purified, separated, and sanctified. It is true that these things are difficult and unbearable for human nature, unless the Spirit of the Lord moves on these waters and the darkness of this abyss, so that it becomes light.

Hence the whole folly of this matter is that a person does not submit to the counsel of God, but asks to be helped in a way that he chooses and at a time that is convenient for him. And in doing so, he gives the 'unnameable mountain' a name he has chosen, and profanes the holy mountain of God by touching it with his thought. He is like a horse or a mule, who follows his master as long as he feels and understands him, but will not follow him beyond his own limits, because he does not live by faith but by his own reason.

The Dark Night of the Soul
John of the Cross (1542–1591)

Author Juan de Yepes y Álvarez was born near Avila and, like his compatriot Teresa, was of Jewish heritage. He was raised by a widowed mother and the family experienced extreme poverty. He received some basic education before joining a Carmelite community in 1563 and then studied theology and philosophy at the University of Salamanca, being ordained priest in 1567. Later that year he met Teresa of Avila during a visit to Medina del Campo, where she was establishing a new convent under her reformed rule. Juan began to work closely with Teresa and in 1568 established the first of his own reformed communities, taking for himself the name 'de la Cruz' (of the Cross). As the reforms became more widespread hostile opposition arose from within the order itself and from Dominican overseers. In 1577 Juan was kidnapped and taken to the monastery in Toledo where he was imprisoned and tortured for not denouncing the reforms. It was during this time that he composed

The Spiritual Canticle. He escaped the following year and was nursed back to health by Teresa's community in Toledo. He then began a ministry of oversight of the increasing number of reformed Carmelite communities, which involved much travelling within Spain. His health continued to be fragile and he died at the age of 49. His writings are in the form of poems with commentary: *Spiritual Canticle, Dark Night of the Soul, Living Flame of Love,* and *Ascent of Mount Carmel*.

Language Andalusian Spanish. The original manuscript is lost but there are several reliable contemporary copies. The translation below is by E. Allison Peers.

Date Unknown, but probably c.1578.

Genre and context It seems likely that the concerns of this poem are informed by Juan's horrendous experience of beatings and solitary confinement in the dark, but his spirituality was already one of privation and austerity, very much focused on the crucified and suffering Christ whom he famously depicted in a drawing. The poem makes use of paradox but also draws on the erotic themes of the Song of Songs. In his lengthy accompanying commentary Juan explains that it refers to the whole life of faith that involves voluntary hardship and detachment (as in the reformed rule) and also unsought periods of adversity and suffering.

The Dark Night of the Soul

On a dark night,
Kindled in love with yearnings – oh, happy chance!–
I went forth without being observed,
My house being now at rest.

In darkness and secure,
By the secret ladder, disguised – oh, happy chance!–
In darkness and in concealment,
My house being now at rest.

In the happy night,
In secret, when none saw me,
Nor I beheld aught,
Without light or guide, save that which burned in my heart.

This light guided me
More surely than the light of noonday
To the place where he (well I knew who!) was awaiting me–
A place where none appeared.

Oh, night that guided me,
Oh, night more lovely than the dawn,
Oh, night that joined Beloved with lover,
Lover transformed in the Beloved!

Upon my flowery breast,
Kept wholly for himself alone,
There he stayed sleeping, and I caressed him,
And the fanning of the cedars made a breeze.

The breeze blew from the turret
As I parted his locks;
With his gentle hand he wounded my neck
And caused all my senses to be suspended.

I remained, lost in oblivion;
My face I reclined on the Beloved.
All ceased and I abandoned myself,
Leaving my cares forgotten among the lilies.

The Spiritual Espousals (extract)
John Van Ruysbroeck (1293–1381)

Author See p. 137.

Language See p. 137.

Date See p. 137.

Genre and context This section comes towards the end of the Book on yearning for God, leading into Book III and beginning to talk in the negative language that, in varying ways for the writers in this chapter, stands for union with the divine.

> ### The Spiritual Espousals Book II 'The Life of Yearning for God'
> ### Part 4: 'To meet him': How we shall Meet God Spiritually through Means and without Means
>
> **The union without mean in a threefold manner**
>
> *… The first manner: setting us free from distractions*
>
> Sometimes the fervent man turns inward, in his singleness, according to his delectable inclination, above all works and above all virtues, with a single perception of delectable love. And here he meets God without mean. And out of the unity of God there shines in him a single light, and this light reveals to him darkness, nakedness and nothing. In the darkness, he will be seized, and he will fall into a lack of manner, as it were into a trackless waste. In the nakedness he will lose his observation and perception of all things, and he will be formed again and transfused with a single clarity. In the nothing all his works will fail him, for in the working of the unfathomable love of God he will be conquered. And in the delectable inclination of his spirit he conquers God, and becomes one spirit with Him. And in this union in the Spirit of God he comes to a delectable savour, and possesses the Divine Being. And he is filled full, according to the sinking away of his self into his essential being, with the unfathomable delights and riches of God.

Further reading

Between Cross and Resurrection: A theology of Holy Saturday by Alan E. Lewis. Grand Rapids, MI: Eerdmans, 2001.

God Within: The mystical tradition of northern Europe by Oliver Davies. London: Darton, Longman & Todd, 2006.

The Mysticism of the Cloud of Unknowing by William Johnston. New York: Fordham University Press, 2000.

Ruysbroeck by Evelyn Underhill. London: Alicia Editions, 2021.

Sadness, Depression, and the Dark Night of the Soul: Transcending the medicalisation of sadness by Glòria Durà-Villà. London: Jessica Kingsley, 2017.

A Turbulent, Seditious and Factious People: John Bunyan and his church by Christopher Hill. London: Verso Books, 2016.

The Wound of Knowledge: Christian spirituality from the New Testament to St. John of the Cross by Rowan Williams. London: Darton, Longman & Todd, 2014.

9

Breaking Through

... when Jesus had been baptized, just as he came up from the water, suddenly the heavens were opened to him and he saw the Spirit of God descending like a dove and alighting on him. And a voice from heaven said, 'This is my Son, the Beloved, with whom I am well pleased.'
(Matthew 3.16–17)

Jesus answered, 'Do you believe because I told you that I saw you under the fig tree? You will see greater things than these.' And he said to him, 'Very truly, I tell you, you will see heaven opened and the angels of God ascending and descending upon the Son of Man.'
(John 1.50–51)

But filled with the Holy Spirit, [Stephen] gazed into heaven and saw the glory of God and Jesus standing at the right hand of God. 'Look,' he said, 'I see the heavens opened and the Son of Man standing at the right hand of God!'
(Acts 7.55–56)

After this I looked, and there in heaven a door stood open! And the first voice, which I had heard speaking to me like a trumpet, said, 'Come up here, and I will show you what must take place after this.' At once I was in the spirit, and there in heaven stood a throne, with one seated on the throne!
(Revelation 4.1–2)

... I will go on to visions and revelations of the Lord. I know a person in Christ who fourteen years ago was caught up to the third heaven – whether in the body or out of the body I do not know; God knows. And I know that such a person – whether in the body or out of the body I do not know; God knows – was caught up into Paradise and heard things that are not to be told, that no mortal is permitted to repeat.
(2 Corinthians 12.1b–4)

The readings in the previous chapter all expressed aspects of being caught up into the mystery of God from darkness into darkness. The crucifixion is never far away from the thoughts of these writers, and the experience of wounding was made explicit in the extracts from Gregory the Great, John Bunyan and John of the Cross. Somehow the journey that leads one into a unifying encounter with God of the sort described in these texts cannot by-pass the cross (John 14.6). This idea is reiterated forcefully by Benet Canfield, the sixteenth-century English mystic, in a chapter from his work *The Rule of Perfection* entitled 'The passion not to be forsaken for contemplation of the Godhead alone':

> ... many there be who casting one glance at the passion, long straight to mount to the Godhead; Others disrespecting the passion are, as they think, directly transported to the Deity by a certain transcendence of the mind, which for the most part I suspect rather natural then supernatural; and imaginary then real.[1]

Christ's cross is also his glory (John 12.28–33). It is therefore not surprising that the wounds and piercings that form such an important part of the passion accounts also have their place in the literature on Christian contemplation. Piercings are literally poignant. Wounds open up new spaces. They signify breaking through from one domain to another: breaking through the body's physical barrier as in the stigmata of Francis and others; breaking through psychological defences as in John of the Cross' description of his desire for Christ as the wounding of arrows that is only to be healed by one who is also wounded;[2] breaking through the cloud of unknowing with a 'sharp dart of longing love';[3] breaking through the veil which separates the reality of earthly existence from the ultimate reality of heaven.

This breaking through has what the psychologist and philosopher William James referred to as a 'noetic' quality, something he understood to be a distinctive mark of mystical experience; it refers to the individual's utter conviction that they have directly encountered deepest truth that could be accessed in no other way.[4] This is not the same as the sorts of imaginative 'as if' encounter with Christ explored in Chapter 6. Often it feels revelatory: being given a glimpse of another place or a taste of another time, of the bringing the future into the present.

This may seem quite a long way from the process of bereavement that has so far framed the readings in this book, but there are some perhaps unexpected points of connection. Loss, particularly traumatic loss, has a way of confronting us with the fact that reality is not as we had assumed: 'I thought that love would last forever: *I was wrong.*' It can force us to take a different perspective, to become aware of a bigger picture, and to gain insights that can only come through this sort of direct and deeply troubling experience. These insights can carry a profound sense of knowing and, in navigating what is

---

1 Benet Canfield, 1609, *The Rule of Perfection*. Part 3, Chapter XX, London, 1646 printing, p. 221.
2 *Spiritual Canticle.*
3 *The Cloud of Unknowing*, Chapter VI.
4 W. James, 1902, *The Varieties of Religious Experience*, Longmans, Green, Lecture XVI.

so often a paradoxical path through them, we find ourselves profoundly changed.

Sometimes the insights gained are visionary: an assurance that the deceased is in a good place, a shrinking of the distance between us and them, a fore-taste of a future reunion. The Christian doctrine of the communion of saints honours such visionary insights; it is well-expressed in the bidding prayer for the traditional Christmas service of nine lessons and carols written by Eric Milner-White in 1918 and surely influenced by his experience as an army chaplain in the Great War: 'those who rejoice with us, but upon another shore and in a greater light, that multitude which no man can number, whose hope was in the Word made flesh, and with whom we for evermore are one.'

The readings in this chapter are again arranged in three groups. They each present a different perspective on the shrinking of the distance between earth and heaven. The first group picks up where Chapter 8 left off, promoting the negation of concepts as a means of 'piercing' or 'plunging into' divine realities; the second talks in terms of a heavenly ascent on the part of the believer; the third describes the opening of heaven so that it can be seen plainly from earth by the eye of faith. In several of the readings the insights achieved occur in a context of affliction or loss.

9.1 Piercing the veil

The Book of Divine Consolation and
Sermon for Ascension Day (extracts)
Meister Eckhart (c.1260–1328)

Author See p. 118.

Language Middle High German. The translations below are by Oliver Davies and Maurice O'C. Walshe.

Date *The Book of Divine Consolation* c.1308; sermon date uncertain.

Genre and context *The Book of Divine Consolation* was written for Queen Agnes of Hungary (1281–1364) to offer spiritual comfort following a bereavement. She had suffered the loss of several close family members, but the most likely context is the assassination of her father, Duke Albrecht of Austria. In the section below Eckhart sets out the life of faith as one of achieving progressively more intimate connection with God through a process of detachment. This was something Agnes almost certainly pursued herself during her long period of widowhood, largely spent in a convent she had founded. The *Sermon for Ascension Day* describes this progression to the divine in the much more dramatic language of *durchbruch* (breaking through), and the reality that is attained as beyond words and concepts.

The Book of Divine Consolation

From Part 1

Now I say further that all suffering comes from our love for what misfortune takes from us. If the loss of external things causes me pain, then this is a clear sign that I love external things and thus, in truth, love suffering and despair. Is it surprising then that I suffer, since I love and seek suffering and despair? My heart and my affections assign to creatures that goodness which is God's possession.

From Part 3

… Augustine says that the first stage of the inner or new man is achieved when we live according to the example of good and holy people, even though we still clutch at chairs and lean against the walls and we still drink at the breast.

The second stage comes when we no longer consider external images, even those of good men and women, but run and hasten towards the teaching and counsel of God and divine wisdom, turning our back on the world and our face towards God. Then we clamber off our mother's lap and smile at our heavenly Father.

The third stage is reached when we increasingly withdraw from our mother, removing ourselves more and more from her lap, shedding concern and fear so that even if it were in our power to inflict evil and injustice on all people without difficulty, we would not desire to do so, since through our love we are so bound to God in eager devotion that he finally establishes and leads us in joy and sweetness and blessedness to where all that is unlike God and alien to him is hateful to us.

The fourth stage comes when we grow and become ever more rooted in love and in God, so that we are prepared to take upon ourselves any trial, temptation, unpleasantness and suffering willingly and gladly, eagerly and joyfully.

The fifth stage is when we live altogether at peace in ourselves, quietly resting in the overflowing wealth of the highest and unutterable wisdom.

The sixth stage comes when we are stripped of our own form and are transformed by God's eternity, becoming wholly oblivious to all transient and temporal life, drawn into and changed into an image of the divine, and have become God's son. Truly, there is no stage higher than this, and here eternal peace and blessedness reign, for the end of the inner man and the new man is eternal life.

Sermon Sixteen 16 (Q29)
Acts 1.4 'he ordered them not to leave Jerusalem, but to wait there for the promise of the Father.'

… No one can receive the Holy Spirit because he lives above time in eternity. In things temporal, the Holy Ghost can be neither received nor given. When a man turns from temporal things and into himself, he there perceives a heavenly light, a light that comes from heaven. It is beneath heaven, but it comes from heaven. In this light man finds satisfaction, and yet it is corporeal: they say it is material. A piece of iron, whose nature is to fall, will rise against its nature and hang suspended to a lodestone in virtue of the master force the stone has received from heaven. Wherever the stone turns, the iron will turn with it. The spirit does the same: not fully satisfied with this light, it presses right through the firmament and drives through heaven till it reaches that spirit that revolves the heavens, and from the revolution of the heavens all things in the world grow and green. Still the mind is not satisfied till it pierces to the apex, to the primal source where spirit has its origin. This (human) spirit knows neither number nor numberlessness: there is no numberless number in the malady of time. No one has any other root in eternity, where there is 'nobody' without number. This spirit must transcend number and break through multiplicity, and God will break through him: and just as He breaks through into me, so I break through in turn into Him. God leads this spirit into the desert and into the unity of Himself, where He is simply One and welling up in Himself. This spirit is in unity and freedom.

... Here some folk will say, 'You are telling us wondrous things, but we perceive them not.' I regret that too. This state is so noble yet so common, that you have no need to purchase it for a penny or a halfpenny. If your intention is right and your will is free, you have it. He who has thus abandoned all things on the lower plane where they are mortal, will recover them in God, where they are reality. Whatever is dead here is alive there, and all that is dense matter here is spirit there in God.

... Our Lord ascended into heaven, beyond all light, beyond all understanding and all human ken. The man who is thus translated beyond all light, dwells in eternity? Therefore St. Paul says, 'God dwells in a light to which there is no approach' (1 Timothy 6.16), and that is in itself pure unity. Therefore a man must be slain and wholly dead, devoid of self and wholly without likeness, like to none, and then he is really God-like. For it is God's character, His nature, to be peerless and like no man. That we may be thus one in the oneness that is God Himself, may God help us. Amen.

On Mystical Theology (extract)
Pseudo-Dionysius (fifth–sixth century)

Author The author presents himself as Dionysius the Areopagite, an Athenian philosopher and member of the city council converted by Paul (Acts 17.34), thus giving himself the authority of one known to the apostles. This meant that his works were revered and carefully preserved by the church; and they were very influential. However, from the Renaissance onwards his identity came under critical scrutiny, and it is now agreed, on the basis of the Neoplatonist and Christian references in his works, that he was writing some time in the late fifth to early sixth century and that he was probably of Syrian origin. He is sometimes known as Pseudo-Denys.

Language Greek. The translation below is by Colm Luibhéid and Paul Rorem.

Date Early sixth century.

Genre and context *On Mystical Theology* is one of four treatises, the others being *On the Celestial Hierarchy*, *On the Divine Names* and *On the Ecclesiastical Hierarchy*. In these works the author lays out a complicated account of reality that, as the names of two of the treatises suggest, is highly hierarchical in nature, in line with the Neoplatonic character of his thinking. While these take a 'top down' perspective, *On Mystical Theology* is presented from the bottom up, with the progress of the faithful likened to Moses' ascent of Mount Sinai. It is addressed to Paul's co-worker, Timothy (a contemporary of the actual Areopagite) and mentions the teachings of the Apostle Bartholomew, possibly referring to a non-canonical Gospel attributed to him but since lost. Like the readings in Chapter 8, it uses the imagery of darkness, and is concerned with the laying aside of conceptual thinking and language in order to meet with the divine. But its imagery is more violent, involving a breaking away from statements about God, either affirmative or negative 'beyond unknowing', and a 'plunging' into another reality.

On Mystical Theology
Chapter 1

1.Trinity!! Higher than any being,
any divinity, any goodness!
Guide of Christians in the wisdom of heaven!
Lead us up beyond unknowing and light,
up to the farthest, highest peak
of mystic scripture,
where the mysteries of God's Word
lie simple, absolute and unchangeable
in the brilliant darkness of a hidden silence.
Amid the deepest shadow they pour overwhelming light
on what is most manifest.
Amid the wholly unsensed and unseen
they completely fill our sightless minds
with treasures beyond all beauty.

For this I pray; and, Timothy, my friend, my advice to you as you look for a sight of the mysterious things, is to leave behind you everything perceived and understood, everything perceptible and understandable, all that is not and all that is, and, with your understanding laid aside, to strive upward as much as you can toward union with him who is

---

beyond all being and knowledge. By an undivided and absolute abandonment of yourself and everything, shedding all and freed from all,
you will be uplifted to the ray of the divine shadow which is above
everything that is …

3. This, at least, is what was taught by the blessed Bartholomew. He
says that the Word of God is vast and minuscule, that the Gospel is
wide-ranging and yet restricted. To me it seems that in this he is extraordinarily shrewd, for he has grasped that the good cause of all is both
eloquent and taciturn, indeed wordless. It has neither word nor act of
understanding, since it is on a plane above all this, and it is made manifest only to those who travel through foul and fair, who pass beyond the
summit of every holy ascent, who leave behind them every divine light,
every voice, every word from heaven, and who plunge into the darkness where, as scripture proclaims, there dwells the One who is beyond
all things. It is not for nothing that the blessed Moses is commanded to
submit first to purification and then to depart from those who have not
undergone this. When every purification is complete, he hears the many
voiced trumpets. He sees the many lights, pure and with rays streaming
abundantly. Then, standing apart from the crowds and accompanied by
chosen priests, he pushes ahead to the summit of the divine ascents. And
yet he does not meet God himself, but contemplates, not him who is
invisible, but rather where he dwells. This means, I presume, that the
holiest and highest of the things perceived with the eye of the body or
the mind are but the rationale which presupposes all that lies below the
Transcendent One. Through them, however, his unimaginable presence
is shown, walking the heights of those holy places to which the mind at
least can rise. But then he [Moses] breaks free of them, away from what
sees and is seen, and he plunges into the truly mysterious darkness of
unknowing. Here, renouncing all that the mind may conceive, wrapped
entirely in the intangible and the invisible, he belongs completely to him
who is beyond everything. Here, being neither oneself nor someone else,
one is supremely united to the completely unknown by an inactivity of
all knowledge, and knows beyond the mind by knowing nothing.

9.2 'Lift up your hearts'[5]

Pseudo-Dionysius' picture of the life of faith as a mountainous ascent into the clouds resonates with the upward trajectory of readings in this section, all of which feature journeys in which individuals are lifted up beyond themselves away from this earth into the clouds and the dazzling light beyond. Accounts of heavenly ascents are characteristic of Jewish literature between the two Testaments, and the New Testament book of Revelation also features such a journey. There is often a guide on the journey who provides commentary and interpretation. The ascent feels like flight rather than ambulation, and offers a new perspective on life 'below', yet it can also provide a sense of home or resting place, reflecting the idea that the Christian has in some sense already risen to a heavenly home (Colossians 3.2–3).

The Divine Comedy (extract)
Dante Alighieri (c.1265–1321)

Author Dante was born in Florence into a family of the mercantile political class. This was a time of the emergence of city states in Italy, jockeying for power, and complex alliances. Dante's family were supporters of the Guelphs, a party that supported the pope against the Holy Roman Emperor. He saw military service with them and, after victory over their opponents, held political positions in Florence and also began to write. The Guelphs split into two parties, distinguished by their attitude to the role of the pope in Florence's affairs. The conflict between them was bitter and violent, Dante was essentially on the losing side, and from 1302 was living in exile on pain of death. He moved from place to place, becoming deeply disillusioned with politics and engaging more deeply with scholarship; he spent his final years in Ravenna. Dante is famous for his unrequited passion for Beatrice, a girl he met when they were both children and claimed to have loved at first sight. However, he was promised in marriage to someone else and anyway barely knew Beatrice who was also married to another and died in her twenties. She is the inspiration for his 1294 work *The New Life* and also appears in *The Divine Comedy*.

Language Tuscan Italian. The translation below is by Tony Kline.

Date c.1321 (first published 1472).

Genre and context This is a narrative poem in three parts which was written over a period of about twelve years and shows the development of ideas and

---

5 These words, traditionally known as the *Sursum Corda*, signal the beginning of the prayer of consecration in Holy Communion. In the Orthodox tradition they reflect the belief that the whole congregation is about to begin an ascent to the heavenly places.

style that might be expected over that time. Its literary form, theological content and vivid visual imagery had a major influence on subsequent European culture, and its local Tuscan dialect became established as standard Italian. It tells the story of Dante's journey down to hell and then up through purgatory to paradise from Good Friday until the following Wednesday of 1300 (a year that was a key in the charges that led to his exile). Dante's guide through hell and purgatory is the Roman poet Virgil. Beatrice is his guide through heaven. The genre is a subject of much scholarly debate: is it fantasy, an allegory or the literal account of a series of visionary experiences? In his correspondence with his patron, Cangrande Della Scala, Dante indicated that it can be read at multiple levels. The work is the product of the final years of Dante's life in exile, a period dominated by loss; it is a redemptive story and appears in part to be an apologia for the genuine and orthodox nature of his Christian faith. In the passage below Dante is journeying with Beatrice through the 'spheres of heaven' (the planets, each of which stands for a virtue) and has ascended beyond the sun to Mars. Here he sees a cross formed from the souls of warriors who have defended the faith, expressing the virtue of fortitude; to his surprise, Christ himself appears on the cross and Dante hears the souls singing his praise as the Warrior King. The meaning of the final sentences is debated, but may well refer to the anticipation of further divine revelation, more beautiful even than Beatrice, as he continues his ascent.

Paradiso
Canto I

1–36 Dante's Invocation

The glory of Him, who moves all things, penetrates the universe, and glows in one region more, in another less. I have been in that Heaven that knows his light most, and have seen things, which whoever descends from there has neither power, nor knowledge, to relate: because as our intellect draws near to its desire, it reaches such depths that memory cannot go back along the track.

Nevertheless, whatever, of the sacred regions, I had power to treasure in my mind, will now be the subject of my labour.

Canto XIV

67–139 The Fifth Sphere: Mars: Fortitude

Look around! A shining dawn, of equal brightness, beyond what was there, like a whitening horizon. And, as at twilight new things to see begin to appear, in the heavens, so that the vision seems real, and unreal, so, there, I began to see newly arrived beings, making a third circle, out beyond the other two rims. O true sparks of the sacred exhalation, how sudden and glowing, in front of my eyes, which, overcome, could not withstand it!

But Beatrice showed herself so lovely and smiling to me, it must be left among those sights that my memory cannot follow. From that my eyes recovered their power to raise themselves, and I saw myself carried, along with my Lady, to a higher fortune. I saw clearly that I was lifted higher, by the burning smile of that planet, which seemed to me redder than usual.

I made sacrifice to God, of my heart, and in that speech which is the same for all of us, as fitted this newly given grace: and the ardour of the sacrifice was not yet gone from my chest, before I knew the prayer had been accepted, and with favour, since splendours appeared to me, inside two rays, so radiant and red, that I exclaimed: 'O Helios, who glorifies them so!' As the Milky Way gleams between the poles of the Universe, decked with greater and lesser lights, so white as to set the very sages questioning, so those constellated rays made the ancient sign, in the depth of Mars, that crossing quadrants make in a circle.

Here my memory outruns my ability, since Christ flashed out so on that Cross, that I can find no fitting comparison. But whoever takes up his cross and follows Christ, will forgive me for what I leave unspoken, when he sees Christ white within that glow. From cusp to cusp, from summit to base, there were lights moving, that sparkled intensely, in meeting one another, and passing. So we see, here, motes moving through a ray, that sometimes penetrates the shadow people contrive, with art and ingenuity, against the sunlight, straight, curved, fast or slow, long or short, changing in appearance.

And as harp and viol, tuned in many-chorded harmony, make a sweet chime, to one who cannot separate the notes, so a melody enraptured me, from the lights that appeared, gathered along the Cross, though I could not follow the hymn. I clearly knew it was of high praise, since there came to me the words: '*Rise and conquer*,' as to one who hears but does not understand. And I was so enamoured of it, there, that there had been nothing, till then, that tied me in such sweet chains.

Perhaps it may be too bold to say so, as if it slighted the joy of those lovely eyes, gazing into which my longing finds rest, but he who recognises how those living seals of all beauty have ever greater effect the higher the region, and that I had not yet turned towards them, may excuse me from my self-accusation, and can see I speak the truth: for that sacred joy is not excluded here, that as it climbs grows purer.

The Life of Teresa of Jesus (extract)
Teresa of Avila (1515–1582)

Author See p. 81.

Language Spanish. The original manuscript still exists. The translation below is by E. Allison Peers.

Date c.1565.

Genre and context The book was written in response to a command by Teresa's confessor, Domingo Bàññez, but she seems to have been working on an autobiography for several years before this official request, the final version taking a further three years. Teresa's preferred title was *Of the Mercies of God*, reflecting her desire to turn attention from her spiritual practices and mystical experiences towards the grace of God given to her, a sinner. In the extract below she offers an account of what was happening during the regular trances that she began to experience during this period, and which were witnessed and documented by others. It is a combination of simple description of something rather like what we would now call an out of body experience, together with an attempt to make theological sense of it. Detachment is a key lynchpin of Carmelite spirituality, and uplifting of the soul (understood by Teresa to be fully embodied rather than a psychological phenomenon) loosens it from the earthly ties that would otherwise bind it.

The Life of Teresa of Jesus
Chapter XX

I should like, with the help of God, to be able to describe the difference between union and rapture, or elevation, or what they call flight of the spirit, or transport – it is all one. I mean that these different names all refer to the same thing, which is also called ecstasy …

But as we are giving Him thanks for this great blessing, and doing our utmost to draw near to Him in a practical way, the Lord gathers up the soul, just (we might say) as the clouds gather up the vapours from the earth, and raises it up till it is right out of itself (I have heard that it is in this way that the clouds or the sun gather up the vapours) and the cloud rises to Heaven and takes the soul with it, and begins to reveal to it things concerning the Kingdom that He has prepared for it. I do not know if the comparison is an exact one, but that is the way it actually happens …

You realize, I repeat, and indeed see, that you are being carried away, you know not whither. For, though rapture brings us delight, the weakness of our nature at first makes us afraid of it, and we need to be resolute and courageous in soul, much more so than for what has been described …

On other occasions the soul seems to be going about in a state of the greatest need, and asking itself: 'Where is thy God?' … It seems as though it were on the threshold of death, save that this suffering brings with it such great happiness that I know of nothing with which it may be compared. It is a martyrdom, severe but also delectable; for the soul will accept nothing earthly that may be offered it, even though it were the thing which it had been accustomed to enjoy most: it seems to fling it away immediately. It realizes clearly that it wants nothing save its God; but its love is not centred upon any particular attribute of Him: its desire is for the whole of God and it has no knowledge of what it desires. By 'no knowledge', I mean that no picture is formed in the imagination; and, in my opinion, for a great part of the time during which it is in that state, the faculties are inactive: they are suspended by their distress, just as in union and rapture they are suspended by joy …

And now comes the distress of having to return to this life. Now the soul has grown new wings and has learned to fly. Now the little bird has lost its unformed feathers. Now in Christ's name the standard is raised on high; it would seem that what has happened is nothing less than that the captain of the fortress has mounted, or has been led up, to the highest of its towers, and has reared the standard aloft there in the name of God. From his position of security he looks down on those below. No longer does he fear perils; rather he desires them, for through them, as it were, he receives the assurance of victory. This becomes very evident in the little weight now given by the soul to earthly matters, which it treats as the worthless things that they are …

I believe myself that a soul which attains to this state neither speaks nor does anything of itself, but that this sovereign King takes care of all that it has to do. Oh, my God, how clear is the meaning of that verse about asking for the wings of a dove and how right the author was – and how right we shall all be! – to ask for them! It is evident that he is referring to the flight taken by the spirit when it soars high above all created things, and above itself first of all; but it is a gentle and a joyful flight and also a silent one.

When it looks upon this Divine Sun, the brightness dazzles it; when it looks at itself, its eyes are blinded by clay. The little dove is blind. And very often it remains completely blind, absorbed, amazed, and dazzled by all the wonders it sees. From this it acquires true humility, which will never allow it to say anything good of itself nor will permit others to do so. It is the Lord of the garden, and not the soul, that distributes the fruit of the garden, and so nothing remains in its hands, but all the good that is in it is directed towards God; if it says anything about itself, it is for His glory. It knows that it possesses nothing here; and, even if it so wishes, it cannot ignore this; for it sees it by direct vision, and, willy-nilly, shuts its eyes to things of the world, and opens them to an understanding of the truth.

Steal away to Jesus
Wallace Willis (c.1820–1880)

Author Wallace Willis was a member of the native American Choctaw nation. A freedman, his compositions are said to have been heard by Revd Alexander Reid, who promoted them via the Fisk Jubilee Singers. Other compositions include 'Swing low, Sweet Chariot'.

Language American English.

Date 1870s.

Genre and context This American spiritual uses language from Psalm 77 and alludes to Paul's discussion of the resurrection of believers in 1 Corinthians 15 and 1 Thessalonians 4.16–18, in which he asserts that at the sound of the trumpet they will be carried up into the clouds. Much has been made of the potential coded language signalling escape of enslaved individuals from plantations under cover of stormy weather. However, the song's first meaning may have been simply devotional: the expression of the desire for respite from a situation of chronic privation and loss by stealing away to a quiet place to pray, and there to experience a foretaste of the liberation provided by death and resurrection.

Steal away to Jesus

Refrain:
Steal away, steal away,
steal away to Jesus!
Steal away, steal away home,
I ain't got long to stay here.

1. My Lord, He calls me,
He calls me by the thunder;
The trumpet sounds within my soul;
I ain't got long to stay here.

2. Green trees are bending,
Poor sinners stand a trembling;
The trumpet sounds within my soul;
I ain't got long to stay here.

3. My Lord, He calls me,
He calls me by the lightning;
The trumpet sounds within my soul;
I ain't got long to stay here.

9.3 The open heaven

The readings in this section describe heavenly visions in which God graciously parts the skies and/or reaches down to earth.

Life of Antony (extract)
Athanasius of Alexandria (c.296–373)

Author Athanasius was born in in the region of Alexandria in Egypt to a Christian family. He was well educated and initially served as secretary to Bishop Alexander who ordained him deacon in 319. It is likely that during this time Athanasius got to know Antony, who lived a solitary life in the desert south of Alexandria. In 325 Athanasius attended the first Council of Nicaea in his capacity of bishop's secretary and quickly became drawn into the doctrinal conflict with Arius centred on the status of Christ in relation to the Father, a conflict that would dominate his life. When Alexander died in 328 Athanasius became bishop of Alexandria. He remained bishop (on and off) for the rest of his life but underwent several periods of exile as the result of politicized theological conflicts with followers of Arius. Apart from the *Life of Antony*, he is best known for his theological writings on the Incarnation and for the first formal statement on the contents of the New Testament.

Language Greek. The translation below is by Carolinne White from a Latin version by Evagrius of Antioch dating from around 370.

Date c.356.

Genre and context This is quite different from Athanasius' theological treatise. It was a new genre and became a model for biographies of revered Christian figures. It appears to have been written during Athanasius' third exile in which he withdrew to the desert area and lived the life of a monk. It was perhaps prompted by the death of Antony (251–356) shortly after he arrived. Nearly everything that is known about Antony is based on the *Life* which, following its translation by Evagrius, quickly became a best-seller and strongly influenced the development of monasticism. However, some of Antony's own letters (originally written in Coptic) still exist. The move to the desert by early Christians was at least in part a flight from persecution under various Roman regimes, but once there they pursued lives of varying degrees of solitude and asceticism. Antony is said to have been at the extreme end of this spectrum, and is remembered for his battles with the devil, vividly recounted by Athanasius. The extract below is from early in Antony's desert life, as he begins to take his own path following a period as a disciple of older hermits and is strengthened by a direct encounter with the heavenly Christ.

Life of Antony

VIII. Then the holy Antony, considering that a servant of God ought to take as his model the way of life of the great Elijah and to use it as a mirror to organize his own life, moved away to some tombs situated not far from the settlement. He asked one of his friends to bring him food at regular intervals. And when this brother had shut him up in one of the tombs, Antony remained there alone. But the devil was afraid that, as time went on, Antony might cause the desert to become inhabited, so he gathered together his minions and tortured Antony by beating him all over. The intensity of the pain deprived Antony of the ability both to move and to speak, and later he himself would often tell how his injuries had been so serious that they were worse than all the tortures devised by men …

IX. … the devil, the enemy of the good, was amazed that after so many beatings Antony dared to return. He gathered his dogs together and tearing himself to pieces in his fury, he said, 'You see how Antony is overcome neither by the spirit of fornication nor by physical pain, and on top of it all he challenges us insolently. Take up all your weapons; we must attack with greater force. Let him feel, let him feel; he must understand who it is that he is provoking.' He spoke and all those listening to him agreed with his exhortation, because the devil has countless ways of causing harm. Then there was a sudden noise that caused the place to shake violently: holes appeared in the walls and a horde of different kinds of demons poured out. They took on the shape of wild animals and snakes and instantly filled the whole place with spectres in the form of lions, bulls, wolves, vipers, serpents, scorpions and even leopards and bears, too. They all made noises according to their individual nature: the lion roared, eager for the kill; the bull bellowed and made menacing movements with his horns; the serpent hissed; the wolves leaped forward to attach; the spotted leopard demonstrated all the different wiles of the one who controlled him. The face of each of them bore a savage expression and the sound of the fierce voices was terrifying. Antony, beaten and mauled, experienced even more atrocious pains in his body, but he remained unafraid, his mind alert. And though the wounds of his flesh made him groan, he maintained the same attitude and spoke as if mocking his enemies. 'If you had any power, one of you would be enough for the fight, but since the Lord has robbed you of your strength, you are broken and so you attempt to use large numbers to terrify me, although the fact that you have taken on the shapes of unreasoning beasts is itself a proof of your weakness.' And he went on confidently,

'If you have any influence, if the Lord has granted you power over me, look, here I am: devour me. But if you cannot, why do you expend so much useless effort? For the sign of the cross and faith in the Lord is for us a wall that no assault of yours can break down.' They made numerous threats against the holy Antony but gnashed their teeth because none of their attempts were successful – on the contrary they made fools of themselves rather than of him.

X. Jesus did not fail to notice his servant's struggle but came to protect him. When at last Antony raised his eyes, he saw the roof opening above him and, as the darkness was dispelled, a ray of light poured in on him. As soon as this bright light appeared, all the demons vanished and the pain in Antony's body suddenly ceased. Furthermore, the building which had been destroyed a moment earlier was restored. Antony immediately understood that the Lord was present. Sighing deeply from the bottom of his heart, he addressed the light that had appeared to him, saying 'Where were you, good Jesus? Where were you? Why were you not here from the beginning to heal my wounds?' And a voice came to him saying. 'Antony, I was here, but I was waiting to watch your struggle. But now, since you have bravely held your own in this fight, I will always help you and I will make you famous throughout the world.' When he heard this, Antony stood up and prayed; he felt so greatly strengthened that he realised he had received more strength now than he had before he lost it. Antony was thirty-five years old at the time.

Hymn of Divine Love 2 (extracts)
Symeon the New Theologian

Author See p. 71.

Language Greek. See p. 71.

Date 1009–1022.

Genre and context See pp. 71–2. This hymn may refer to Symeon's first mystical vision (p. 71). Characteristically, it uses the experience of light and radiance to signify the immanence of God. Despite its hymnic genre and experiential feel, it is making a substantial and controversial theologico-political claim: direct access to the divine is still possible for some believers despite the end of the apostolic age. Such a revelatory experience is understood to give the believer authority to speak on matters of theology, bypassing the teaching of the Church, which is simply reworking the tradition handed down to it from the apostles. This dangerous claim has been made by many who have undergone mystical or charismatic experiences (see p. 16), and it usually got them into trouble with the magisterium of the day. Symeon was no exception in this respect.

Hymn of Divine Love 11: 1–9, 30–43, 55–78

What is this new and marvellous thing that is happening, even now?
For even now, God wishes to appear to sinners:
He who of old ascended on high and was seated upon the throne
In his Father's heaven, and remains hidden.
For he was hidden from the eyes of the divine apostles
And, as we have heard, after that it was only Stephen
Who saw the heavens opened, and then said:
'I see the Son standing at the right hand of the glory
Of the Father.' …

Even to think of it makes me tremble. How can I write it
down in words?
Which hand could minister it? Which pen could inscribe it?
What word could express ? What tongue could voice?
What lips could ever speak, of the things seen
Happening in me? Accomplished over an entire day?
What is more: both in that same night, and in that very darkness,
I was gazing on Christ, terrifyingly opening the heavens to me;
Christ himself who stooped down and manifested himself to me,
Together with the Father and the Spirit, in the thrice-holy light,
Which is one [light] in the three, and three [lights] in the One.
They are, altogether, the light, and the three are one single light
Which throws a light upon my soul greater than that of the sun
And enlightens my spiritual consciousness, which had formerly
lain in darkness…

And, to a certain degree, I have learned things which are
incomprehensible
And now, from far off, I can see beautiful and imperceptible things.
Yet the inaccessibility of the light, and the unbearable
nature of the glory,
So greatly astounds me, and I am overwhelmed by fear,
Especially since it is only a single drop from the ocean's depth
that I look at.
But even from one drop, the whole nature of water is revealed
Both as to its quality and as to its form,

Just as we can 'tell the whole garment from the edge of its hem',
Or, as the saying goes about the lion: 'By its paw you will know
the beast';
Just so did I see; my lips kissing the totality by this little part.
It is He himself whom I worship, the Christ, my God,
And I gained the understanding, a small encouragement,
That I would not be cast into the fire, not consumed there,
As the prophet says, as wax is by the flame,
By the fact that I was so far from that Unapproachable Fire,
Standing in the middle of darkness, and hidden within it,
And thence, dizzily, looking as if through a tiny hole.
Engaged in all of this, with my mind in much turmoil,
Seeming, as it did to me, that I was staring into heaven and
Shivering lest I might be given even more, and become completely
swallowed up,
It was then I found Him, whom I had seen from afar,
The same whom Stephen saw when the heavens were opened,
And, later on, the same whose vision blinded Paul.
He was completely, most truly, like a fire in the middle of my heart.

Book of Divine Works (extract)
Hildegard of Bingen (c.1098–1179)

Author Hildegard was born into a large family in Bermersheim in what is now the German Rhineland. As a young child she was chronically unwell and, perhaps because of her health condition, she began to experience recurrent cosmic visions which persisted throughout her life. At some point in her middle childhood, her parents, who were of the nobility, offered her as an oblate to the community of nuns attached to the local Benedictine monastery at Disibondenberg. By the time she was 14 she had made her profession along with her friend and mentor, Jutta, who taught her to read and write. She remained in the monastery for nearly 40 years, by which time she had become the leader of the female community. However, she was eager to establish a convent independent of the oversight of the Abbot at Disibondenberg and her last years there were marked by conflict with religious authorities and finally dramatic illness when her request was refused. Eventually in 1150 she founded her independent and more austere community in Rupertsberg and then a second in Elbingen in 1165. Hildegard was extraordinarily gifted, and despite what appears to have been a limited education, she wrote many works of theology in the form of letters or sermons (she undertook four preaching tours across the land), together with treatises on natural philosophy and her system of medicine. She played the psaltery (a zither-like instrument) and was a prolific composer of sacred vocal music. Hildegard is perhaps most famous for her visions which she described, illustrated (often in the form of mandalas) and interpreted theologically in her three-volume work *Know the Ways of the Lord (Scivias)* and again in *Book of the Rewards of Life* and *Book of Divine Works*.

Language Latin. Contemporary manuscripts survived into modern times. The translation below is by Nathaniel M. Campbell.

Date 1162–1173.

Genre and context Hildegard was assisted by her friend and confessor Volmar, a member of the Disibondenberg monastic community, with whom she had discussed her visions over many years. He encouraged her in her writing, particularly when she struggled with the pain and ill-health that appear to have been inextricably bound up with her visionary experience, and he edited her work. The book arose from Hildegard's meditation on the prologue to John's Gospel – on the Word as Creator and incarnate Redeemer. It documents ten visions towards the end of her life and draws together her previous thinking on what is essentially theological cosmology. Hildegard explicitly describes her visions as rational rather than ecstatic (unlike Teresa's from three centuries later): a bird's-eye view of the scope of ultimate reality.

Book of Divine Works
Part III, Vision 3

1. And I also saw three images as if in the middle of the aforementioned southern stretch. Two were standing in the clearest fountain, encircled and crowned with a round, perforated stone; and they were as if rooted in it, as when trees sometimes seem to grow in the water's midst. The one was dressed in purple, the other in white, and they gleamed so brightly that I could not completely look upon them. The third meanwhile was standing outside the fountain upon its stone rim, clothed in brilliant white. Her face shone with such stark radiance that it turned back my face. And before these images appeared the blessed ranks of the saints like a cloud, upon whom they gazed lovingly.

2. And the first image spoke: 'I am Divine Love, the radiance of the living God. Wisdom has done her work with me, and Humility, who is rooted in the living fountain, is my helper, and Peace accompanies her. And through that radiance that I am, the living light of the blessed angels blazes. For as a ray of light shines from its source, so this radiance enlightens the blessed angels; and it cannot but shine, as no light can

exist without its flash. For I have composed humankind, who was rooted in me like a shadow, just as an object's reflection is seen in water. So too I am the living fountain, because all that was made existed in me like a shadow. In accordance with this shadow, humankind was made with fire and water, as I too am fire and living water. So too humans have the ability in their souls to ordain each thing as they will.

'Indeed, every animal possesses this shadow, and that which gives each one life is like a shadow, moving this way and that. In rational animals, these are thoughts, but not in beasts, for their life is guided only by their senses, by which they know what to avoid and what to seek. But only the soul, breathed by God, is rational.

'My radiance also overshadowed the prophets, who foretold things to come by holy inspiration, as all things God wished to make were foreshadowed in him before they came to be. But rationality speaks with sound, and sound is like thought, and word like work. From this shadow, moreover, came forth the writing of *Scivias* through the form of a woman who was but a shadow of strength and health, since such powers were not active within her.

'And so the living fountain is the Spirit of God, which he distributes unto all his works. They live because of him and have vitality through him, as the shadow of all things appears in water. And there is nothing that can clearly see this source of its life; rather, it can only sense what causes it to move. As water makes what is in it to flow, so too the soul is the living breath ever streaming in a human being, and it makes him to know, to think, to speak, and to work as if by streaming forth.

'Wisdom also distributes in this reflected shadow all things in equal measure, so that one thing should not exceed another in weight, nor should one thing be able to be moved by another contrary to its nature. For she overcomes and restrains every wicked plot of the devil, because she existed before the beginning of all beginnings, and after their ending she will remain, mightiest in her own power, and nothing will be able to stand against her. Never has she called upon any for help, nor has she lacked for anything, for she was the first and the last. She answers to none, for she is the first and fashioned the direction of all things. In herself and through herself she established all things with gentle kindness, and these no enemy can destroy, for she oversees with excellence the beginning and end of her works, all of which she fully appointed to reign also with her.

'She looked too upon her work, which she had set in order and right proportion in the shadow of the living water, when through the afore-mentioned unlearned womanly form, she revealed certain natural powers of various things, the writing of Scivias and certain other profound mysteries, which she saw in true vision, even as she became weak and debilitated.'

Letter to Anna Flaxman (extract)
William Blake (1757–1827)

Author William Blake was born in London to a humble Nonconformist family; for reasons that are unclear he was nevertheless baptized as an Anglican. From an early age Blake experienced visions in which the ordinary world about him appeared transfigured. Much of his education was undertaken by his mother, Catherine, and the Bible was a key resource for his thinking and imagery. A gifted artist, he was apprenticed to an engraver in 1772 and retained this profession all his life. His studies at the Royal Academy had the effect of making him oppose the English artistic establishment, just as he would also come to oppose the political and religious establishments. He married Catherine Boucher in 1783. Four years later his younger brother Robert died aged 25. Blake saw Robert's spirit leave his body at the moment of death and later Robert appeared to him in a dream in which he disclosed the method of illuminated printing that William would go on to develop as a vehicle for his visual art and poetry. Blake's work deals with interlocking themes of social justice, cosmology, depth psychology and the Christian gospel, increasingly presented in visionary mythic form. He had a number of patrons who championed his work, but he never achieved popular success in his lifetime; its themes and images were perhaps too challenging and strange for his contemporaries. His numerous works include *Songs of Innocence and Experience*, *The Marriage of Heaven and Hell*, a collection entitled *The Lambeth Prophecies*, *Jerusalem the Emanation of the Giant Albion* and illustrations to Dante's *Divine Comedy* and the biblical book of Job.

Language English.

Date 1800.

Genre and context Blake lived in London for nearly all his life but from 1800 to 1803 he and his wife occupied a cottage in Felpham in Sussex under the patronage of William Hayley. John Flaxman was another patron and fellow artist to whom Blake wrote on his arrival, 'Felpham is a sweet place for study, because it is more spiritual than London. Heaven opens here on all sides her golden gates'. The poem below is from a letter written by the Blakes to Flaxman's wife Anna, asking her to persuade her husband to visit him. It is rich in biblical allusions and documents a visionary experience or perhaps an almost continuous visionary consciousness which was to continue for much of Blake's time in Felpham. Notice the comforting mention of Blake's deceased brother.

To my dear Friend, Mrs. Anna Flaxman
Hercules Buildings Lambeth, 14th September 1800

THIS song to the flower of Flaxman's joy,
To the blossom of hope for a sweet decoy;
Do all that you can, or all that you may,
To entice him to Felpham and far away.

Away to sweet Felpham, for Heaven is there;
The Ladder of Angels descends thro' the air;
On the turret its spiral does softly descend,
Thro' the village then winds, at my cot it does end.

You stand in the village and look up to Heaven;
The precious stones glitter on flights seventy-seven;
And my brother is there, and my friend and thine
Descend and ascend with the bread and the wine.

The bread of sweet thought and the wine of delight
Feed the village of Felpham by day and by night,
And at his own door the bless'd Hermit does stand,
Dispensing unceasing to all the wide land.

Further reading

Blake and the Bible by Christopher Rowland. New Haven, CT: Yale University Press, 2010.

Carmelite Prayer: A tradition for the twenty-first century by Keith J. Egan. Mahwah, NJ: Paulist Press.

Dante the Theologian by Denys Turner. Cambridge: Cambridge University Press, 2002.

Hildegard of Bingen: An integrated vision by Anne King-Lenzmeier. Collegeville, MN: Michael Glazier.

'Hymns of Divine Eros' of St Symeon the New Theologian by John Anthony McGuckin. Yonkers: Saint Vladimir Seminary Press, 2024.

The Desert Fathers: Sayings of the early Christian monks by Benedicta Ward. London: Penguin, 2003.

The Dionysian Mystical Theology by Paul Rorem. Minneapolis, MN: Fortress Press, 2015.

The Life of St Teresa of Avila by Carlos Eire. Princeton, NJ: Princeton University Press, 2019.

10

Placing

Then Jacob woke from his sleep and said, 'Surely the LORD is in this place – and I did not know it!' And he was afraid, and said, 'How awesome is this place! This is none other than the house of God, and this is the gate of heaven.' So Jacob rose early in the morning, and he took the stone that he had put under his head and set it up for a pillar and poured oil on the top of it. He called that place Bethel …
(Genesis 28.16–19a)

When the LORD saw that [Moses] had turned aside to see, God called to him out of the bush, 'Moses, Moses!' And he said, 'Here I am.' Then he said, 'Come no closer! Remove the sandals from your feet, for the place on which you are standing is holy ground.'
(Exodus 3.4–5)

'In my Father's house there are many dwelling places. If it were not so, would I have told you that I go to prepare a place for you? And if I go and prepare a place for you, I will come again and will take you to myself, so that where I am, there you may be also. And you know the way to the place where I am going.'
(John 14.2–4)

Who is to condemn? It is Christ Jesus, who died, yes, who was raised, who is at the right hand of God, who indeed intercedes for us. Who will separate us from the love of Christ?
(Romans 8.34–35a)

God put [his] power to work in Christ when he raised him from the dead and seated him at his right hand in the heavenly places, far above all rule and authority and power and dominion, and above every name that is named, not only in this age but also in the age to come.
(Ephesians 1.20–21)

In Chapter 9 we saw that one of the insights achieved from breakthrough experiences can be a conviction that our deceased loved ones are in a 'better place'. This is certainly part of Blake's vision in which he sees his greatly missed youngest brother, Robert, and it is suggested in Dante's literary reunion with his beloved but long-dead Beatrice. This can be understood as a special case of the 'continuing bonds' theory of grief mentioned in Chapter 6. In order to maintain a continuing bond with the deceased we need to know were she or he is now, and this involves a process of placing.

First, in addition to caring for the remains discussed in Chapter 5, there is a need to place them with dignity in the proper location. Sometimes the deceased will have left directions about this; for many people this seems to be an important aspect of preparing to die. When no directions have been given the process of deciding where to lay the deceased can be a cause of family debate and tension. The modern practice of cremation followed by disposal of ashes can complicate things further. There is often a significant delay between the funeral and the final placing or scattering of ashes; family members can seem to be dragging their feet. During that limbo period, significant psychological processing may be happening; and this cannot be rushed. Something similar seems to be going on in the stop-start process of clearing the house or room where a loved one resided. There are significant moments along the way; for example, the point at which their residual familiar smell no longer permeates the dwelling.

Along with these practical physical actions of burial and house clearance, there is a psychological placing of the person somewhere new. As we find places for their bodily remains and possessions, we 'lay them to rest', and as we find a place for them in our mental topography we too can reach a place of peace. We re-draw our mental landscape; we re-draw the landscape of friends and family members, welcoming new people while maintaining an honoured place for those who have gone, and perhaps seeing their traces in the faces of others; and we redraw the geographical landscape: 'Here she departed.' 'Here he lies.' 'He loved it here.' 'When I am here, she feels close.' 'The new baby has his ears!'

In a similar way in the history of Christian spirituality, characterized as it is by a longing for the Jesus who walked this earth and then departed it, unexpected encounters with Christ in the natural world become the occasion for re-drawing the landscape. It becomes populated with signals of transcendence, marking what Celtic spirituality calls the 'thin places'. Indeed, the journeying of the pilgrims considered in Chapter 7 was to some of these thin places; places where Jesus had walked, or his disciples' remains had been laid to rest, or where heavenly visions had been experienced so that the place was transfigured and became 'holy ground' (as with Blake's vision at Felpham).

Many traditions assert that the whole of creation including the ordinary routines of human daily life can be seen in this way. Jesuit spirituality is perhaps most strongly associated with this approach. Jerome Nadal (1507–1580), a close companion of Ignatius of Loyola, recounted Ignatius' repeated injunctions to 'see and contemplate in all things, actions, and conversations the presence of God and the love of spiritual things, to remain a contemplative even in the midst of action.'[1] Writing a little later in a related tradition, François de Sales (see Chapter 11) encourages the cultivation of an awareness of God's immanence in prayer through:

> ... a lively and attentive apprehension of the omnipresence of God, which means that God is in everything and everywhere, and that there is not any place or thing in this world where he is not most assuredly present; so that just as the birds, wherever they fly, always encounter the air, so, wherever we are, we find God present.[2]

---

1 J. de Guibert, 1972, *The Jesuits: Their spiritual doctrine and practice*, Chicago, IL: Institute of Jesuit Sources, pp. 2–3.

2 François de Sales, 1948, *Introduction to the Devout life*. Part II. Chapter II, Allan Ross (tr.), Westminster, MD: The Newman Press.

10.1 Christ in nature

Hymn on the Nativity 4 (extract)
Ephrem the Syrian (c.306–373)

Author Ephrem was born in Nisibis (Nusaybin in present-day Turkey). The city was on the border of the Roman Empire, highly diverse but with a growing Christian community. He was baptized as a youth and is thought to have joined an early form of monastic community, at some point being ordained as a deacon. He was appointed a teacher of theology by Jacob, Bishop of Nisibis and founded a theological school. When Nisibis fell to the Persians in 363, Ephrem moved west to Edessa, an established centre of Christianity, reportedly working in its school of theology, establishing a women's choir to sing his hymns. and continuing his diaconal duties, which probably resulted in his death from plague.

Language Syriac. Earliest manuscripts date from the early sixth century. The translation below is by Kathleen McVey.

Date Probably before 337.

Genre and context The hymns were written to be sung but they are very long and heavy with theological content; they are clearly intended for catechesis as much as worship. The Council of Nicaea had been held in 325, and Bishop Jacob had been a signatory, but there were many competing versions of Christianity around. Ephrem's hymns assert the new Nicene orthodoxy in this context. Much of this concerns the nature of Christ in the light of the incarnation. The extract below addresses the question of where the pre-existent Creator Logos was while the human Jesus walked this earth.

Hymn 4 on the Nativity
Stanzas 143, 149–159, 165–171

Glory to that voice that became a body,
and to the lofty word that became flesh.

He was lofty but he sucked Mary's milk,
and from his blessings all creation sucks.
He is the Living Breast of living breath;
by his life the dead were suckled and they revived.
Without the breath of air no one can live;
without the power of the Son no one can rise.

Upon the living breath of the One Who vivifies all
depend the living beings above and below.
As indeed he sucked Mary's milk,
He has given suck – life to the universe.
As again he dwelt in His mother's womb,
in His womb dwells all creation.
Mute He was as a babe, yet He gave
to all creation His commands.
For without the First-born no one is able
to approach Being, for he alone is capable of it.
Indeed the thirty years that He was on earth,
who was guiding all creation?
Who was receiving all offerings?
the praise of those on high and those below?
He was entirely in the depths and in the heights;
He was entirely in all and entirely in each one.

Thus although all of him was dwelling in the womb,
His hidden will was supervising all.
For He saw that all of Him was hanging on the cross
but His power made all creation tremble.
For His power darkened the sun and shook the earth;
Graves were torn open and the dead emerged.
See, indeed, that He was entirely on the cross
while yet He remained entirely everywhere.
In the same way He had been entirely in the womb,
while yet He remained entirely everywhere.
While indeed he was on the cross, He revived the dead;
just so, while He was a babe, He was forming babes.
While he was dead, He was opening graves;
while He was in the womb, he was opening wombs.

Canticle of the Sun
Francis of Assisi (c.1181–1226)

Author Francesco di Pietro di Bernardone was born in Assisi in Umbria, Italy, into a wealthy family. As a young man he entered the family business of fine cloth merchandising and enjoyed a hedonistic lifestyle which included military enterprises, one of which ended in a year's imprisonment. When he was about 25 he began to embrace a life of poverty as part of a spiritual quest. He undertook a pilgrimage to Rome and also wandered the

Umbrian countryside. It was here in the ruined chapel of San Damiano that he experienced a vision of the crucified Christ who called him by name and commanded him to repair the building, which Francis attempted to do using appropriated family funds. There then followed a period of conflict with his abusive father, which ended with Francis publicly renouncing both his father and his inheritance. For the next two years he lived as a penitential beggar, managing to rebuild San Damiano and several other small chapels with donated stones. He began the practice of nursing lepers. In 1208, in response to the account of Jesus' sending out the Twelve in Matthew 10 (the Gospel read at Mass that day) he took up an intentionally itinerant ministry of preaching, healing and poverty that conformed to this gospel pattern, as did the formation of a group of twelve brothers that soon followed. The group travelled to Rome to seek recognition as a distinctive religious order, the 'Lesser Brothers' (*Friars Minor*). This was granted by Pope Innocent III in 1210, and the order rapidly expanded in numbers. Francis' passion for evangelism led him to travel widely, including a trip to Egypt during the Fifth Crusade. Here he had a cordial audience with the Sultan and is said to have preached to his retinue. Francis had been given free access to Mount Verna north of Assisi in 1213, and he habitually retreated there. It was here, two years before his death, that he experienced a vision of Christ crucified carried by a six-winged seraph; as the vision faded the wounds of Christ appeared on his body (see p. 73). Francis wrote relatively little: two versions of his rule, *Canticle of the Sun*, some liturgical texts and prayers, and his final *Testament*.

Language Umbrian Italian. Manuscripts exist from shortly after Francis' death. The translation below is by Bill Barrett.

Date 1224–1226.

Genre and context This was composed when Francis was ill and blind following receipt of the stigmata. It is thought to be the first attributed poem in the Umbrian language (Francis was not proficient in Latin), though it was originally a song rather than a poem – a sacred version of the troubadour ballads Francis had enjoyed as a young man, which he is said to have sung with those nursing him. Despite his itinerant ministry, Francis had a very strong sense of the sacredness of place and of his part in the created order. The song's implicit theology is unpacked in the next reading by his follower, Bonaventure. It is clearly influenced by 'The song of the Three' (Daniel 3.52–87 NJB).

Canticle of the Sun

Most high, all powerful, all good Lord! All praise is yours, all glory, all honour, and all blessing. To you, alone, Most High, do they belong. No mortal lips are worthy to pronounce your name.

Be praised, my Lord, through all your creatures, especially through my lord Brother Sun, who brings the day; and you give light through him. And he is beautiful and radiant in all his splendour! Of you, Most High, he bears the likeness.

Be praised, my Lord, through Sister Moon and the stars; in the heavens you have made them, precious and beautiful.

Be praised, my Lord, through Brothers Wind and Air, and clouds and storms, and all the weather, through which you give your creatures sustenance.

Be praised, My Lord, through Sister Water; she is very useful, and humble, and precious, and pure.

Be praised, my Lord, through Brother Fire, through whom you brighten the night. He is beautiful and cheerful, and powerful and strong.

Be praised, my Lord, through our sister Mother Earth, who feeds us and rules us, and produces various fruits with coloured flowers and herbs.

Be praised, my Lord, through those who forgive for love of you; through those who endure sickness and trial. Happy those who endure in peace, for by you, Most High, they will be crowned.

Be praised, my Lord, through our Sister Bodily Death, from whose embrace no living person can escape. Woe to those who die in mortal sin! Happy those she finds doing your most holy will. The second death can do no harm to them.

Praise and bless my Lord, and give thanks, and serve him with great humility.

The Soul's Journey into God (extract)
Bonaventure (c.1217–1274)

Author See p. 72.

Language Latin. The translation below is by Ewert Cousins.

Date c.1259.

Genre and context *The Soul's Journey into God* is part theological treatise and part spiritual manual, shifting between poetry and prose, and divided into seven chapters. Bonaventure recounts that in the autumn of 1259, having been Minister General of the Franciscan order for two years, he felt the need to retreat from these demands and, following in the steps of Francis and around the time of the thirty-third anniversary of his death, went to Mount Verna to spend time in prayer and contemplation. As he meditated on the six-winged seraph that had appeared to Francis, he had an epiphany: he came to understand the six wings as stages on a journey to divine contemplation, and Christ crucified as the goal of that journey. Bonaventure was more highly educated and intellectually inclined than his master, and he places Francis' simple and biblical hymn to nature in a broader theological context, clearly influenced by the tradition of ascent that began with Pseudo-Dionysius (see Chapter 9). The journey to God begins with close observation of the natural world in an essentially scientific way in order to see it accurately. The extract below is from the second stage in which nature is looked at with the eye of faith and seen to bear traces of Christ, to be patterned on him, even to be his very reflection. The insight that came to Bonaventura in his sacred place was that all of nature is sacred because Christ can be found within it.

The Soul's Journey into God
Chapter II: On Contemplating God in his
Vestiges in the Sense World

1. Concerning the mirror of things
perceived through sensation,
we can see God
not only through them as through his vestiges,
but also in them
as he is in them
by his essence, power and presence.

This type of consideration is higher than the previous one;*
therefore it holds second place
as the second level of contemplation
by which we are led to contemplate God
in all creatures
which enter our minds through our bodily senses.

7. All these are vestiges in which we can see our God. For the species which is apprehended is a likeness generated in a medium and then impressed upon the organ itself. Through this impression, it leads to its source, namely the object to be known. This clearly suggests that the Eternal Light generates from itself a coequal Likeness or Splendour, which is consubstantial and coeternal. It further suggests that he who is *the image of the invisible God* (Colossians 1.15) and *the brightness of his glory and the image of his substance* (Hebrews 1.3), who is everywhere through his initial generation, as the object generates its likeness in the entire medium, is united by the grace of union to an individual of rational nature, as the species is united to the bodily organ. Through this union he leads us back to the Father as to the fountain-source and object. If, therefore, all things that can be known generate a likeness of themselves, they manifestly proclaim that in them as mirrors we can see the eternal generation of the Word, the Image and Son, eternally emanating from God the Father.

* nature viewed scientifically *Ed.*

10.2 The domestic transfigured

The Book of Margery Kempe (extract)
Scribe(s) of Margery Kempe (c.1373–c.1438)

Author Margery was born in King's Lynn to a middle-class family. Her father, John Brunham, was a merchant and also mayor. In 1394 she married John Kempe, by whom she had at least 14 children. After the birth of her first child, Margery suffered a great deal of mental anguish that included demonic visions, but also comforting visions of Christ and his mother. Her devotional life intensified and she became known for long outbursts of weeping and shaking during prayer. She adopted many of the marks of the religious life: a vow of chastity, dressing in white, pilgrimage and public pronouncement on matters of faith, including to senior churchmen. She sought spiritual direction concerning her visions from Julian of Norwich (see Chapter 6), who she said affirmed them, but was also tried for heresy on a number of occasions, though never convicted.

Language Middle English. The extract below is my rendition.

Date 1430s, with earliest surviving manuscript dating from 1450s.

Genre and context *The Book* is written by at least one scribe to Margery's dictation, presumably because she was not literate. It is a form of sacred autobiography (Margery refers to herself as 'the creature') and also acts as an apologia. There is emphasis on her personal, literally close, relationship with Christ, often in a domestic setting. In these extracts Margery presents Christ not so much as a romantic lover but as a 'homely' husband, with whom she is intimate and comfortable. She also describes taking his mother a hot drink to comfort her on Good Friday (a detail removed by later editors), strongly identifying with the anguish of Mary's maternal loss and her search for the absent Jesus.

The Book of Margery Kempe
Book 1, Chapters XXXVI, LXXVII, LXXX1

XXXVI

… And if I were on earth as bodily as I was before I died on the Cross, I should not be ashamed of thee, as other men be, for I should take thee by the hand amongst the people, and make thee great cheer, so that they should well know that I loved thee right well …

'For It is fitting for the wife to be homely with her husband. Be he ever so great a lord, and she ever so poor a woman when he weddeth her,

---

yet they must he together and rest together in joy and peace. Right so must it be between thee and Me, for I take no heed what thou hast been, but what thou wouldst be, and oftentimes have I told thee that I have clean forgiven thee all thy sins. Therefore I must needs be homely with thee, and he in thy bed with thee.'

LXXVII

… Then answered our Lord to her and said, 'I pray thee, daughter, give Me nothing but love Thou mayest never please Me better than to have Me ever in thy love, nor shalt thou ever, many penance that thou mayest do on earth, please Me so much as by loving Me. And, daughter, if thou wilt be high in Heaven with Me, keep Me always in thy mind as much as thou mayest, and forget Me not at thy meat, but think always that I sit in thy heart and know every thought that is therein, both good and ill, and that I perceive the least thinking and twinkling of thine eye.'…

LXXXI

When Our Lord was buried. Our Lady fell down in a swoon as she would have come from the grave, and Saint John took her up in his arms, and Mary Magdalene went on the other side to support and comfort Our Lady, as much as they could or might. Then the said creature, desiring to abide still by the grace of Our Lord, mourned, wept, and sorrowed with loud crying for the tenderness and compassion that she had of Our Lord's death, and many a lamentable desire that God put into her mind for the time Wherefore the people wondered on her, having great marvel what ailed her, for they knew full little the cause She thought she would never have departed thence, but desired to have died there, and been buried with Our Lord.

Later the creature thought she saw Our Lady go homeward again, and as she went, there came many good women to her and said, 'Lady, woe are we that your Son is dead, and that our people have done Him so much despite.'

And then Our Lady bowing her head, thanked them full meekly with cheer and countenance, for she could not speak, her heart was so full of grief.

Then the creature thought, when Our Lady was come home and was laid down on a bed, that she made for Our Lady a good caudle, and brought it her to comfort her, and then Our Lady said unto her, 'Take it away, daughter. Give me no food, but mine own Child.' The creature answered, 'Ah, Blessed Lady, ye must needs comfort yourself and cease of your sorrowing.'

'Ah, Daughter, where should I go, or where should I dwell without sorrow? I tell thee, certainly was there never woman on earth who had such great cause to sorrow as I have, for there was never a woman in this world who bore a better Child, or a meeker to His mother, than my Son was to me.'

And she thought she heard Our Lady crying anon with a lamentable voice, and saying, 'John, where is my Son Jesus Christ?'...

Then the creature was left still with Our Lady and thought it a thousand years till the third day came, and that day, she was with Our Lady in a chapel where Our Lord Jesus Christ appeared unto her, and said, '*Salve, sancta parens.*'

The Temple (extracts)
George Herbert (1593–1633)

Author George Herbert was born in the town of Montgomery in Wales, into a wealthy and politically powerful family. His father died when he was three and his godfather, the poet John Donne, played a significant role in his early life. He was educated at Westminster School and Trinity College, Cambridge. He excelled at his studies in classical languages, was elected a Fellow of Trinity College and later appointed Public Orator for the University of Cambridge. It appears that he had political ambitions; in 1624 he became member of parliament for his home town, but this was short-lived, and he continued in his academic post, still very much in contact with Donne, who was by then Dean of St Paul's Cathedral in London. Five years later Herbert married and was also ordained as a priest in the Church of England. His parish of Fugglestone St Peter with Bemerton consisted of two small village churches. It was near Salisbury and Herbert spent a proportion of his time at the cathedral where, as a proficient lutist and violist, he participated in the music-making. He died of tuberculosis at the age of 39. Apart from some academic Latin writings from his time at Cambridge and *The Temple*, Herbert wrote *The Country Parson* and *Outlandish Proverbs*.

Language English.

Date 1633. The poems that form *The Temple* were written and re-edited over a number of years. On his deathbed Herbert entrusted the manuscript to Edmund Duncan, who was visiting him on behalf of his old friend, Nicholas Ferrar, with the request that Ferrar publish them if he thought them worthy. Ferrar's nieces immediately made a clear calligraphy copy. The title of the collection appears to have been chosen by Ferrar. The book was produced at

Cambridge in collaboration with the University authorities and published by Thomas Buch and Roger Daniel. Many editions followed.

Genre and context *The Temple* is composed of 164 poems, arranged in three sections: 'The Church Porch', a preparatory liminal section; 'The Church', made up of 150 poems mirroring the book of Psalms and with a structure broadly reflecting the church's year; and 'The Church Militant' which is eschatological in character. There are many thematic connections between the poems. Herbert's style is radically simple and free from literary ornament. The two poems below (both from 'The Church') explore the immanence of God in the ordinary active life of daily prayer and domestic chores.

The Temple
Prayer (1)

Prayer the Church's banquet, Angels' age,
God's breath in man returning to his birth,
The soul in paraphrase, heart in pilgrimage,
The Christian plummet sounding heav'n and earth;
Engine against th' Almighty, sinners' tower,
Reversed thunder, Christ-side-piercing spear,
The six-days world-transposing in an hour,
A kind of tune, which all things hear and fear;
Softness, and peace, and joy, and love, and bliss,
Exalted Manna, gladness of the best,
Heaven in ordinary, man well dressed,
The milky way, the bird of Paradise,
Church-bells beyond the stars heard, the soul's blood,
The land of spices; something understood.

The Elixir

Teach me, my God and King,
In all things thee to see,
And what I do in anything
To do it as for thee:

Not rudely, as a beast,
To run into an action;
But still to make Thee prepossessed,
And give it his perfection.

A man that looks on glass,
On it may stay his eye;
Or if he pleaseth, through it pass,
And then the heav'n espy.

All may of Thee partake:
Nothing can be so mean,
Which with his tincture (for thy sake)
Will not grow bright and clean.

A servant with this clause
Makes drudgery divine:
Who sweeps a room, as for Thy laws,
Makes that and th' action fine.

This is the famous stone
That turneth all to gold:
For that which God doth touch and own
Cannot for less be told.

Journal (extract)
Susanna Wesley (1670–1742)

Author Susanna Annesley was born in London to a Nonconformist clergy-man and his second wife. As a girl she was well educated by the standards of the time and encouraged to think independently and critically. Ironically, this led to her early decision in 1682 to join the Church of England. In 1688 she married Samuel Wesley, an Anglican clergyman. The marriage was not without its tensions; Samuel was twice imprisoned for debt and there was even a year's separation in 1702 due to Samuel and Susanna supporting different claimants to the English throne (William II and Charles Stuart respectively). The couple had 19 children, of whom ten survived to adulthood, including John and Charles (see Chapter 6). Susanna undertook their early education herself. In 1712, when her husband was absent and had left the parish in the charge of a curate she considered incompetent, Susanna offered alternative Sunday sermons (mainly from her father and husband's stock) in her kitchen. These proved popular and attracted large numbers, but the practice was also highly controversial. Nevertheless Susanna stoutly defended it as a necessary ministry to the community, and the openness of Methodism to lay preaching and women's ministry is in part attributed to her stance. Susanna wrote many letters, meditations and extended commentaries on the Apostles' Creed, the Lord's Prayer, and the Ten Commandments.

Language English.

Date c.1711–1715.

Genre and context This is a devotional journal, a typical mode of written self-expression for women of that time, but it goes beyond simple piety to wrestle with theological and social questions of the day. It was arranged around a thrice daily 'examination of conscience', strikingly similar to Ignatius of Loyola's practice of the *Examen* (see Chapter 12). Susanna wrote the journal at a period in her life when she was raising her children and living with the constant stress of her husband's mismanagement of finances.

Journal entry for one (unspecified) day

Morn

God cannot be properly said to be present more in one place than another. He fills heaven and earth and all the imaginary spaces beyond this universal system of beings.

Q: Why then is it so often said that God dwelleth in the heavens, that he sitteth in heaven, etc.?

A: This is not to be understood of his essential presence, which cannot possibly be circumscribed or determined to one place more than another, but all such expressions I humbly conceive signify the manifestations that he is pleased to make of his glory to those blessed spirits that inhabit those happy regions of light and love. Besides, we must consider that the human nature of the Son of God must be in some place, as all other bodies are, and in that human nature dwells the fulness of the Godhead therefore.

Noon

'Praise God, my Soul, and all. that is within me bless his holy Name!' Thankfully recognize the mercies of this day hitherto. The assistance of his Holy Spirit in family devotions, the disposition and ability to speak of him, to instruct the children, to perform all domestic duties, the health and preservation of yourself and family from all ill accidents, terrors and dangers. Surely the tribute of our praise is an indispensable and pleasing duty. Heartily thank the omnipotent Goodness that he hath preserved you from all presumptuous sins and trust in and rely on Jesus Christ for the supply of your deficiencies and firmly believe that, as almighty God imputed Adam's sin to all his posterity, so he will, upon account of the perfect obedience his only Son paid to the divine laws in our nature, accept of our sincere, though otherwise imperfect, obedience. Glory be to thee, O Lord!

Even

You had long hoped and expected by your care, frugality and industry to have provided amply for the ensuing summer; and thought that such a sum which you believed you should receive upon account would infallibly prevent the pressures you lay under last year. Upon review of incomes and exits you find yourself greatly disappointed and that all your prospect of ease and plenty was but a dream, and after all you are like to be involved in greater difficulties than your boasted prudence could foresee. This hath somewhat discomposed your mind and hath disposed it to that anxiety about the things of this world that in obedience to the command of Jesus Christ you have resolvedly avoided for some time. What are your thoughts upon this occasion? I think myself highly obliged to adore and praise the unsearchable wisdom and boundless goodness of almighty God for this dispensation of his providence towards me. For I clearly discern there is more of mercy in this disappointment of my hopes than there would have been in permitting me to enjoy all that I had desired, because it hath given me a sight and sense of some sins which before I could not have imagined I was in the least inclined to, viz., of idolatry and covetousness and want of practical subjection to the will of God.

Q: How were you guilty of idolatry in these expectations?

Parochial and Plain Sermons (extract)
John Henry Newman (1801–1890)

Author John Henry Newman was born into a middle-class family in London. He attended Great Ealing School, a leading public school of the time, and at the age of 15 he underwent a conversion experience and embraced a Calvinist form of evangelical Christianity. He studied at Oxford University, not entirely successfully, but was elected as a fellow of Oriel College, and in 1825 was ordained as a priest in the Church of England. In 1828 he became Vicar of the University Church of St Mary the Virgin. He began to leave his earlier evangelicalism behind and by 1833, following recovery from a severe illness contracted abroad which he interpreted as signalling that he still had work to do for God, he was ready to join with like-minded colleagues in the launch of what would come to be known as the Oxford Movement. The ideas were disseminated through *Tracts for the Times*, which he edited, and by his sermons. Central to them was a rediscovery of personal holiness; the importance of church tradition and clearly articulated doctrine; the sacramental nature of reality, particularly times and seasons, and the expression of this in liturgical ritual. Newman was increasingly drawn to the Roman Catholic

Church and was finally received into it in 1845, having resigned his living two years earlier. He lived most of the rest of his life in Birmingham as part of a community of the Oratory of Saint Philip Neri. In 1879 he was made a cardinal by Pope Leo XIII. He took a lead in defending the English Roman Catholic Church from the hostile criticism to which it was subjected at the time, most notably through a series of public lectures on 'The Present Position of Catholics in England' in 1851. Newman was a prolific writer in a number of genres. His most famous works are *The Dream of Gerontius*, *Apologia Pro Vita Sua* (his spiritual autobiography), *A Grammar of Assent* and *The Idea of a University*.

Language English.

Date Preached some time between 1834 and 1843.

Genre and context These sermons were preached while Newman was vicar of the University Church in Oxford. This was a time when he was rediscovering old English Catholic spirituality that he understood to be deeply intertwined with the rhythms and duties of ordinary everyday life: his friend John Keble's 'trivial round and common task'.[3]

Parochial and Plain Sermons VIII
Sermon XI: Doing Glory to God in Pursuits of the World

'Whether, therefore, ye eat or drink, or whatsoever ye do, do all to the glory of God' (1 Corinthians 10:31).

... surely it is possible to 'serve the Lord,' yet not to be 'slothful in business;' not over devoted to it, but not to retire from it. We may do *all things* whatever we are about to God's glory; we may do all things *heartily*, as to the Lord, and not to man, being both active yet meditative; and now let me give some instances to show what I mean...

Thankfulness to Almighty God, nay, and the inward life of the Spirit itself, will be additional principles causing the Christian to labour diligently in his calling. He will see God in all things. He will recollect our Saviour's life. Christ was brought up to a humble trade. When he labours in his own, he will think of his Lord and Master in His. He will recollect that Christ went down to Nazareth and was subject to His parents, that He walked long journeys, that He bore the sun's heat and the storm, and had not where to lay His head. Again, he knows that the Apostles had various employments of this world before their calling; St. Andrew and

---

3 'New every morning is the love' from J. Keble, 1827, *The Christian Year*, Oxford: Oxford University Press.

St. Peter fishers, St. Matthew a tax-gatherer, and St. Paul, even after his calling, still a tent-maker. Accordingly, in whatever comes upon him, he will endeavour to discern and gaze (as it were) on the countenance of his Saviour. He will feel that the true contemplation of that Saviour lies *in* his worldly business, that as Christ is seen in the poor, and in the persecuted, and in children, so is He seen in the employments which He puts upon His chosen, whatever they be; that in attending to his own calling he will be meeting Christ; that if he neglect it, he will not on that account enjoy His presence at all the more, but that while performing it, he will see Christ revealed to his soul amid the ordinary actions of the day, as by a sort of sacrament. Thus he will take his worldly business as a gift from Him, and will love it as such …

May God give us grace in our several spheres and stations to do His will and adorn His doctrine; that whether we eat and drink, or fast and pray, labour with our hands or with our minds, journey about or remain at rest, we may glorify Him who has purchased us with His own blood!

10.3 Material artefacts charged with cosmic significance

The Dream of the Rood (extracts)
Anonymous

Author Unknown.

Language Old English. The translation below is by Richard Hamer.

Date Eighth–tenth century. An extract is carved on the eighth-century Ruthwell Cross, a stone monument from the old Anglo-Saxon kingdom of Northumbria, but this may be later than the cross itself. The earliest manuscript is from the tenth century.

Genre and context The poem is 156 lines long (with variations in different translations) and tells the story of a dream in which the narrator sees a tree covered in jewels which they take to signify victory and power, but then the tree begins to tell its own story and reveals itself as the rood (cross) of Christ. In line with this, Christ is presented as a heroic warrior who has done battle with sin and death and defeated them. The cross identifies itself as the place of Christ's suffering and death, but now transformed into the place of glory and victory; a tree of life and the means of connection with Christ for all who trust in it. The mode of presentation is similar to epic English warrior poetry of the age, but the place-memory of the rood as the means of telling the Christian story is unique.

The Dream of the Rood

Hear while I tell about the best of dreams
Which came to me the middle of one night
While humankind were sleeping in their beds.
It was as though I saw a wondrous tree
Towering in the sky suffused with light,
Brightest of beams; and all that beacon was
Covered with gold. The corners of the earth
Gleamed with fair jewels, just as there were five
Upon the cross-beam. Many bands of angels,
Fair throughout all eternity, looked on.
No felon's gallows that, but holy spirits,
Mankind, and all this marvellous creation,
Gazed on the glorious tree of victory.
And I with sins was stained, wounded with guilt.
I saw the tree of glory brightly shine
In gorgeous clothing, all bedecked with gold.

The Ruler's tree was worthily adorned
With gems; yet I could see beyond that gold
The ancient strife of wretched men, when first
Upon its right side it began to bleed.
I was all moved with sorrows, and afraid
At the fair sight. I saw that lively beacon
Changing its clothes and hues; sometimes it was
Bedewed with blood and drenched with flowing gore,
At other times it was bedecked with treasure.
So I lay watching there the Saviour's tree,
Grieving in spirit for a long, long while,
Until I heard it utter sounds, the best
Of woods began to speak these words to me: ...
[The tree tells its story]
'... Now you may understand, dear warrior,
That I have suffered deeds of wicked men
And grievous sorrows. Now the time has come
That far and wide on earth men honour me,
And all this great and glorious creation,
And to this beacon offers prayers. On me
The Son of God once suffered; therefore now
I tower mighty underneath the heavens,
And I may heal all those in awe of me.
Once I became the cruellest of tortures,
Most hateful to all nations, till the time
I opened the right way of life for men.
So then the prince of glory honoured me,
And heaven's King exalted me above
All other trees, just as Almighty God
Raised up His mother Mary for all men
Above all other women in the world.
Now, my dear warrior, I order you
That you reveal this vision to mankind,
Declare in words this is the tree of glory
On which Almighty God once suffered torments
For mankind's many sins, and for the deeds
Of Adam long ago. He tasted death
Thereon; and yet the Lord arose again
By his great might to come to human aid.
He rose to heaven. And the Lord Himself,
Almighty God and all His angels with Him,
Will come onto this earth again to seek

Mankind on Doomsday, when the final Judge
Will give His verdict upon every man,
What in this fleeting life he shall have earned.
Nor then may any man be without fear
About the words the Lord shall say to him.
Before all He shall ask where that man is
Who for God's name would suffer bitter death
As formerly He did upon the cross.
Then they will be afraid, and few will know
What they may say to Christ. But there need none
Be fearful if he bears upon his breast
The best of tokens. Through the cross each soul
May journey to the heavens from this earth,
Who with the Ruler thinks to go and dwell.'

Life of Malachy (extract)
Bernard of Clairvaux

Author For Bernard, see p. 86. Malachy (Máel Máedóc Ua Morgair) was born in Armagh, Ireland, in 1095 and ordained priest in 1119. He oversaw reform in his diocese to bring it into conformity with Roman Catholic order and liturgical practice. He subsequently became Bishop of Armagh, Connor and Down, and in 1134 primate of all Ireland. It was at this time that Malachy first visited Clairvaux. The Abbey was intentionally designed to be simple and austere, marked out as a sacred space described by Bernard as 'Jerusalem', a place where heaven and earth meet. Malachy was so deeply impressed by the architecture, community and, above all, by Bernard himself that he determined to join them; but he was not granted permission by Pope Innocent II, who no doubt had other plans for him, having recently made him papal legate. Instead in 1142 Malachy returned to Ireland, taking five brothers with him, in order to establish a Cistercian community, Mellifont Abbey in County Louth. In 1148 Malachy again visited Clairvaux en route to Rome, but fell ill and died there.

Language Latin. The translation below is by Hugh Jackson Lawlor.

Date 1149.

Genre and context This is a sacred biography of the first Irish-born man to be canonized by the church (in 1190) that reads at times like a eulogy. There is no doubt that Bernard and Malachy were extraordinarily close. Bernard is reported to have worn Malachy's habit for his funeral oration. When he died five years later, he was buried next to Malachy in the same habit. Bernard's admiration for his colleague is very evident in the work. This extract describes Malachy's desire to build a Cistercian oratory in Ireland, to bring the ordering of place that he had experienced in Clairvaux to his native land. The vision he experiences shows him how this can be done in a way that respects its distinctive topographical situation near Strangford Lough in County Down.

Life of Malachy
Chapter VIII

61. (34)... It seemed good to Malachy that a stone oratory should be erected at Bangor like those which he had seen constructed in other regions. And when he began to lay the foundations the natives wondered, because in that land no such buildings were yet to be found.

63. ... And there is no doubt that that was the work of God, because Malachy had foreseen it by God's revelation. He had first consulted with the brothers concerning that work; and many on account of their lack of means were unwilling to assent to it. Anxious therefore and doubtful what he should do, he began to inquire earnestly in prayer what was the will of God.

And one day coming back from a journey, when he drew near to the place he viewed it some way off; and lo, there appeared a great oratory, of stone and very beautiful. And paying careful attention to its position, form and construction, he took up the work with confidence, having first however related the vision to a few of the elder brothers. Indeed so carefully did he adhere to all his attentive observations regarding place and manner and quality that when the work was finished that which was made appeared closely similar to that which he had seen, as if he also as well as Moses had heard the saying, *Look* that *thou make all things according to the pattern shewed to thee in the mount.* By the same kind of vision there was shown to him before it was built, not only the oratory, but also the whole monastery, which is situated at Saul.

On Noah's Moral Ark (extracts)
Hugh of St Victor (c.1096–1141)

Author Hugh's origins are unknown. He probably came from Belgium or Germany. Following a short period as a member of a community of canons regular in the German town of Halberstadt, he joined the Abbey of St Victor in Paris, a centre of scholarship at the time. He eventually rose to become the head of the community. Hugh was a prolific writer of systematic theology and biblical exegesis, but also wrote on contemplation and mysticism, and had an interest in nature, philosophy and the arts. Apart from the *Noah's Ark* trilogy, his most famous works are *On the Sacraments of the Christian Faith*, *On the Study of Reading* and *On the Celestial Hierarchy*, a commentary on the Pseudo-Dionysius (see Chapter 9).

Language Latin. The translation below is by an unknown sister of the Community of St Mary the Virgin, Wantage.

Date 1125.

Genre and context *Noah's Ark* consists of three volumes: 'On Noah's Moral Ark', 'On Noah's Mystical Ark' and 'On the World's Vanity'. It is a theological treatise based on an allegorical reading of the story of Noah in Genesis 6—8. The first volume is a written form of a presentation Hugh had made at a colloquium. There was at that time a traditional way of interpreting the size and shape of the ark. Hugh agreed with this regarding size but departed from it with respect to shape, presenting it for the first time in the form it appears today in nursery stories and toys – a boat with a house on top. The life of faith is set out spatially as a series of storeys, knowing the good, doing the good and being good, within a structure that has Christ at its centre holding it together and giving it life, ascended to heaven at the top and present to the believers below, constantly drawing them upwards.

Noah's Moral Ark

Book I, Chapter XIV: Of the ark of the Church, and the meaning of its length and breadth and height. Of the three storeys, the cubit, and the hundred years that the ark took to build

It remains for us to see what the ark of the Church may be. And, to put it more exactly, the Church is herself the ark, which her Noah, our Lord Jesus Christ, the Helmsman and the Haven, is guiding through the tempests of this present life, and leading through Himself unto Himself.

Book II, Chapter VIII: The meaning of the three storeys, the cubit, and the pillar set up in the midst of the ark of the understanding, that is to say, of wisdom

The three storeys in the ark of the understanding denote three kinds of thoughts, right, profitable, necessary. If, therefore, I have begun to love to meditate upon the Scriptures, and have always been ready to ponder the virtues of the saints, and the works of God, and whatever else there is that serves to improve my conduct and stimulate my spirit, then I have already begun to be in the first storey of the ark. But if I neglect to imitate the good I know, then I can say that my thought is right, but unprofitable. For it is good that I should think what I do think and know what I know about others, but it profits me nothing if I do not take it to myself as a pattern for living. For another person's virtue is of no profit to me, if I neglect to copy it as far as I am able. 'A treasure hid, and knowledge hid, what profit is in either?' I hide my knowledge, if I do not put into practice the good that I know; and therefore it cannot profit me that, knowing, I feign not to know.

But if I have taken pains not only to know, but also to perform good and profitable actions, and if my heart's preoccupation is to see how by self-control and a right way of living I can make my own the virtues which I love and admire in others, then I can say that my thought is profitable, then I have gone up to the second storey. My heart is now more at one with itself; in consequence, it does not gad about among vain and profitless things.

There remains the third kind of thought, that when I have begun to do the works of the virtues, I should labour to have the virtues themselves – that is to say, that I should possess within myself the virtue which I show in outward works. Otherwise it will not be much good for me to have performed the works, unless I have also the virtues of the works. If, then, I direct the thought of my heart to this end, that I may strive to show inwardly before the eyes of God whatever good appears in me outwardly to human sight, then I have gone up into the third storey, where the essential virtues are to be found. But among all these there is one that is supremely necessary, namely, charity, which unites us to God; and that is why the ark is gathered into one at the top, that even now we should be thinking of the One, looking for the One, desiring the One, even our Lord Jesus Christ.

So in the first storey there is knowledge, in the second works, in the third virtue, and at the top the reward of virtue, Jesus Christ our Lord.

These steps if you change the order to 'knowledge, discipline, and goodness' you have in the psalm where it says, 'Teach me goodness, discipline, and knowledge, O Lord Jesus Christ.'

The pillar set up in the middle of the ark to the height of thirty cubits, to which the entire structure leans, and the top whereof measures a single cubit from corner to corner, this is the tree of life which was planted in the midst of paradise, namely, our Lord Jesus Christ, set up in the midst of His Church for all believers alike as the reward of work, the End of the journey, and the victor's crown. He it is who rose from earth and pierced the heavens, who came down to the depths, yet did not leave the heights, who is Himself both above and below, above in His majesty, below in His compassion, above that He may draw our longings thither, below that He may offer us His help. Below He is among us, above He is above us. Below is what He took from us, above is what He sets before us.

Further reading

The Architecture of Medieval Churches: Theology of love in practice I by John A. H. Lewis. London: Routledge, 2017.

The Cross and Creation in Christian Liturgy and Art by Christopher Irvine. London: SPCK, 2013.

For Thy Great Pain Have Mercy on my Little Pain by Victoria MacKenzie. London: Bloomsbury, 2013.

Hearts Aflame: Prayers of Susanna, John and Charles Wesley by Michael McMullen. Leigh: Triangle, 1995.

Music at Midnight: The life and poetry of George Herbert by John Drury. London: Penguin, 2014.

Newman: The heart of holiness by Roderick Strange. London: Hodder & Stoughton, 2020.

A Priest to the Temple or the Country Parson, with selected poems by Ronald Blythe. Norwich: Canterbury Press, 2003.

The Theology of Hugh of St Victor: An interpretation by Boyd Taylor Coolman. Cambridge: Cambridge University Press, 2010.

The Way Back to God: The spiritual theology of Bonaventure by Douglas Dales. Cambridge: James Clarke, 2019.

11

Doing What He Would Want

Then the righteous will answer him, 'Lord, when was it that we saw you hungry and gave you food, or thirsty and gave you something to drink? And when was it that we saw you a stranger and welcomed you, or naked and gave you clothing? And when was it that we saw you sick or in prison and visited you?' And the king will answer them, 'Truly I tell you, just as you did it to one of the least of these who are members of my family, you did it to me.'
(Matthew 25.37–40)

You also must be ready, for the Son of Man is coming at an unexpected hour … Blessed is that slave whom his master will find at work when he arrives.
(Luke 12.40, 43)

Little children, I am with you only a little longer. You will look for me; and as I said to the Jews so now I say to you, 'Where I am going, you cannot come.' I give you a new commandment, that you love one another. Just as I have loved you, you also should love one another. By this everyone will know that you are my disciples, if you have love for one another.
(John 12.33–35)

Be imitators of me, as I am of Christ.
(1 Corinthians 11.1)

… let us run with perseverance the race that is set before us, looking to Jesus the pioneer and perfecter of our faith, who for the sake of the joy that was set before him endured the cross, disregarding its shame, and has taken his seat at the right hand of the throne of God.
(Hebrews 12.1b–3)

God abides in those who confess that Jesus is the Son of God, and they abide in God. So we have known and believe the love that God has for us. God is love, and those who abide in love abide in God, and God abides in them … We love because he first loved us.
(1 John 4.15–16, 19)

Just as we come to associate particular places and objects with lost loved ones, having a sense of being close to them in certain locations or when handling treasured possessions such as a special book or piece of china, we may also see them in others. This may be because of physical resemblance passed down through genes or familiar habits and values passed down through instruction or imitation.

Additionally, an important part of mourning is trying to do what the deceased would have wanted, certainly with respect to funeral arrangements and the disposal of the estate, but often more broadly in trying to live one's life in accordance with their character or in promoting certain values that they exemplified. When we violate these, we talk about a person 'turning in his grave', as if there is a legacy to which we failed to be faithful. Sometimes we even ask, 'What would mum have done in this situation?'; and there is evidence that this sort of thinking can help people make wise decisions.[1]

These patterns of seeing likeness and doing alike are also there in the Christian life. Much is centred on the believer becoming more like Christ through imitation, but also on being attentive to the likeness of Christ in other human beings and, furthermore treating them as if they were Christ himself. The discernment of Christ in others is closely connected with an awareness of Christ in nature, explored in Chapter 10; it is especially evident in Franciscan spirituality's smooth move from contemplation of nature to standing in solidarity with the weak, the poor and the oppressed.

This chapter begins with readings concerned with this seeing of Christ in the other, before moving on to 'What would Jesus [have us] do?' In both these areas the work of the Spirit is understood to be vital, working in cooperation with the believer on a transformative process that goes beyond emulating Christ to identifying with him.

---

1 U. Staudinger and P. Baltes, 2006, 'Interactive minds: A facilitative setting for wisdom-related performance?' *Journal of Personality & Social Psychology*, 71, pp. 746–62.

11.1 Seeing Christ in humanity

Funeral oration for Basil of Caesarea (extracts)
Gregory of Nazianzus (329–390)

Author Gregory was born near Nazianzus in what is now Turkey, where his father was bishop. Gregory was an able student and studied Greek philosophy and rhetoric at a number of prestigious centres, including Athens, where he first met Basil of Caesarea. His father wanted him to be ordained as a priest, but he resisted this, preferring the life of an ascetic, and pursued this for a year with Basil, who persuaded him to reconsider, and he returned to Nazianzus to be ordained priest in 361. For the next ten years, Basil and Gregory worked closely together to combat Arianism and uphold the doctrine agreed at the Council of Nicaea. In 370, Basil became Bishop of Caesarea and two years later he ordained Gregory Bishop of Sasima. This was primarily a tactical move, aimed at shoring up Basil's influence in the area, resented by Gregory and undercut when he effectively became Bishop of Nazianzus as his father's health began to fail later the same year. This gave him a forum to apply his strong rhetorical skills in the form of the extended sermonic 'orations' for which he would later become famous. However, once Gregory's parents had died, he withdrew to Seleucia to embrace the monastic existence he had always craved, and it was while he was here, or possibly en route to Constantinople at Basil's behest, that he received news of his friend's death (for more on Basil see Chapter 12).

Language Greek. The translation below is by Charles Gordon Browne and James Edward Swallow. Gregory's works were preserved, edited and quickly translated into Latin so that they were soon disseminated across the Roman Empire.

Date 381.

Genre and context This very long oration is in the form of a Greek *'encomium'* (essentially a eulogy). It (or perhaps a portion of it) was delivered three years after Basil's death in 378, possibly on the anniversary. Gregory was prevented from attending the funeral by his absence in Seleucia or Constantinople and by his own poor health. The oration describes Basil's life as a seamless integration of theological study, prayerful contemplation, excellence in liturgy and skilful political influence to enable the establishment of structures and systems for supporting those in need. The extracts below concerns Basil's actions during the famine of 368 and his radical attitude to the treatment of people with leprosy. The motivation for this is expressed in Basil's Rule in which, in response to a question about the correct attitude towards the sick, he answers, 'As offering our service to the Lord himself who said: *When you did this to the least of these, my brothers, you did it to me'* (Rule Question 36, see

p. 222). In fact, for Basil *both* serving Christ in others *and* imitating the actions of Jesus in the Gospels are important; the extract concludes with a reference to imitating Christ. For all three Cappadocian Fathers, serving the sick and poor was understood as a route to participation in the divine nature (*theosis* or deification) because, to paraphrase Gregory of Nyssa, 'you become what you copy'.

Funeral oration for Basil of Caesarea

34. Of his care for and protection of the Church, there are many other tokens; his boldness towards the governors and other most powerful men in the city: the decisions of disputes, accepted without hesitation, and made effective by his simple word, his inclination being held to be decisive: his support of the needy, most of them in spiritual, not a few also in physical distress: for this also often influences the soul and reduces it to subjection by its kindness; the support of the poor, the entertainment of strangers, the care of maidens; legislation written and unwritten for the monastic life: arrangements of prayers, adornments of the sanctuary, and other ways in which the true man of God, working for God, would benefit the people: one being especially important and noteworthy. There was a famine, the most severe one ever recorded ...

35. ... by his word and advice he opened the stores of those who possessed them, and so, according to the Scripture dealt food to the hungry, and satisfied the poor with bread, and fed them in the time of dearth, and filled the hungry souls with good things. And in what way? For this is no slight addition to his praise. He gathered together the victims of the famine with some who were but slightly recovering from it, men and women, infants, old men, every age which was in distress, and obtaining contributions of all sorts of food which can relieve famine, set before them basins of soup and such meat as was found preserved among us, on which the poor live. Then, imitating the ministry of Christ, Who, girded with a towel, did not disdain to wash the disciples' feet, using for this purpose the aid of his own servants, and also of his fellow servants, he attended to the bodies and souls of those who needed it, combining personal respect with the supply of their necessity, and so giving them a double relief.

63. What more? He however it was, who took the lead in pressing upon those who were men, that they ought not to despise their fellowmen [lepers], nor to dishonour Christ, the one Head of all, by their inhuman treatment of them; but to use the misfortunes of others as an opportunity

---

of firmly establishing their own lot, and to lend to God that mercy of which they stand in need at His hands. He did not therefore disdain to honour with his lips this disease, noble and of noble ancestry and brilliant reputation though he was, but saluted them as brethren, not, as some might suppose, from vainglory, (for who was so far removed from this feeling?) but taking the lead in approaching to tend them, as a consequence of his philosophy, and so giving not only a speaking, but also a silent, instruction. The effect produced is to be seen not only in the city, but in the country and beyond, and even the leaders of society have vied with one another in their philanthropy and magnanimity towards them. Others have had their cooks, and splendid tables, and the devices and dainties of confectioners, and exquisite carriages, and soft, flowing robes; Basil's care was for the sick, and the relief of their wounds, and the imitation of Christ, by cleansing leprosy, not by a word, but in deed.

Treatise on the Love of God (extract)
Francis de Sales (1567–1622)

Author François Bonaventura de Sales was born in the Haute Savoie region of France to a noble and long-established family. At the age of eleven he left home for Paris to study at the College de Claremont, a Jesuit foundation. He showed an early interest in theology, but in 1586 participated in a discussion on predestination that convinced him that he was personally damned. A period of great mental and spiritual distress ensued but was resolved when he consecrated himself to the Blessed Virgin Mary, took a vow of chastity and became a tertiary of the Minim order of friars. He completed his university education in Padua and, now qualified as a lawyer, returned to his home town. Despite his parents' hope that he would take up a political role, François chose instead to relinquish his rights as oldest son and heir and was ordained to the priesthood in 1593. Due to family influence, François immediately took up a senior position in the Diocese of Geneva, whose seat was actually in Annecy due to the fact that Geneva was at that time under Calvinist control. Ironically, this position, together with his high level of education and polish, meant that he took on several political and diplomatic missions in the border struggles between France and Switzerland in the area, coming close to losing his life on some occasions. In 1602 he became Bishop of Geneva, exercising a highly effective ministry with a special concern for nurturing the spirituality of lay people. In accordance with his baptismal names, he had a lifelong association with the Franciscan order, especially the Capuchins. François specialized in spiritual direction and wrote many letters which have survived; apart from the *Treatise*, his most famous works are *The Introduction to the Devout Life* and the *Conferences*.

Language French. The translation below is by Henry Benedict Mackey OSB.

Date 1616.

Genre and context The *Introduction to the Devout Life* was published in 1609 and was aimed at developing devotion to God in its lay readership. It is written to 'Philothea', the soul who longs to love God. The *Treatise* is essentially a sequel presented in the form of systematic enquiry, and this time is addressed to 'Theotimus', the soul who loves God and wants to understand this love better. Following on from his early crisis, François seems to have embraced an almost exclusively positive approach to faith, treating it as a path to consolation rather than an escape from condemnation, of finding freedom from self in the love of others. In this extract he counsels attentiveness to the family resemblance between human beings and their Creator.

Treatise on the Love of God
Book X

Chapter XI. How Holy Charity Produces the Love of our Neighbour

As God created man to his own image and likeness, so did he appoint for man a love after the image and resemblance of the love which is due to his own divinity. Thou shalt love the Lord thy God, with thy whole heart, and with thy whole soul, and with thy whole mind. This is the greatest, and the first commandment. And the second is like to this: Thou shalt love thy neighbour as thyself. Why do we love God, Theotimus? 'The cause for which we love God,' says St Bernard, 'is God Himself;' as though he had said: we love God because he is the most sovereign and infinite goodness. And why do we love ourselves in charity? Surely because we are the image and likeness of God; and whereas all men are endowed with the same dignity, we love them also as ourselves, that is, as being holy and living images of the divinity. For it is on that account that we belong to God by so strict an alliance and so sweet a dependence of love, that he makes no difficulty to call himself our father, and to call us his children; it is on that account that we are capable of being united to his divine essence by the fruition of his sovereign goodness and felicity; it is on that account that we receive his grace, that our spirits are associated to his most Holy Spirit, and made in a manner participant of his divine nature, as St Leo says. And therefore the same charity which produces the acts of the love of God, produces at the same time those of the love of our neighbour. And even as Jacob saw that one same ladder touched heaven and earth, serving the angels both for descending and ascending, so we know that one same charity extends itself to both the love of God and our neighbour, raising us to the union of our spirit with God, and bringing us back again to a loving society with our neighbours; always, however, on the understanding that we love our neighbour as being after the image and likeness of God, created to have communication with the divine goodness, to participate in his grace, and to enjoy his glory.

Theotimus, to love our neighbour in charity is to love God in man, or man in God; it is to hold God alone dear for his own sake and the creature for the love of him. The young Tobias, accompanied by the angel Raphael, having met with Raguel his relative, by whom, however, he was unknown, – Raguel had no sooner set eyes upon him, says the Scripture, but turning himself towards his wife: Anna, look, look, said he, how like is this young man to my cousin? ... And Raguel went to him, and kissed him with tears, and weeping upon his neck, said: a blessing be upon thee, my son, because thou art the son of a virtuous man. And Anna his wife and Sara their daughter wept, through tenderness of affection. Do you not observe that Raguel, without knowing the younger Tobias, embraces, caresses, kisses him, and weeps for joy over him. Whence proceeds this love but from that which he had for the old Tobias, the father, whom this child did so much resemble? A blessing be upon thee, said he; but why? certainly not because thou art a good youth, for that as yet I know not, but because thou art son, and like, to thy father, a good and most virtuous man.

Ah! then, Theotimus, when we see a neighbour who is created to the image and likeness of God, ought we not to say one to another: Observe and see this creature, how he resembles the Creator? Might we not cast ourselves upon his neck, to caress him and weep over him with love? Should we not bless him a thousand and a thousand times? And why? For the love of him? No verily: for we know not whether he be worthy of love or hatred in himself; but wherefore then? O Theotimus! for the love of God, who has made him to his own image and likeness, and consequently capable of participating in his goodness, in grace and in glory. For the love of God, I say, from whom he is, whose he is, by whom he is, in whom he is, for whom he is, and whom he resembles in a most particular manner. Wherefore the love of God not only oftentimes commands the love of our neighbour, but itself produces this love and pours it into man's heart, as its resemblance and image: for even as man is the image of God, so the sacred love of man towards man, is the true image of the heavenly love of man towards God.

Discourse on Christian Charity (extract)
Jonathan Edwards (1703–1758)

Author Jonathan Edwards was born in Connecticut, USA, the son of a scholarly Congregationalist minister and devout mother. He was a precocious child with a great love of and interest in nature, and began his studies at Yale aged only 13, graduating four years later. Here he became very influenced by contemporary developments in science and empiricist philosophy. He underwent a deep intensification of his personal faith at this time and decided to train as a minister. He was ordained in 1727, initially working as an assistant to his maternal grandfather, Solomon Stoddard, a highly influential New England figure, and on his death took charge of his prestigious congregation in Northampton. In 1731 Edwards delivered a lecture in Boston reasserting the Calvinist doctrine of predestination. This was followed by a series of sermons developing the theme and which marked the beginning of a revival referred to as 'The great awakening' in which thousands of people underwent 'conversion' experiences, first in his parish and then across New England. His fame spread, helped by the publication of his key sermons, and in 1740 he was visited by George Whitefield (see Chapter 6). However, there were ongoing problems: some individuals who believed they were selected for eternal damnation killed themselves; some of his converts were found in the possession of 'impure publications'; there was increasing unease from conservative churches at the histrionic behaviour of many of those attending his services. Eventually in 1750 his congregation requested that he resign. After a period in ministry in Massachusetts, he was invited to become President of what is now Princeton University but died of complications of a smallpox vaccination when he had only been in post for a month. Edwards wrote on a wide range of topics in theology, philosophy, spirituality and natural history. His most famous works are his sermon 'Sinners in the Hands of an Angry God' and treatises on Calvinist doctrine and the process of conversion including *Religious Affections* and *Faithful Narrative of the Surprising Work of God in the Conversion of Many Hundred Souls in Northampton.*

Language English.

Date 1739.

Genre and context This is one of several essays originally written as single manuscripts and collected and prepared for publication by Edwards' son under the title 'Miscellaneous Discourses on Important Theological Subjects' which covered aspects of doctrine, biblical knowledge and ethics. It can be seen that Edwards was as interested in the ongoing Christian life of his congregants as he was in their initial conversion.

On Deuteronomy 15.7–12
The Duty of Charity to the Poor, Explained and Enforced

II. God tells us, that he shall look upon what is done in charity to our neighbours in want, as done unto him; and what is denied unto them, as denied unto him. 'He that hath pity on the poor lendeth to the Lord.' God hath been pleased to make our needy neighbours his receivers. He in his infinite mercy hath so interested himself in their case, that he looks upon what is given in charity to them, as given to himself; and when we deny them what their circumstances require of us, he looks upon it that we therein rob him of his right.

Christ teaches us, that we are to look upon our fellow-Christians in this case as himself, and that our giving or withholding from them, shall be taken, as if we so behaved ourselves towards him. There Christ says to the righteous on his right hand, who had supplied the wants of the needy, 'In that ye have done it to one of the least of these my brethren, ye have done it unto me.' In like manner he says to the wicked who had not shown mercy to the poor, 'Inasmuch as ye did it not unto one of the least of these, ye did it not to me.' – Now what stronger enforcement of this duty can be conceived, or is possible, than this, that Jesus Christ looks upon our kind and bountiful, or unkind and uncharitable, treatment of our needy neighbours, as such a treatment of himself?

If Christ himself were upon earth, and dwelt among us in a frail body, as he once did, and were in calamitous and needy circumstances, should we not be willing to supply him? Should we be apt to excuse ourselves from helping him? Should we not be willing to supply him so, that he might live free from distressing poverty? And if we did otherwise, should we not bring great guilt upon ourselves? And might not our conduct justly be very highly resented by God? Christ was once here in a frail body, stood in need of the charity, and was maintained by it; 'And certain women which had been healed of evil spirits and infirmities, Mary called Magdalen, out of whom went seven devils, and Joanna the wife of Chuza, Herod's steward, and Susanna, and many others, which ministered unto him of their substance.' So he still, in many of his members, needs the charity of others.

As Kingfishers Catch Fire
Gerard Manley Hopkins (1844–1889)

Author Gerard Manley Hopkins was born in Stratford, Essex (as was – now east London). He was raised as an Anglican but converted to Roman Catholicism in 1866 while studying classics at Oxford. As part of this process he consulted John Henry Newman (see Chapter 10). Two years later he entered the Jesuit novitiate, and it was during his training that he discovered the writings of the medieval theologian Duns Scotus (d. 1308). These offered a sacramental view of nature that grounded Hopkin's intuition that the world reflects the beauty of Christ. He was ordained as a priest in 1877. He worked as a teacher and lecturer in classics as well as a parish priest in several locations across Britain before finally becoming Professor of Greek and Latin at University College, Dublin, where he remained until his death from typhoid at the age of 44. Throughout his adult life he struggled with the tension between his primary vocation as a priest and his identity as a poet (and also as an artist and musician.) He was ambivalent about his poetry, often seeing it as a self-indulgent distraction, but also recognizing it as expressing a God-given talent. His poems were published posthumously, edited by his friend Robert Bridges.

Language English.

Date 1877.

Genre and context Hopkins said that his poetry was meant to be heard rather than read. It relies on what he called 'sprung rhythm', which gives it a freer and more musical feel than the poetic tradition he inherited. He elaborated this by placing accents over syllables that should be stressed. This poem, which dates from the year of his ordination, explores the vocation of every creature to be what it is, and for human beings to become Christ, an idea also expressed in *As Nature is a Heraclitean Fire* (1888).

As Kingfishers Catch Fire

As kingfishers catch fire, dragonflies draw flame;
As tumbled over rim in roundy wells
Stones ring; like each tucked string tells, each hung bell's
Bow swung finds tongue to fling out broad its name;
Each mortal thing does one thing and the same:
Deals out that being indoors each one dwells;
Selves – goes itself; *myself* it speaks and spells,
Crying *Whát I dó is me: for that I came.*

I say móre: the just man justices;
Keeps grace: thát keeps all his goings graces;
Acts in God's eye what in God's eye he is –
Chríst – for Christ plays in ten thousand places,
Lovely in limbs, and lovely in eyes not his
To the Father through the features of men's faces.

11.2 What would Jesus do?

The Philokalia (extracts)
Maximos the Confessor (c.580–662)

Author Little is known about Maximos' early life. He was born somewhere in the Roman-Byzantine empire and was highly educated, probably at Constantinople. While still a young man, he held senior civil administrative positions under the Emperor Heraclitus. At some point after 610, Maximos relinquished his life at the centre of political power and entered the monastic community in Philippicus in Chrysopolis, and then in 624–625 joined the Monastery of St George at Cyzicus, where he was able to devote himself to study and writing. However, this was a time of threats to the empire from all sides, and after only a few months the area was invaded by the Persians and the whole monastery was evacuated. Maximos ended up in Carthage in 630. Here he seems to have been engaged in extensive study, bringing together teachings from the very early Church Fathers with insights from somewhat later writers such as Pseudo-Dionysius and the Cappadocian Fathers with his own training in Aristotelian philosophy, and was regularly sought out for advice on theological questions (much of his writing reflects this). From around 640, circumstances required Maximos to become involved in a bitter controversy concerning the divine and human nature(s) of Christ. He was at first successful in defending the positions of the Councils of Nicaea and Chalcedon against a number of variants, and he played an important part in the Lateran Council of 645 in Rome. However, following Emperor Heraclitus' death, there was a struggle for succession; the new emperor, Constans II, opposed the position of the Lateran Council and arrested both the pope and Maximos. Maximos was condemned as a heretic in 658 and again in 662 when his tongue and right hand were cut off so that he could no longer communicate his ideas. He unsurprisingly died shortly afterwards in captivity in Georgia. Despite the fact that he was abandoned at the end, his disciples treasured and preserved his writings, and he is the figure to whom most space is devoted in the *Philokalia*.

Language Greek. The translation below is by G. E. H. Palmer, Philip Sherrard and Kallistos Ware.

Date The original versions date from the 620s–630s. However, as noted in Chapter 2, the *Philokalia* was published in 1782, and the degree of editorial changes made at this time remains unknown.

Genre and context This is from the early period of Maximos' writings. The *Four Hundred Texts on Love* are arranged in four 'centuries' modelled on the four Gospels. The connection between imitating Christ and partaking of the divine nature draws on the thought of the Cappadocian Fathers described earlier in this chapter. The extracts from *Treatise on the Lord's Prayer* and *Two Hundred Texts on Theology* show how the possibility of deification rests on the fully human nature, energy and will of Christ, the truth for which Maximos died.

Four Hundred Texts on Love
Fourth Century

55. He who loves Christ is bound to imitate Him to the best of his ability. Christ, for example, was always conferring blessings on people; He was long-suffering when they were ungrateful and blasphemed Him; and when they beat Him and put Him to death, He endured it, imputing no evil at all to anyone. These are the three acts which manifest love for one's neighbour. If he is incapable of them, the person who says that he loves Christ or has attained the kingdom deceives himself. For 'not everyone who says to Me: "Lord, Lord" shall enter into the kingdom of heaven; but he that does the will of My Father' (Matthew 7:21); and again, 'He who loves Me will keep My commandments' (cf. John 14:15, 23).

90. Only God is good by nature (cf. Matthew 19:17), and only he who imitates God is good in will and purpose. For it is the intention of such a person to unite the wicked to Him who is good by nature, so that they too may become good. That is why, though reviled by them, he blesses; persecuted, he endures; vilified, he supplicates (cf. 1 Corinthians 4:12–13); put to death, he prays for them. He does everything so as not to lapse from the purpose of love, which is God Himself.

Treatise on the Lord's Prayer

... The Logos bestows adoption on us when He grants us that birth and deification which, transcending nature, comes by grace from above through the Spirit. The guarding and preservation of this in God depends on the resolve of those thus born: on their sincere acceptance of the grace bestowed on them and, through the practice of the commandments, on their cultivation of the beauty given to them by grace. Moreover, by emptying themselves of the passions they lay hold of the divine to the same degree as that to which, deliberately emptying Himself of His own sublime glory, the Logos of God truly became man.

Two Hundred Texts on Theology and the Incarnate Dispensation of the Son of God Written for Thalassios

II.18. He who prays must never stand still on the steep ascent that leads to God. Just as he has to progress upwards from strength to strength in the practice of the virtues and to rise in his contemplation of spiritual truths from glory to glory (cf. 2 Corinthians 3:18), and to pass from the letter to the spirit of Holy Scripture, so he must advance in a similar manner within the realm of prayer. He must raise his intellect and the resolve of his soul from what is human to what is divine, so that his intellect can follow Jesus the Son of God, who has passed through the heavens (cf. Hebrews 4:14) and who is everywhere. For He has passed through all things for us by the dispensation of His incarnation, so that we, by following Him, may pass through all that is sequent to Him and so come to be with Him, provided we apprehend Him not according to the limitations to which He accommodated Himself in His incarnation but according to the majesty of His natural infinitude.

First Rule of the Lesser Brothers (extract)
Francis of Assisi (c.1181–1226)

Author See p. 177.

Language Latin. Many manuscripts exist. The translation below is by Paschal Robinson OFM.

Date 1221.

Genre and context The earliest written version of the Rule dates from 1209. This was approved by Pope Innocent III but without a papal bull. No record of this Rule survives. It was added to over the ensuing years by Francis in consultation with others as his own ideas developed and in the light of the emerging needs of a growing community of friars. It reached a settled form in 1221, and the extract below is taken from this version. Nevertheless, as the order continued to expand, it proved unwieldy, and it was drastically edited (possibly under papal direction) to form the Rule of 1223 which was confirmed by Pope Honorius III and remains in use today.

First Rule of the Lesser Brothers
Chapter IX. Begging Alms

Let all the brothers strive to follow the humility and poverty of our Lord Jesus Christ, and let them remember that we should have nothing else in the whole world, except as the Apostle says: Having food and clothing, we are content with these. They must rejoice when they live among people considered of little value and looked down upon, with the sick and the lepers, and the beggars by the wayside. When it is necessary, they may go for alms. Let them not be ashamed and remember, moreover, that our Lord Jesus Christ, the Son of the all powerful living God, set His face like flint and was not ashamed. He was poor and a stranger and lived on alms. He, the Blessed Virgin, and His disciples. When people revile them and refuse to give them alms, let them thank God for this, because they will receive great honour before the tribunal of our Lord Jesus Christ for such insults. Let them realize that a reproach is imputed not to those who suffer it but to those who caused it. Alms are a legacy and a justice to the poor that our Lord Jesus Christ acquired for us. The brothers who work at acquiring them will receive a great reward, and enable those who give them to gain and acquire one; for those who give; for all that people leave in the world will perish, but they will have a reward from the Lord for the charity and almsgiving they have done.

Let Each one confidently make known his needs to another that the other might discover what is needed and minister to him. Let each one love and care for his brother as a mother loves and cares for her son, in those matters in which God has given them grace. And let the one who eats not spurn the one who does not eat. Let the one who does not eat not judge the one who eats.

Whenever a need arises, all the brothers, wherever they may be, are permitted to consume whatever food people can eat, as the Lord says of David who ate the loaves of offering that only the priests could lawfully eat. Let them remember what the Lord says: Be careful that your hearts do not become drowsy from carousing, drunkenness and the anxieties of daily life, and that day catches you by surprise; for the day will assault everyone who lives on the face of the earth as a trap. Similarly, in time of an obvious need, all the brothers may do as the Lord has given them the grace to satisfy their needs, 'because necessity has no law.'

Summa Theologica (extract)
Thomas Aquinas (1225–1274)

Author See p. 66.

Language Latin. The translation below is by Alister McGrath.

Date 1270s.

Genre and context The *Summa* is a textbook, written for seminarians and educated lay people, setting out the Christian faith in systematic form. It is in three parts, with the last unfinished at the time of Thomas' death. It is a work of enormous scope covering theology, ethics, and what would now be called political economy and psychology. Each part is divided into topics set out in a Socratic question and answer format. Part II is devoted to questions of virtue and ethics. This extract concerns 'acts of mercy' that Thomas saw as a key part of the Christian life. The list of these acts almost certainly predates him and is based in the parable of the sheep and the goats in Matthew 25. It is not so much concerned with the cultivation of virtue as a route to deification, talking instead of being united with Christ in a relationship of love and resembling him in charitable behaviour – both to like him and be like him.

Summa Theologica II.II

Question 30
4. Whether mercy is the greatest of the virtues?

… We worship God by external sacrifices and gifts, not for his own benefit, but for that of ourselves and our neighbour. God does not need our sacrifices, but he wants them to be offered to deepen our devotion and to benefit our neighbour. So mercy, through which we meet the needs of others, is a sacrifice that is acceptable to God, in that this leads directly to our neighbour's wellbeing, according to Hebrews 13:16: 'Do not forget to do good and to share with others, for with such sacrifices God is pleased.'

From the perspective of external works, the essence of the Christian religion consists in mercy. However, the inward love of charity, by which we are united to God, is of greater importance than both love and mercy for our neighbour. Charity makes us like God by uniting us to him in a bond of love: for this reason, it surpasses mercy, which makes us like God through a similarity of works.

213

Question 32

1. Whether almsgiving is an act of charity?

… External acts belong to the virtue which motivates those acts. Now the motive for giving alms is to relieve someone who is in need. For this reason, some have defined alms as being 'an action by which something is given to the needy, out of compassion and for God's sake.' The motive for this is mercy … So it is clear that almsgiving is, properly speaking, an act of mercy. This is clear from its very name, for in Greek (eleemosyne) it is derived from 'having mercy (eleein)' as is the case with the Latin term miseratio. And since mercy is an effect of charity … it follows that almsgiving is an act of charity through the medium of mercy.

2. Whether the different kinds of almsdeeds are appropriately numbered?

… We consider there are seven physical almsdeeds – namely, to give food to the hungry, to give drink to the thirsty, to clothe the naked, to harbour the harbourless, to visit the sick, to ransom the captive, and to bury the dead; all of which are expressed in the following verse: 'To visit, to quench, to feed, to ransom, clothe, harbour or bury.'

Again, we consider there are seven spiritual alms – namely, to instruct the ignorant, to counsel the doubtful, to comfort the sorrowful, to reprove the sinner, to forgive injuries, to bear with those who trouble and annoy us, and to pray for everyone. These are all contained in the following verse: 'To counsel, reprove, console, pardon, forbear, and pray' (in that this 'counsel' includes both advice and instruction).

This distinction between types of almsdeeds is appropriate for the various needs of our neighbours. Some affect the soul, and are relieved by spiritual almsdeeds, while others affect the body, and are relieved by physical almsdeeds. Physical need occurs either during this life or afterwards. If it occurs during this life, it is either a common need in respect of things needed by all, or it is a special need that arises from some accident. In the first case, the need is either internal or external. The internal need is twofold: the first – hunger – is relieved by solid food, so that we should feed the hungry; while the other – thirst – is relieved by liquid food, so that we should give drink to the thirsty. The common need with regard to external help is twofold; one in respect of clothing, so that we should clothe the naked: while the other concerns a dwelling place, so that we need to 'harbour the harbourless.' If there is a special need, it either results from an internal cause, like sickness, so that we have to visit the sick; or it results from an external cause, so that we have to 'ransom the captive.' After this life we give burial to the dead.

In the same way, spiritual needs are relieved by spiritual acts in two ways. First by asking for help from God through prayer, by which one person prays for others; and second, by giving human assistance, which can take three forms. First, in order to relieve some deficiency on the part of the intellect. If this deficiency lies in the speculative intellect, the remedy is applied by instruction. If it lies in the practical intellect, the remedy is applied by counselling. Second, there may be a deficiency in respect of the appetitive power, especially by way of sorrow, which is remedied by comforting. Third, the deficiency may be due to an inordinate act; and this can be considered in three ways. First, in respect of the sinner, in that this sin proceeds from a disordered will, the remedy takes the form of reproof. Secondly, in respect of the person sinned against; and if the sin is committed against ourselves, we apply the remedy by pardoning the injury. If it is committed against God or our neighbour, it is not in our power to pardon it, as Jerome observes in his Commentary on Matthew 18.15. Thirdly, in respect of the result of a disordered act, on account of which the sinner is an irritation to those who live with him, despite his intentions; in this case the remedy is applied by bearing with him, especially with regard to those who sin out of weakness, according to Romans 15:1: 'We that are stronger, ought to bear the infirmities of the weak,' and not only because they are infirm and consequently troublesome on account of their unruly actions, but also by bearing any other burdens of theirs with them, according to Galatians 6:2: 'Bear one another's burdens.'

Social Purity (extract)
Josephine Butler (1828–1906)

Author Josephine Grey was born in Northumberland and grew up in a socially progressive political family. As a woman, she was well educated by the standards of the time. In her late teens, she developed an intensely personal form of spirituality that she saw as being in tension with the formal character of contemporary Anglicanism. Following a visit to Ireland in 1847, where she directly observed the effects of the great famine, this faith incorporated a passion for social justice, conceived in terms of the coming of the kingdom of God. In 1852 she married George Butler, an Oxford academic and priest, who shared much of her political and spiritual perspective. George held senior positions in schools at Cheltenham and Liverpool, where the couple continued their practice begun in Oxford of taking sick and destitute prostitutes into their homes, later continued through the establishment of hostels. At this time Josephine began her political campaigns for women's rights. These were focused on access to higher education and suffrage, and the abolition of trafficking of women and girls in the sex trade. She was involved for many years in the campaign to repeal the Contagious Diseases Acts, which was finally successful in 1886, and then for measures to stamp out the procurement of child prostitutes, addressed by the Criminal Law Amendment Act of 1885. In later life she campaigned for these advances to be applied across the British Empire, specifically in India.

Language English.

Date May 1879.

Genre and context This is the transcript of a public lecture given in Cambridge to the Committee of the Social Purity Alliance (an anti-prostitution campaign group). Butler critically engages with a theory promulgated by the social historian William Lecky, that prostitution was necessary to maintain the middle-class notion of holy matrimony that had emerged at that period. The theory held that male fidelity to virginal and sexually repressed brides from the upper classes could only be maintained by ready access to prostitutes drawn from the lower classes. Despite their allegedly vital social role, prostitutes were nevertheless to be despised and feared as carriers of sexually transmitted disease. In challenging this Butler berates the church for forgetting Jesus and doing the opposite of what he would do.

Social Purity

It will be useful to consider first what it is that lies at the root of the evil which we are gathered together here today to consider, with a view to opposing it. The root of the evil is the unequal standard in morality; the false idea that there is one code of morality for men and another for women ...

Some will tell me that this is the inevitable rule, and that the sternest possible reprobation of the *female* sinner, as being the most deeply culpable, has marked every age and all teaching in which the moral standard was high. No! – not every age, nor all teaching! There stands on the page of history one marked exception; and, so far as I know, one only – that of Christ.

I will ask you the question of today, therefore, in this connection, 'What think ye of Christ?' Come with me into his presence. Let us go with Him into the temple; let us look at Him on the occasion when men rudely thrust into his presence a woman, who with loud-tongued accusation they condemned as an impure and hateful thing. 'He that is without sin among you, let him first cast a stone at her.' At the close of that

---

interview, He asked, 'Woman, where are those thine accusers?' It was a significant question; and we ask it again today. Where, and *who*, are they? In what state are *their* consciences? Beginning from the eldest even to the youngest, they went out, scared by the searching presence of Him who admitted not for one moment that God's law of purity should be relaxed for the stronger, while imposed in its utmost severity on the weaker.

Almost as soon as that holy Teacher had ascended into the heavens, Christian society and the Church itself began to be unfaithful to his teaching; and man has too generally continued up to this day to assert, by speech, by customs, by institutions, and by laws, that, in regard to this evil, the woman who errs is irrevocably blighted, while the man is at least excusable. As a floating straw indicates the flow of the tide, so there are certain expressions that have become almost proverbial, and till lately have passed unchallenged in conversation and in literature, plainly revealing the double standard which society has accepted. One of these expressions is, 'He is only sowing his wild oats;' another is, that 'a reformed profligate makes a good husband.' The latter is a sentiment so gross that I would not repeat it, if it were not necessary to do so – as a proof of the extent of the aberration of human judgment in this matter.

Here we are at once brought into contact with the false and misleading idea that the essence of right and wrong is in some way dependent on sex. We never hear it carelessly or complacently asserted of a young woman that '*she* is only sowing her wild oats.' This is not a pleasant aspect of the question; but let us deal faithfully with it. It is a fact, that numbers even of moral and religious people have permitted themselves to accept and condone in man what is fiercely condemned in woman.

And do you see the logical necessity involved in this? It is that a large section of female society has to be told off – set aside, so to speak, to minister to the irregularities of the excusable man. That section is doomed to death, hurled to despair; while another section of womanhood is kept strictly and almost forcibly guarded in domestic purity …

Obviously, then, the essence of the great work which we propose to ourselves, is to Christianize public opinion, until, both in theory and practice, it shall recognize the fundamental truth that the essence of right and wrong is in no way dependent upon sex, and shall demand of men precisely the same chastity as it demands of women.

Further reading

A Heart Lost in Wonder: The life and faith of Gerard Manley Hopkins by Catharine Randall. Grand Rapids, MI: Eerdmans, 2020.

Heart Speaks to Heart: The Salesian tradition by Wendy Wright. London: Darton, Longman & Todd. 2004.

Josephine Butler: A guide to her life, faith and social action by Rod Garner. London: Darton, Longman & Todd, 2009.

Making Room: Recovering hospitality as a Christian tradition by Christine Pohl. Grand Rapids, MI: Eerdmans, 1999.

Practical Theology: Spiritual direction from Thomas Aquinas by Peter J. Kreeft. San Francisco, CA: Ignatius Press, 2014.

Saint Francis of Assisi by G. K. Chesterton. 1923. (Several editions available.)

A Short Life of Jonathan Edwards by George M. Marsden. Grand Rapids, MI: Eerdmans, 2008.

Three Wise Men from the East: The Cappadocian fathers and the struggle for orthodoxy by Patrick Whitworth. Durham: Sacristy Press, 2015.

12

Remembering

I thank my God every time I remember you, constantly praying with joy in every one of my prayers for all of you, because of your sharing in the gospel from the first day until now.
(Philippians 1.3–5)

'But when he came to himself he said, "How many of my father's hired hands have bread enough and to spare, but here I am dying of hunger! I will get up and go to my father..."'
(Luke 15.17–18a)

Then he said, 'Jesus, remember me when you come into your kingdom.' He replied, 'Truly I tell you, today you will be with me in Paradise.'
(Luke 23.42–43)

For I received from the Lord what I also handed on to you, that the Lord Jesus on the night when he was betrayed took a loaf of bread, and when he had given thanks, he broke it and said, 'This is my body that is for you. Do this in remembrance of me.' In the same way he took the cup also, after supper, saying, 'This cup is the new covenant in my blood. Do this, as often as you drink it, in remembrance of me.' For as often as you eat this bread and drink the cup, you proclaim the Lord's death until he comes.
(1 Corinthians 11.23–26)

I am grateful to God – whom I worship with a clear conscience, as my ancestors did – when I remember you constantly in my prayers night and day. Recalling your tears, I long to see you so that I may be filled with joy. I am reminded of your sincere faith, a faith that lived first in your grandmother Lois and your mother Eunice and now, I am sure, lives in you. For this reason I remind you to rekindle the gift of God that is within you through the laying on of my hands; for God did not give us a spirit of cowardice, but rather a spirit of power and of love and of self-discipline.
(2 Timothy 1.3–7)

The readings in Chapter 7 were concerned with various forms of return to the past, something that can be an important part of grief and mourning. This chapter is concerned with remembering. While it might seem that 'return' and 'remembering' are different words for the same thing, this book understands return as one of the things we do in order to remember. That is, remembering is the *goal* of the grief process. That is why it is the topic of the final chapter of Part II.

Remembering is here understood as a form of reconstitution. This does involve return, but it is much more than that: it is the putting back together of what has been *dis*membered by loss, tragedy or trauma. Of course, things will never be the same as they were; healthy reconstitution incorporates the experience of loss, but it does so in such a way that life can be lived well in its light.

This sort of remembering begins after the acute shock and practical demands of loss have receded. This is perhaps why memorial services tend to take place some time after the bereavement itself. They may also be repeated at key anniversaries; this is a normal part of Eastern Orthodox Christian mourning rites and the 'year's mind' of Catholic tradition. Remembering is never fully completed, though it may be more intense and acute at certain points in the life of an individual or community.

Remembering tends to be a social process:[1] it helps to have others to remind you of details that have slipped your mind or to give an alternative perspective. Memories can differ and some negotiation may be necessary to arrive at a story that is coherent and acceptable to everyone involved. Often there will be smiles and even laughter, and, in the context of bereavement, a sense of closeness as treasured memories of a loved one are retrieved, shared and polished.

Memorial services are a formal and socially recognized way of doing this and are sometimes described as thanksgiving for a person's life. This makes complete sense. In the Christian tradition remembering and giving thanks are very closely linked. Throughout the New Testament epistles, some of which are quoted at the start of this chapter, remembering someone in prayer is inseparable from giving thanks for them. Most significantly, the Eucharist is a combination of remembering Jesus' life and death and giving thanks to God for it.

The Eucharist embraces many, if not all, the themes of the previous chapters in this book. For example, it involves *lament* at our own sin and the state of the world; *return* in the re-telling of the story of Jesus' life and death; a heavenly *ascent* as worshippers are invited to lift their hearts and join in with the praise of the angels; intentional *placing* of the bread and wine on the Communion Table, but more profoundly the placing of and by God as *body* and blood in the eating and drinking of these elements.

---

1 For a fuller discussion see J. Collicutt, 2015, *The Psychology of Christian Character Formation*, London: SCM Press, chapter 5, and for an exploration of how this works in funeral and memorial services see R. R. Ganzevoort, 2010, 'Minding the wisdom of ages: Narrative approaches to pastoral care in the elderly', *Practical Theology*, 3, pp. 331–40.

Perhaps the most overlooked element of the Eucharist comes at the beginning, known in the Church of England *Common Worship* service as 'The Gathering'. This formally acknowledges the coming together of scattered individuals to form a body – the body of Christ, 'lovely in limbs and eyes not his'. The pieces are picked up and, as the service proceeds, woven together again, paradoxically in broken bread and wine outpoured. And at the end, just as in a healthy grieving process, it should feel possible to move forward, more fully oneself, more secure in one's identity and vocation as a community of faith and as individuals.

The texts in this chapter are arranged in three sections. First, remembering with appreciation, which can be understood as a form of praise, for 'We praise what we first appraise. What we appreciate we "see as precious."'[2] Second, remembering as a reconstitution of the community as it intentionally gathers to remember, or the reconstitution of the self through retelling and deep reflection on its story in the light of God's story. Third, as a keeping of Christ constantly in mind in order to be ready for the reunion when he returns.

Ancient understandings of memory and related concepts such as 'recollection', 're-presenting', 'intellect' and 'mindfulness', were varied and not the same as those of modern psychology (though there are many points of contact), and most of these texts are not written in English. This should be borne in mind when trying to interpret them, and attention should be paid to the overall flow of the argument rather than single words. The process of remembering that they describe is embodied but primarily spiritual rather than psychological (though this distinction is a product of modernity that their authors would not have recognized).

---

2 R. Daniels, 2016, *The Virgin Eye: Towards a contemplative view of life*, Watford: Instant Apostle, p. 159.

12.1 Remembering with appreciation

Rule of Basil (extract)
Basil of Caesarea (330–378)

Author Basil was the older brother of Gregory of Nyssa (Chapter 7) and is the senior 'Cappadocian father'. He was initially educated by his father (also called Basil), an eminent Christian lawyer and rhetorician, and following his death, underwent a classical education in Constantinople and Athens (where he met Gregory of Nazianzus – see Chapter 11). In 356 he cut short his studies to return home, possibly due to the death of his younger brother, Naucratius, who had drowned while living as an ascetic in the Cappadocian wilderness. Basil began to pursue a successful career, following in his father's footsteps, but was challenged by his older sister, Macrina, to embrace the path of asceticism and, following visits to ascetics in Egypt, Syria and Mesopotamia, he went to live in the retreat vacated by his dead brother in 358. However, he remained engaged with the wider church and the doctrinal controversies that were dividing it in the period after the Council of Nicaea, being in the forefront of resistance to Arianism. In parallel with this he pursued a bottom-up agenda of renewal and reform of the ascetic movement, drawing on cenobite principles established by Pachomius (Chapter 5). He promoted small religious communities across the area which were dedicated to living out biblical principles and sound theology. While he was doing this, his older sister Macrina and younger brother Peter were setting up an ascetic community in his family home. It was in this context that he developed the first version of his *Rule*, 'The Small *Asketikon'*. In 365 Basil was called back to Caesarea by its bishop, his friend Eusebius, to be ordained priest, and on Eusebius' death in 370 he became bishop. As observed in Gregory of Nazianzus' funeral oration (p. 200), he brought significant political and practical skills to this role, and is credited with founding the first centre for health and social care, the *Basiliad*, located just outside the city. His political skills were also required to manage the continuing conflict with his Arian opponents, which was still raging when he died eight years after his consecration. Apart from his *Asketika*, Basil wrote many letters and sermons, the theological treatise *On the Holy Spirit* and a lengthy work refuting Arianism.

Language Greek, but quickly translated into Latin, Syriac and other languages. The manuscript history is very complicated. The original text of the Small *Asketikon* did not survive. The translation below, by Anna Silvas, is from a very early Latin version translated from the Greek, possibly with significant editorial changes by Rufinus of Aquileia, a member of a monastic community on the Mount of Olives.

Date Early 360s.

Genre and context During the early 360s Basil journeyed to different ascetic communities and individuals in the Cappadocian area, including the one established in his mother's house, teaching the principles of monastic living. These were in the form of oral question and answer which were written down contemporaneously by scribes. As Basil's career and the monastic movement progressed the *Rule* expanded into a much longer document, 'The Great *Asketikon*', and exerted enormous influence on the development of monasticism. The extract below emphasizes appreciative remembering of God's gifts as a way of coming to love him more deeply. Influenced by his training in Greek philosophy, Basil had a high view of memory as an active force that, through engendering emotions such as delight, maintains a longing for the good. To remember God is a form of perpetual prayer (1 Thessalonians 5.17).

Rule of Basil
Question 14

Question: In what disposition ought one serve God and that disposition itself, what is it?

Response: I consider it a good disposition or mind when there is in us an eager, unquenchable, and unshakable desire to be pleasing to God. Such a disposition is attained through *théorian* or the knowledge through which we are able to look towards and perceive the majesty of the glories of God, and by devout and pure thoughts and through remembrance of the benefits that have been bestowed on us by God. From the recollection of which there arises the soul's love for the Lord her God, so that she loves him with 'all her heart and all her soul and all her mind' (cf. Mark 12:30), like the one who said: 'as the deer that yearns for fountains of water, so my soul yearns for you O God' (Psalm 42:1). Such is the disposition with which we must serve the Lord, fulfilling the saying of the Apostle: 'Who shall separate us from the love of Christ? Shall tribulation or anguish, or persecution, or hunger or nakedness or danger or the sword?' and the rest (Romans 8:35).

Contemplation for Attaining Love
Ignatius of Loyola (c.1491–1556)

Author See p. 110.

Language Spanish. The translation below is by Joseph Munitiz SJ and Philip Endean SJ.

Date See p. 110.

Genre and context This is part of an appendix to the *Spiritual Exercises* which consists of supplementary material designed to enrich them, but it can be understood to be the climax or goal of the exercises. The objective is to look at the world and the self with such a degree of appreciative wonder that a response of love for their creator and redeemer is naturally evoked. It is a disciplined exercise in 'bringing to memory, seeing, and considering' with gratitude very much in the tradition of Basil.

Contemplation for Attaining Love

The preparatory prayer is to ask God Our Lord for grace that all my intentions, actions and operations may be directed purely to the service and praise of His Divine Majesty.

Preamble 1 The composition, which here is to see how I am before God Our Lord, and before the angels and the saints who intercede for me.

Preamble 2 To ask for what I want. Here it will be to ask for interior knowledge of all the good I have received so that acknowledging this with gratitude, I may be able to love and serve His Divine Majesty in everything.

Point 1 This is to bring to memory the benefits received – creation, redemption, and particular gifts – the pondering with great affection how much God Our Lord has done for me, and how much He has given me of what He has; and further, how according to His divine plan, it is the Lord's wish, as far as He is able, to give me Himself; then to reflect and consider within myself what, in all reason and justice, I ought for my part to offer and give to His Divine Majesty, and that is to say, everything I have, and myself as well, saying, as one making a gift with great love:

'Take Lord, and receive all my liberty, my memory, my understanding, and my entire will, all that I have and possess. You gave it all to me; to you Lord I give it all back. All is yours, dispose of it entirely according to your will. Give me the grace to love you,' for that is enough for me.

Point 2 To see how God dwells in creatures – in the elements – giving being, in the plants, causing growth, in the animals, producing sensation, and in humankind, granting the gift of understanding – and so how He dwells also in me, giving me being, life and sensation, and causing me to understand. To see how He makes a temple of me, as I have been created in the likeness and image of His Divine Majesty. Again, to reflect within myself in the way indicated in Point 1, or in some other way I feel to be better. The same procedure is to be followed in each of the following points.

Point 3 To consider how God works and labours on my behalf in all created things on the face of the earth, i.e. 'He behaves in the same way as a person at work',* as in the heavens, elements, plans, fruits, cattle, etc, He gives being, conserves life, grants growth and feeling, etc. Then to reflect within myself.

Point 4 To see how all that is good and every gift descends from on high; so, my limited power descends from the supreme and infinite power above, and similarly justice, goodness, pity, mercy, etc, as rays descend from the sun, and waters from a fountain. Then to finish reflecting within myself, as has been said.

Colloquy End with a colloquy and Our Father.

* A Latin idiom of the time. *Ed.*

12.2 Remembering as a reconstitution of the self

Anaphora of St Basil (extract)
Basil of Caesarea (330–378)

Author See p. 222.

Language Coptic. The translation below is by Ronald Jasper and Geoffrey Cuming.

Date c.357.

Genre and context As part of his work of renewing and reforming church practice, Basil paid a good deal of attention into improving and standardizing prayers. Most of this work did not survive in its original form but was highly influential on the subsequent development of Christian liturgy. However, there are some very early manuscripts of a Eucharistic prayer (in several versions). The earliest of these is in Coptic and therefore likely to have been used in those cenobite monastic communities that Basil developed in Egypt. 'Anaphora' refers to a form of rhetoric in which a phrase is repeated several times for effect. Here the phrase 'Remember, Lord' is repeated. It is a request to God to hold his people in mind, but it follows on from an act of remembrance on their part; remembrance of Jesus according to his instruction and with the intention of being re-membered as his body. In what appear to be later expanded editions of this prayer it is set in a wider narrative of God's creation, loving-kindness, and saving power. Again, memory is understood to engender emotions; adoration and longing for the coming of Christ and a holy transformation of the character of the community and its individual members through the work of the Spirit.

Anaphora of St Basil

[Jesus] left us this great mystery of godliness: for when he was about to hand himself over to death for the life of the world, he took bread, blessed, sanctified, broke, and gave it to his holy disciples and apostles, saying, 'Take, eat from this, all of you; this is my body, which is given for you and for many for forgiveness of sins. Do this for my remembrance.'

Likewise also the cup after supper: he mixed wine and water, blessed, sanctified, gave thanks, and again gave it to them, saying, 'Take, drink from it, all of you; this is my blood which is shed for you and for many for forgiveness of sins. Do this for my remembrance. For as often as you eat this bread and drink this cup, you proclaim my death until I come.'

We also remembering his holy sufferings, and his resurrection from the dead, and his return to heaven, and his session at the right hand of the

---

Father, and his glorious and fearful coming (again), have set forth before you your own from your own gifts, this bread and this cup. And we, sinners and unworthy and wretched, pray you, our God, in adoration, that in the good pleasure of your goodness your Holy Spirit may come upon us and upon those gifts that are set before you, and may sanctify them and make them holy of holies.

Make us worthy to partake of your holy things for sanctification of soul and body, that we may become one body and one spirit, and may have a portion with all the saints who have been well-pleasing to you from eternity.

Remember, Lord, also your one, holy, catholic, and apostolic Church: give it peace for you purchased it with the precious blood of Christ. [There follow six more petitions, each beginning 'Remember, Lord ...']

Confessions, Book X (extracts)
Augustine of Hippo (354–430)

Author See p. 63.

Language and translator Latin. The work quickly became popular, and several manuscript versions were circulating in Augustine's lifetime. The oldest preserved manuscript dates from the sixth century. The earliest printed versions date from the fifteenth century. Scholars disagree as to how much Augustine's original text suffered from editorial interference in its early printed form. The translation below is by Henry Chadwick.

Date c.397–400.

Genre and context The *Confessions* are 'apologetic' in both senses of the word: saying sorry but also offering an explanation for the past and justification for the present. Augustine's consecration as bishop had been controversial and he had many critics; the *Confessions* is written in part to answer them. The Donatists, an influential group in north Africa at the time, argued that Augustine's past life made him morally unfit to be a priest; several mainstream Catholic leaders suspected that he had not really abandoned his previous beliefs and was intent on setting up Manichean cells in his locality; as an African he had always been the object of some suspicion in Italy. But, as noted on p. 14, the work is far more than an apology; it is a model for the Christian life of discipleship, a profoundly personal account of intimacy with God, and a work of theology in its own right.

These extracts are taken from Book X, in which Augustine presents the journey into God as a yearning arising from a kind of inchoate remembering, based on the journey home of the prodigal son. It is no accident that he chooses the genre of 'memoir' to communicate this.

Confessions
Book X

viii (15)* This power of memory is great, very great, my God. It is a vast and infinite profundity. Who has plumbed its bottom? This power is that of my mind and is a natural endowment, but I myself cannot grasp the totality of what I am. Is the mind, then, too restricted to compass itself, so that we have to ask what is that element of itself which it fails to grasp? Surely that cannot be external to itself; it must be within the mind. How then can it fail to grasp it? This question moves me to great astonishment. Amazement grips me. People are moved to wonder by mountain peaks, by vast waves of the sea, by broad waterfalls on rivers, by the all-embracing extent of the oceans, by the revolutions of the stars. But in themselves they are uninterested. They experience no surprise that when I was speaking of these things, I was not seeing them with my eyes. On the other hand, I would not have spoken of them unless the mountains and waves and rivers and stars (which I have seen) and the ocean (which I believe on the reports of others) I could see inwardly with dimensions just as great as if I were actually looking at them outside my mind. Yet when I was seeing them, I was not absorbing them in the act of seeing with my eyes. Nor are the actual objects present to me, but only their images. And I know by which bodily sense a thing became imprinted on my mind.

xx (29) How then am I to seek for you, Lord? When I seek for you, my God, my quest is for the happy life. I will seek you that 'my soul may live' (Isaiah 55.3), for my body derives life from my soul, and my soul derives life from you. How then shall I seek for the happy life? It is not mine until I say: 'It is enough, it is there.' But then I ought to say how my quest proceeds; is it by remembering, as if I had forgotten it and still recall that I had forgotten? Or is it through an urge to learn something quite unknown, whether I never had known it or had so forgotten it that I do not even remember having forgotten it? …

xxiii (32) Far be it from me, Lord, far from the heart of your servant who is making confession to you, far be it from me to think myself happy, whatever be the joy in which I take my delight. There is a delight which is given not to the wicked (Isaiah 48:22), but to those who worship you for no reward save the joy that you yourself are to them. That is the authentic happy life, to set one's joy on you, grounded in you and caused by you. That is the real thing, and there is no other. Those who think the happy life is found elsewhere, pursue another joy and not the true one. Nevertheless their will remains drawn to some image of the true joy.

xxiv (35) See how widely I have ranged, Lord, searching for you in my memory. I have not found you outside it. For I have found nothing coming from you which I have not stored in my memory since the time I first learnt of you. Since the day that I learnt of you, I have never forgotten you. Where I discovered the truth there I found my God, truth itself, which from the time I learnt it, I have not forgotten. And so, since the time I learnt of you, you remain in my consciousness, and there I find you when I recall you and delight in you. These my holy delights you have given me, in your mercy looking upon my poverty.

xxvii (38) Late have I loved you, beauty so old and so new: late have I loved you. And see, you were within and I was in the external world and sought you there, and in my unlovely state I plunged into those lovely created things which you made. You were with me, and I was not with you. The lovely things kept me far from you, though if they did not have their existence in you, they had no existence at all. You called and cried out loud and shattered my deafness. You were radiant and resplendent, you put to flight my blindness. You were fragrant, and I drew in my breath and now pant after you. I tasted you, and I feel but hunger and thirst for you. You touched me, and I am set on fire to attain the peace which is yours.

---

* Small Roman numerals denote chapters (present in early printed editions) and Arabic numerals denote paragraphs (introduced in the seventeenth century). *Ed.*

Of the Lord's Supper (extract)
Ulrich Zwingli (1484–1531)

Author Huldrych (Ulrich) Zwingli was born in Wildhaus in a mountainous area in the region of Zurich. He was of peasant heritage, but his father had risen to the position of magistrate in the town. At the age of ten he was sent to school in Basel where he developed a love of music and the humanities that were flowering as part of the northern Renaissance. He continued his studies in Berne and the University of Vienna before returning to Basel, where he began to study theology more seriously along with the humanities. Here he came under the influence of Thomas Wyttenbach (1472–1526), which sowed the seeds of his later positions on the supremacy of the Bible and the doctrine of salvation by grace through faith. He was ordained priest in 1506 and served as the pastor of Glarus and surrounding villages, where he stayed for ten years. During this time, he taught himself Greek in order to read the New Testament in line with the Renaissance principle of going back to the source. He continued his biblical and patristic studies when he moved to the parish of Einsiedeln, and then to the Great Minster at Zurich, which gave him a much higher national profile as a preacher, thinker and also accomplished musician. He preached expository sermons on the Bible, spoke out against financial and theological corruption in the church and gradually began a programme of reforming the Swiss church. This programme was both theological and administrative, aiming to give a sense of coherence and national identity to the potentially fragmented collection of cantons. By 1524 he had married Anna Reinhard and written a large number of works promoting the Swiss Reformation and disputing with Reformation thinkers in other parts of Europe, particularly with Lutheran understandings of the Eucharist. However, his reforming agenda was coming under threat, first from Catholic resistance within Switzerland, which was successfully quashed in a military clash in 1529; second from the Holy Roman Emperor, Charles V, who was not so easily dealt with. Zwingli responded by seeking alliances with the German Lutherans and sympathetic movements in Venice and France. However, these were all unsuccessful. Fearing invasion by the Emperor, Zwingli pressed neighbouring cantons to amalgamate with Zurich, but this instead provoked them to attack the city. He acted as chaplain to the defending army and was killed in the battle.

Language Swiss German. The translation below is by Alister McGrath.

Date 1526.

Genre and context This is a pamphlet in the vernacular, one of several written to disseminate Zwingli's ideas, already set out in scholarly Latin publications, to the general public. This pamphlet focuses on his understanding of the Eucharist. His aim was to develop a new sacramental theology that was not dependent on a literal understanding of the presence of Christ in the bread and wine for which he could find no evidence in his reading of the New Testament. In order to do this, he moves from a physical to a psychological approach, placing particular emphasis on the role of memory, the potential of material objects to act as symbols and be invested with meaning, and the group solidarity and identity that come from communal remembrance. It is a liminal piece, standing on the threshold of modernity.

Of the Lord's Supper
Third Article

As for the anniversaries of what took place only once, we use the same names that were originally given at the time of their occurrence and institution. That is why in our act of remembrance we have retained the words of Christ and of Paul in exactly the same form as these were originally given. Along with them, we have provided the following words of explanation to indicate how these are to be properly understood. 'That our Lord Jesus Christ, on the night on which he gave himself up to death, by which he fulfilled the blood and physical sacrifices of the Old Testament, intended to institute a memorial of his death, grace and redemption. This deliverance and exodus from Egypt was a type of his redemption, and in that deliverance a lamb was slain and eaten as a sign of the Passover and the blood was sprinkled on the side posts and the upper door posts, all which expressly typified and represented the Lord Jesus Christ. In the same way he himself instituted a remembrance of the deliverance by which he redeemed the whole world, so that we might never forget that he submitted his body to death for our sakes, not merely so that we might not forget it in our hearts, but so that we might publicly declare it with praise and thanksgiving, joining together to glorify and proclaim this in the eating and drinking of this sacrament of his sacred passion, which is a representation of Christ's giving of his body and shedding of his blood for our sakes.' And Christ intended the words 'This is (that is, "signifies") my body' and 'this is my blood' to be understood in much the same way as someone might say 'This is my late husband' when she displays her husband's ring. And when we poor creatures give thanks in this way amongst ourselves, we demonstrate that we are those who trust in the Lord Jesus Christ. By keeping this remembrance or thanksgiving, we are one body with all other Christians. Therefore if we are the members of his body, it is necessary that we should live together as Christians, otherwise we are 'guilty of the body and blood of Christ', as Paul says (cf. 1. Corinthians 11:27).

If the sacrament had been administered in this way, it would have been impossible for so much unfaithfulness and arrogance and envy and hatred and for all manner of weeds to take root and to spring up amongst Christian people. For this reason, in Zurich we have allowed the words of Christ to remain unaltered, but we have added some words of explanation to show how these were properly understood by Christ, the disciples and the early Church, as already indicated.

12.3 Remembering as keeping in mind: 'Watch and pray'[3]

In this context remembering is not about the past but about keeping Christ in mind in order to be responsive to the promptings of the Spirit, resist assaults from internal desires or external pressures, and to be poised to greet him.

On Spiritual Knowledge and Discrimination:
One Hundred Texts (extracts)
Diadochos of Photiki (c.400–c.486)

Author Diadochus was Bishop of Photiki in northern Greece. As a bishop, he participated in the Council of Chalcedon in 451 and was a great supporter of its doctrine on the two natures of Christ. It is likely that he was the victim of kidnapping by Vandals and may have ended his life in North Africa.

Language Greek. The translation below is by G. E. H. Palmer, Philip Sherrard and Kallistos Ware.

Date Probably before 467. However, as noted in Chapter 2, the *Philokalia* was published in 1782, and the degree of editorial changes made at this time remains unknown.

Genre and context The *Hundred Texts* are a theological and formational hand-book for the people under Diadichos' care. They express Chalcedon's focus on the nature(s) of Christ and show an equal interest in the nature of human beings and the structure of their inner mental life. Diadochos stands in the tradition of the early Desert Fathers and mothers, for example in seeing the spiritual life as involving a constant fight against demons, but in his writings he introduces certain concepts that would be developed by proponents of the Jesus Prayer and the Hesychasts (see Chapter 7). He was greatly influenced by the ideas of Evagrios of Pontus (345–399) on the importance of non-discursive prayer and inner stillness, but his distinctive contribution was the concept of remembrance of Jesus and the repeated calling on his name as the way to attain these. Remembering Jesus is also a means of banishing unwanted and impure thoughts (rather as in present-day mindfulness practice). Diadochos' approach keeps a loving relationship with Christ at its centre so that it is not simply a meditative technique.

---

3 Matthew 26.41 (RSV).

On Spiritual Knowledge and Discrimination: One Hundred Texts

88. When a man stands out of doors in winter at the break of day, facing the east, the front of his body is warmed by the sun, while his back is still cold because the sun is not on it. Similarly, the heart of those who are beginning to experience the energy of the Spirit is only partially warmed by God's grace. The result is that, while their intellect begins to produce spiritual thoughts, the outer parts of the heart continue to produce thoughts after the flesh, since the members of the heart have not yet all become fully conscious of the light of God's grace shining upon them.

Because some people have not understood this, they have concluded that two beings are fighting one another in the intellect. But just as the man in our illustration both shivers and yet feels warm at the touch of the sun, so the soul may have both good and evil thoughts simultaneously.

Ever since our intellect fell into a state of duality with regard to its modes of knowledge, it has been forced to produce at one and the same moment both good and evil thoughts, even against its own will; and this applies especially in the case of those who have reached a high degree of discrimination. While the intellect tries to think continually of what is good, it suddenly recollects what is bad, since from the time of Adam's disobedience man's power of thinking has been split into two modes. But when we begin wholeheartedly to carry out the commandments of God, all our organs of perception will become fully conscious of the light of grace; grace will consume our thoughts with its flames, sweetening our hearts in the peace of uninterrupted love, and enabling us to think spiritual thoughts and no longer worldly thoughts. These effects of grace are always present in those who are approaching perfection and have the remembrance of the Lord Jesus unceasingly in their hearts.

97. When the heart feels the arrows of the demons with such burning pain that the man under attack suffers as if they were real arrows, then the soul hates the passions violently, for it is just beginning to be purified. It if does not suffer greatly at the shamelessness of sin, it will not be able to rejoice fully in the blessings of righteousness. He who wishes to cleanse his heart should keep it continually aflame through practising the remembrance of the Lord Jesus, making this his only study and his ceaseless task. Those who desire to free themselves from their corruption ought to pray not merely from time to time but at all times; they should give themselves always to prayer, keeping watch over their intellect even when outside places of prayer. When someone is trying

to purify gold, and allows the fire of the furnace to die down even for a moment, the material which he is purifying will harden again. So, too, a man who merely practises the remembrance of God from time to time loses through lack of continuity what he hopes to gain through his prayer. It is a mark of one who truly loves holiness that he continually burns up what is worldly in his heart through practising the remembrance of God, so that little by little evil is consumed in the fire of this remembrance and his soul completely recovers its natural brilliance with still greater glory.

Forty Texts on Watchfulness (extracts)
Philotheos of Sinai (ninth century)

Author Almost nothing is known about Philotheos other than that he was a monk of St Catherine's Monastery on Mount Sinai, possibly the head of the community. He probably lived in the ninth century but may have lived somewhat later.

Language Greek. The translation below is by G. E. H. Palmer, Philip Sherrard, and Kallistos Ware.

Date Unknown, but collected in the *Philokalia*.

Genre and context This is the only surviving text by Philotheos and it stands in the tradition of the monks of Sinai, specifically that of John Klimakos (Climacus) (c.579–649). Like the previous reading by Diadochos, it is concerned with managing unwanted impure thoughts, but it adds the idea of *nepsis* (watchfulness) to Diadochos' idea of remembering. The emphasis on the inner life (a kind of sacred psychology) is based on reading the word *entos* (Luke 17.21) as 'within' whereas it should probably be understood as 'among'. The soul is conceived of a mirror in which the image of Christ is reproduced and gradually becoming more clearly defined (*phōteinographeisthai*) as in a photographic plate; but the plate can be spoiled by impure thoughts. It must be carefully guarded by attentiveness. This is greatly helped by remembering Christ which leads to recollection of fragmented faculties, preparing the individual for contemplation of God in this world or the next.

Forty Texts on Watchfulness

23. At every hour and moment let us guard the heart with all diligence from thoughts that obscure the soul's mirror; for in that mirror Jesus Christ, the wisdom and power of God the Father (cf. 1 Corinthians 1:24), is typified and luminously reflected. And let us unceasingly seek the kingdom of heaven inside our heart (cf. Luke 17:21), the seed (cf. Luke 13:19), the pearl (cf. Matthew 13: 45) and the leaven (cf. Matthew 13:33). Indeed, if we cleanse the eye of the intellect we will find all things hidden within us. This is why our Lord Jesus Christ said that the kingdom of heaven is within us, indicating that the Divinity dwells in our hearts.

26. Be extremely strict in guarding your intellect. When you perceive an evil thought, rebut it and immediately call upon Christ to defend you; and while you are still speaking, Jesus in His gentle love will say: 'Behold, I am by your side ready to help you.' When this whole detachment of the enemy has been put out of action through prayer, again turn your attention to your intellect. There you will see a succession of waves worse than before, with the soul swimming among them. But again, awakened by His disciple, Jesus as God will rebuke the winds of evil (cf. Matthew 8:23–27). Having found respite for an hour perhaps, or for a moment, glorify Him who has saved you, and meditate on death.

27. … by means of certain ploys, keep out all external enemies, and with incorporeal. God-given weapons fight against the thoughts which they produce inside you. Avert sensual pleasure through strenuous vigils, and be sparing in food and drink. Keep the body properly slim so that you reduce the burden of the heart's warfare, with full benefit to yourself. Chastise your soul with the thought of death, and through remembrance of Jesus Christ concentrate your scattered intellect. It is particularly at night that the intellect grows lucid in its radiant contemplation of God and of divine realities.

29. Smoke from wood kindling a fire troubles the eyes; but then the fire gives them light and gladdens them. Similarly, unceasing attentiveness is irksome; but when, invoked in prayer, Jesus draws near, He illumines the heart; for remembrance of Him confers on us spiritual enlightenment and the highest of all blessings.

Letter to Miss Hatton (extract)
John Fletcher (1729–1785)

Author Jean Guillaume de la Fléchère was born in Nyon, Switzerland, into a military family. He was educated in Geneva and then intended to pursue a military career. In 1750 he travelled to England with this intention but instead, spent a year studying English, and then became a tutor to the sons of Thomas Hill, a member of Parliament. While with them in London he first met the Wesleys. He underwent a spiritual awakening and was ordained in the Church of England in 1757. Most of his ministry was as the parish priest of Madeley in Shropshire, where he lived out his firm convictions on social justice and the theological principles of the Methodist movement, while remaining an Anglican. He was a close colleague of the Wesleys and had even been earmarked as the successor to John Wesley as leader of the movement but in the event predeceased him. Fletcher married Mary Bosanquet (1739–1815), a preacher and pastor in her own right, late in his life. She continued his parish ministry after his death. Fletcher wrote several theological treatises, expounding the Arminian position and arguing for its compatibility with Anglicanism, and defending the Methodist concern with personal holiness from the charge of 'justification by works'.

Language English.

Date 1764.

Genre and context A pastoral letter. Fletcher's argument is strikingly similar to that of the previous two readings. This is less surprising than it appears; both Methodism and Philotheos and his inheritors were influenced by the writings of an Egyptian monk, Macarius (300–391), whose works were beginning to be rediscovered in the eighteenth century. But it is probably more directly influenced by the sayings of Brother Lawrence (c.1614–1691), a lay member of a Parisian Carmelite community for whom recollection was a central spiritual practice (see further reading below).

Letter to Miss Hatton
5 March 1764

You ask me some directions to get a mortified spirit. In order to get it, get recollection.

Recollection is a dwelling within ourselves; a being abstracted from the creature, and turned toward God. Recollection is both outward and inward. Outward recollection consists in silence from all idle and super-fluous word; and in solitude, or a wise disentanglement from the world, keeping to our own business, observing and following the order of God for ourselves, and shutting the ear against all curious and unprofitable matters. Inward recollection consists in shutting the door of the senses, in a deep attention to the presence of God, and' in a continual care of entertaining holy thoughts, for fear of spiritual idleness.

Through the power of the Spirit, let this recollection be steady even in the midst of hurrying business; let it be calm and peaceable; and let it be lasting. 'Watch and pray, lest ye enter into temptation.' To main-tain this recollection, beware of engaging too deeply, and beyond what is necessary, in outward things; beware of suffering your affections to be entangled by worldly desire, your imagination to amuse itself with unprofitable objects, and indulging yourself in the commission of what are called 'small faults.'

For want of continuing in a recollected frame all the day, our times of prayer are frequently dry and useless, imagination prevails, and the heart wanders: whereas we pass easily from recollection to delightful prayer. Without this spirit, there can be no useful self-denial, nor can we know ourselves: but where it dwells, it makes the soul all eye, all ear; traces and discovers sin, repels its first assaults, or crushes it in its earliest risings.

In recollection let your mind act according to the drawings of grace, and it will probably lead you either to contemplate Jesus as crucified, and interceding for you, etc., or to watch your senses and suppress your passions, to keep before God in respectful silence of heart, and to watch and follow the motions of grace, and feed on the promises.

But take care here, to be more taken up with the thoughts of God than of yourself; and consider how hardly recollection is sometimes obtained, and how easily it is lost. Use no forced labour to raise a particular frame, nor tire, fret, nor grow impatient if you have no comfort; but meekly acquiesce and confess yourself unworthy of it; lie prostrate in humble submission before God, and patiently wait for the smiles of Jesus.

Further reading

Being Mindful, Being Christian by Roger Bretherton, Joanna Collicutt and Jennifer Brickman. Oxford: Monarch, 2016.

Dementia: Living in the memories of God by John Swinton. London: SCM Press, 2017.

On the Road with Saint Augustine: A real-world spirituality for restless hearts by James K. A. Smith. Ada, MI: Brazos Press, 2019.

The Philokalia and the Inner Life: On passions and prayer by Christopher Cook. Cambridge: James Clarke, 2011.

The Practice of the Presence of God by Brother Lawrence (seventeenth century). Several editions available.

Remembrance, Communion, and Hope: Rediscovering the gospel at the Lord's table by J. Todd Billings. Grand Rapids, MI: Eerdmans, 2018.

Resurrection: Interpreting the Easter gospel by Rowan Williams. London: Darton, Longman & Todd. 2014.

The Shattering of Loneliness: On Christian remembrance by Erik Varden OCSO. London: Bloomsbury, 2018.

Conclusion

Keep us, O Lord,
while we tarry on this earth,
in a serious seeking after you,
and in an affectionate walking with you,
every day of our lives;
that when you come,
we may be found not hiding our talent,
nor serving the flesh,
nor yet asleep with our lamp unfurnished,
but waiting and longing for our Lord,
our glorious God for ever.

Richard Baxter (1691)

13

'Patiently waiting for the smiles of Jesus'

While staying with them, he ordered them not to leave Jerusalem, but to wait there for the promise of the Father. 'This,' he said, 'is what you have heard from me; for John baptized with water, but you will be baptized with the Holy Spirit not many days from now.'
(Acts 1.4–5)

'And see, I am sending upon you what my Father promised; so stay here in the city until you have been clothed with power from on high.' Then he led them out as far as Bethany, and, lifting up his hands, he blessed them. While he was blessing them, he withdrew from them and was carried up into heaven.
(Luke 24.49–51)

The final words of the final reading in Part II bring us back to the beginning of this book: Christian spirituality is about waiting well for a joyous (re)union with Christ. The first Christians expected the return of Jesus within their own lifetimes, but as time progressed the feeling of urgency faded, and attention was increasingly paid to inhabiting an extended period of uncertain duration. Yet the sense of expectation remained; Benedicta Ward points out that the early Desert Fathers and mothers did not go out into the wilderness simply to withdraw from the fleshpots of the town but to await the return of Jesus, to live out the phrase 'Marana tha'. She quotes a contemporary source describing them as 'waiting for Christ as loyal sons watching for their father'.[1]

There were several aspects to this waiting for Christ. The spiritual practice of silence, which is a feature of so many Christian traditions from the Hesychasts to the Quakers is essentially a form of waiting on God.[2] Another, taken up most famously by Benedict of Nursia, is the principle of stability. Being stable should not be mistaken for being static or – worse – stagnant. It is rather the attitude of being poised and ready, so that when called to move, one does not overbalance; this is the 'steady' from 'ready, steady, go!'

Part of this stability is a transformed attitude to time, of which the recitation of the psalms at set points in the day and night became a vital part. For Benedict, and the earlier tradition on which he drew, reciting the psalms is

---

1 B. Ward, 2003, *The Desert Fathers: Sayings of the early Christian monks*, London: Penguin, p. viii.

2 D. MacCulloch, 2014, *Silence: A Christian history*, London: Penguin, pp. 147–8.

a discipline of waiting with joy. The practice of pausing between the lines of each verse suspends this joyful engagement so that it is balanced with anticipatory attentiveness.

Here again there is a link with human loss and grief. Writing about C. S. Lewis' account of his grief on losing his wife, the psychiatrist Colin Murray Parkes also emphasizes suspense and observes: 'The suspense … would seem to indicate the expectation that something is about to happen. To the griever the only happening that seems important is the return of the one who is lost.'[3]

Throughout this book I have drawn connections between the experience of human grief, the ways that people actively cope with loss, and the spiritual ideas, experiences and practices that recur across the history of the church. I have also noted some differences. By far the most important of these is that when Jesus departed from his disciples, he instructed them not to wait for his immediate return but for the coming of the Holy Spirit upon them. This is the 'spirit' bit of Christian spirituality. For the Christian, the practices of lamenting Christ, attending to his body, attaching to him imaginatively, returning to the source, engaging with the reality of his absence, seeking a glimpse of him ascended in glory, finding his traces in this world, living as he would wish, and re-membering ourselves all take place with the support and guidance of the Holy Spirit. If they did not, they would be merely techniques. Nevertheless, the fact that natural human processes play their part is characteristic of the way that God's Spirit cooperates with the human spirit. This idea was first expressed by Paul (Romans 8.16) and developed in later Christian thinking, notably that of Maximos the Confessor. This intimate relationship between divine and human action should perhaps not surprise us, as it is the work of the God who became a human being in Jesus of Nazareth.

The Spirit-powered stability or poise with which the Christian awaits Christ seems to be characterized by an integration of thinking, feeling and acting, itself a sign of the re-membered self. It is interesting that in the field of psychology the term 'stability' denotes the opposite of 'neuroticism'. Some of the readings in this book do seem to push this more secular notion of stability to its limits; they can have a neurotic feel to the modern reader. However, as I have noted elsewhere, 'we are called to be fundamentally integrated and well balanced; but this fundamental stability should, like a roly-poly doll, give us a greater capacity to wobble in a way that may look quite alarming at times.'[4] These writers, including those who may appear 'neurotic', are ultimately known by the fruits they have borne in the church and the world, not simply by their personalities. What they all have in common is a deep reliance on the Bible and a refusal to split theology off from the often complex demands of life in the external world or from the depths of experience in the inner world.

---

3 C. M. Parkes, 1988, *Bereavement: Studies of grief in adult life*, Harmondsworth: Penguin, pp. 75–6.

4 J. Collicutt, 2015, *The Psychology of Christian Character Formation*, London: SCM Press, pp. 143–4.

There is also a keen eschatological awareness evident in anticipation of the return of Christ and/or acute consciousness of their own mortality.

Charles Wesley (1707–1788), the author of the closing reading, is no exception. He was the original founder of the 'Holy Club' that developed into Methodism, but he retained stronger roots in Anglicanism than his brother, John. Like John, Charles experienced an intensification of his faith in 1738, and for the rest of his life had a deep appreciation of the role of the Holy Spirit in the life of the believer. Like Benedict, he saw the importance of marking times and seasons with songs of praise, empowered by the Spirit while waiting on the final reunion with Christ. He wrote several 'Hymns for Whitsunday' (Pentecost), of which this is one.

Whitsunday Hymn 4

Sinners, lift up your hearts,
THE PROMISE to receive!
Jesus himself imparts,
He comes in man to live;
The Holy Ghost to man is given;
Rejoice in God sent down from heaven.

Jesus is glorified,
And gives the Comforter,
His Spirit to reside
In all his members here:
The Holy Ghost to man is given;
Rejoice in God sent down from heaven.

To make an end of sin,
And Satan's works destroy,
He brings his kingdom in,
Peace, righteousness, and joy,
The Holy Ghost to man is given;
Rejoice in God sent down from heaven.

The cleansing blood t' apply,
The heavenly life display,
And wholly sanctify,
And seal us to that day,
The Holy Ghost to man is given;
Rejoice in God sent down from heaven.

Sent down to make us meet
To see his glorious face,
And grant us each a seat
In that thrice happy place,
The Holy Ghost to man is given,
Rejoice in God sent down from heaven.

From heaven he shall once more
Triumphantly descend,
And all his saints restore
To joys that never end,
Then, then, when all our joys are given,
Rejoice in God, rejoice in heaven.

Time and Place Table

Century	North America	Northern Europe	Southern Europe	North Africa	Middle East	Asia Minor
1st			New Testament writers		New Testament writers	New Testament writers
2nd				Tertullian	Ignatius of Antioch	
3rd				Pontius the Deacon/Cyprian		
4th			Ambrose of Milan Egeria	Antony Pachomius Athanasius		Ephrem the Syrian Gregory of Nazianzus Basil of Caesarea Gregory of Nyssa
5th		Patrick of Ireland	Diadochos of Photiki Jerome/Paula	Augustine of Hippo		
6th			Benedict of Nursia Gregory the Great		Pseudo-Dionysius	
7th						Maximos the Confessor
8th		Blathmac, Son of Cú Brettan				
9th		Dream of the Rood			Philotheos of Sinai	
10th						

Century	North America	Northern Europe	Southern Europe	North Africa	Middle East	Asia Minor
11th		Anselm of Canterbury				Symeon the New Theologian
12th		Bernard of Clairvaux Hugh of St Victor (and Malachi of Armagh) Hildegard of Bingen				
13th		Hadewijch	Francis of Assisi Clare of Assisi Bonaventure Thomas Aquinas Jacopone da Todi Angela of Foligno		Hesychasts	
14th		Meister Eckhart John Van Ruysbroeck Henry Suso Julian of Norwich Walter Hilton Cloud author	Dante Alighieri			
15th		Margery Kempe Thomas Kempis				

Century	North America	Northern Europe	Southern Europe	North Africa	Middle East	Asia Minor
16th		Martin Luther Ulrich Zwingli	Ignatius of Loyola Teresa of Avila John of the Cross			
17th		Francis de Sales George Herbert Brother Lawrence Richard Baxter John Bunyan Thomas Traherne				
18th	Jonathan Edwards	Susanna Wesley Christian Friedrich Henrici John Wesley Charles Wesley George Whitefield John Fletcher William Blake				
19th	'Was you there?' Wallace Willis	John Henry Newman John Ruskin Ernst Renan Josephine Butler Gerard Manley Hopkins Thérèse of Lisieux				

Acknowledgements

Every effort has been made to trace all copyright holders, but if any have been overlooked, please get in touch with the publisher.

Title	Author	Translator	Permission
To Mary and her Son	Blathmac, Son of Cú Brettan	James Carney	By kind permission of the Irish Texts Society
Prayer to Christ Meditation on human redemption Prayer of St Paul	Anselm of Canterbury	Benedicta Ward	From *The Prayers and Meditations of St. Anselm with the Proslogion* by Anselm published by Penguin Classics. Copyright © Benedicta Ward 1973. Reprinted by permission of Penguin Books Limited
Rule	Benedict of Nursia	Abbot Parry OSB	By permission of Gracewing Limited
Pentecost sermon	Augustine of Hippo	Edmund Hill OP	By kind permission of The Dominican Council/English Province of the Order of Preachers
The Imitation of Christ	Thomas Kempis	Leo Sherley-Price	From *The Imitation of Christ* by Thomas à Kempis published by Penguin Classics. Copyright © Robert Jeffery 2009. Reprinted by permission of Penguin Books Limited
Hymns of divine love	Symeon the New Theologian	John Anthony McGuckin	By kind permission of John Anthony McGuckin

Title	Author	Translator	Permission
Life of Francis The soul's journey into God	Bonaventure	Ewert Cousins	Excerpts from *Bonaventure*, from Classics of Western Spirituality, translated by Ewert H. Cousins. Copyright 1978 by Paulist Press, Inc., New York/Mahwah, NJ. Used with permission of Paulist Press, www.paulistpress.com
The Memorial of Angela of Foligno	Brother A	Paul LaChance OFM	Excerpts from *Angela of Foligno*, from Classics of Western Spirituality, translated by Paul La Chance, Copyright 1993 by Paulist Press, Inc., New York/Mahwah, NJ. Used with permission of Paulist Press, www.paulistpress.com
Commentary on the Song of Songs	Bernard of Clairvaux	Kilian Walsh OCSO	From the *The Works of Bernard of Clairvaux. Vol.3*, 1976. By permission of Liturgical Press
Letter IV	Hadewijch	Paul Mommaers	From *Hadewijch: The complete letters* translated by Paul Mommaers 2016, by kind permission of Peeters Publishers
Fourth letter to Agnes of Prague	Clare of Assisi	Regis Armstrong OFMCap.	From *Lady Clare of Assisi: Early documents* translated and edited by Regis Armstrong OFMCap. published by New City Press, Hyde Park, NY. Used with permission
Revelations of Divine Love	Julian of Norwich	Clifton Wolters	From *Revelations of Divine Love* by Julian of Norwich published by Penguin Classics. Copyright © Clifton Wolters 1966. Reprinted by permission of Penguin Books
Pilgrimage of Egeria	Egeria	Anne McGowan	From *The Pilgrimage of Egeria: A New Translation of the Itinerarium Egeriae with Introduction and Commentary* by Paul Bradshaw and Anne McGowan, 2018. By permission of Liturgical Press

Title	Author	Translator	Permission
Spiritual Exercises, including Contemplation for attaining love	Ignatius of Loyola	Joseph Munitiz SJ and Philip Endean SJ	From *Personal Writings by Ignatius of Loyola*, Joseph Munitiz published by Penguin Classics. Copyright © Ignatius of Loyola, Joseph Munitiz 1997. Reprinted by permission of Penguin Books
Philokalia	Hesychasts, Maximos the Confessor, Diadochos of Photiki, Philotheos of Sinai	G. E. H. Palmer, Philip Sherrard and Kallistos Ware.	From *The Philokalia Volume 1*, 1983 by G. E. H. Palmer. By permission of Faber & Faber Ltd
Pastoral rule book	Gregory the Great	Henry Davis SJ	Excerpts from *St Gregory the Great Pastoral Care*, from Ancient Christian writers, translated by Henry Davis SJ. Copyright 1978 by Paulist Press, Inc., New York/ Mahwah, NJ. Used with permission of Paulist Press, www.paulistpress.com
The Spiritual Espousals	John Van Ruysbroeck	Eric Colledge	From *The Spiritual Espousals*, translated by Eric Colledge, 1952. By permission of Faber & Faber Ltd
The Scale of Perfection	Walter Hilton	John P. H. Clark and Rosemary Dorward	Excerpts from *Walter Hilton: The Scale of Perfection*, from Classics of Western Spirituality, translated by John P.H. Clark & Rosemary Dorward. Copyright 1991 by Paulist Press, Inc., New York/Mahwah, NJ. Used with permission of Paulist Press, www.paulistpress.com
The Cloud of Unknowing	Anonymous	A. C. Spearing	From *The Cloud of Unknowing and Other Works* published by Penguin Classics. Copyright © A. C. Spearing, 2001. Reprinted by permission of Penguin Books Limited

Title	Author	Translator	Permission
Book of Divine Consolation	Meister Eckhart	Oliver Davies	From *Selected Writings by Meister Eckhart* published by Penguin Classics. Copyright © Oliver Davies 1990. Reprinted by permission of Penguin Books Limited
On mystical theology	Pseudo-Dionysius	Colm Luibheid and Paul Rorem	Excerpts from *Pseudo-Dionysius: The complete works*, from Classics of Western Spirituality, translated by Colm Luibheid & Paul Rorem. Copyright 1987 by Paulist Press, Inc., New York/Mahwah, NJ. Used with permission of Paulist Press, www.paulistpress.com
The Divine Comedy	Dante Alighieri	Tony Kline	Excerpts from *The Divine Comedy* of Dante Alighieri, translated by A. S. Kline, Copyright © 2000. Used with permission
Life of Antony	Athanasius of Alexandria	Carolinne White	From *Early Christian Lives by Athanasius, Gregory, Hilarion, Jerome, Sulpicius Severus* published by Penguin Classics. Copyright © Carolinne White 1998. Reprinted by permission of Penguin Books Limited
Book of Divine Works	Hildegard of Bingen	Nathaniel M. Campbell	From *The Book of Divine Works by* Hildegard of Bingen translated by Nathaniel M. Campbell, 2018. By permission of Catholic University of America Press
Hymn on the nativity	Ephrem the Syrian	Kathleen McVey	Excerpts from *Ephrem the Syrian: Hymns*, from Classics of Western Spirituality, translated by Kathleen McVey. Copyright 1989 by Paulist Press, Inc., New York/Mahwah, NJ. Used with permission of Paulist Press, www.paulistpress.com
Canticle of the sun	Francis of Assisi	Bill Barrett	By kind permission of Revd Dr Laurel Hayes

Title	Author	Translator	Permission
The dream of the rood	Anonymous	Richard Hamer	From *A Choice of Anglo Saxon Verse* by Richard Hamer, 2015. By permission of Faber & Faber Ltd
Noah's ark	Hugh of St Victor	Unknown sister of CSV Wantage	By kind permission of the Community of St Mary the Virgin, Wantage
Rule	Basil of Caesarea	Anna Silvas	From *The Rule of St. Basil in Latin and English: A Revised Critical Edition*, 2013. By permission of Liturgical Press
Anaphora	Basil of Caesarea	Ronald Jasper Geoffrey Cuming	From *Prayers of the Eucharist: Early and Reformed* edited and translated by G. J. Cuming & R. C. D. Jasper, 2018. By permission of Liturgical Press
Confessions	Augustine of Hippo	Henry Chadwick	From *Saint Augustine: Confessions*, translated and edited by Henry Chadwick, 1991. By permission of Oxford Publishing

Index of Bible References

Old Testament

New Testament

Index of Names and Subjects